SAGE was founded in 1965 by Sara Miller McCune to support the dissemination of usable knowledge by publishing innovative and high-quality research and teaching content. Today, we publish over 900 journals, including those of more than 400 learned societies, more than 800 new books per year, and a growing range of library products including archives, data, case studies, reports, and video. SAGE remains majority-owned by our founder, and after Sara's lifetime will become owned by a charitable trust that secures our continued independence.

Los Angeles | London | New Delhi | Singapore | Washington DC | Melbourne

Tour Leadership and Management

Tour Leadership and Management

Shailja Sharma

Assistant Professor, Indian Institute of Tourism and Travel Management, Noida

Nimit Chowdhary

Professor, Department of Tourism, Hotel, Hospitality and Heritage Studies, Jamia Millia Islamia, New Delhi

SAGE | TEXTS

Los Angeles | London | New Delhi
Singapore | Washington DC | Melbourne

First published in 2018 by

SAGE | TEXTS

SAGE Publications India Pvt Ltd
B1/I-1 Mohan Cooperative Industrial Area
Mathura Road, New Delhi 110 044, India
www.sagepub.in

SAGE Publications Inc
2455 Teller Road
Thousand Oaks, California 91320, USA

SAGE Publications Ltd
1 Oliver's Yard, 55 City Road
London EC1Y 1SP, United Kingdom

SAGE Publications Asia-Pacific Pte Ltd
3 Church Street
#10-04 Samsung Hub
Singapore 049483

Published by Vivek Mehra for SAGE Publications India Pvt Ltd, typeset in 10.5/12.5 pt Baskerville by Zaza Eunice, Hosur, Tamil Nadu, India and printed at Sai Printo Pack, New Delhi.

Library of Congress Cataloging-in-Publication Data Available

ISBN: 978-93-528-0737-6 (PB)

SAGE Team: Amit Kumar, Anveshi Gupta, Guneet Kaur Gulati, Shobana Paul and Rajinder Kaur

Contents

Detailed Contents

Preface

Generally speaking, tourism is travel for leisure and fun. It is about holidaying and vacationing. However, in a technical sense, tourism encompasses the activities of tourists travelling for either leisure or business. Even travel for business requires the facilitation of the trip and often some entertainment as an add-on. In either case, travel today is dependent on many associated services. Since time immemorial, people have travelled far and wide for different reasons which include astonishing oneself with a different way of life at a different place. Man has always been excited to discover a new meaning to life—one which is very different from his routine. Every travel is accompanied by some flow of adrenaline, some adventure and some calibrated risk of transcending through the unfamiliar. Travel is, therefore, a lot of interpreting a place and negotiating the lesser known. Given the constraints of time and ability, such travel is often mediated. Visitors require this mediation to interpret the place and also to facilitate their travel. This is the fundamental business of tourism. Most tourism companies are organised around this idea of facilitating travel and mediated interpretation of the visitors' stay.

Tourism today is one of the largest sectors of the economy. Though it is hard to delineate tourism from other economic activities, tourism and allied sectors account for a significant share of a places' economy. In fact, many smaller countries and regions within larger countries are greatly dependent on tourism for their economic growth. It is estimated by WTTC that tourism is growing steadily over the last few years. In 2016, it contributed 10.2 per cent of global GDP which is equal to USD7.6 trillion. In most of the countries, growth of contribution of tourism to the GDP is more than the growth of GDP. Besides these aggregates, the nature of tourism is such that the distribution of wealth is equitable. Thus, tourism ensures growth with equality. In most cases, it is the locals who benefit the most from tourism. Jobs are created locally, disposable incomes of locals increase and quality of life improves with the development of tourism. Tourism contributes almost 1 in 10 jobs globally.

Thus, as the number of visitors to a place increases, it ensures the economic development of the place. Of course, there are social, cultural and environmental impacts of tourism which need to be addressed. As visitors arrive at a destination for a limited time for holiday, they would like to make the most of the opportunity. To be efficient with their holiday, they often require expert advice and support. Call this mediation. Accordingly, tourism as an industry needs a large number of companies that are expert in organising travel and holiday. They offer and deliver travel packages. There are travel companies at home who promote, sell and facilitate travel. Then, at the receiving end, other travel companies receive guests at the destination. They ensure all the promised facilities to the visitors. Often these companies dedicate a responsible individual to accompany the guests to help them understand the place, and make and ensure arrangements and necessary services for them. Even the visitors who book their holidays themselves often require the support of destination experts during their travel. These destination experts are known differently. Many times, they are called tour managers.

Tour managers are, therefore, the experts on the ground who facilitate a visitor's travel at the destination. Many times, outbound companies require these destination managers to accompany clients from home. On other occasions, a tour manager joins the group as they arrive at the destination. Some companies have these tour managers on their payrolls while, in most cases, they are freelancing experts who associate themselves with companies on a case-to-case basis. Thus, while there are companies that engage these tour managers, these tour managers are one-person companies by themselves.

Every place is a potential destination for visitors. Every place has its own specialty, history, geography and legacy. Each place is best understood in the company of an expert, preferably a local. Thus, there are thousands of micro-, small- and medium-sized tourism enterprises in the world. An estimate suggests that more than 98 per cent of tourism companies are micro and small companies. All these companies require tour managers to accompany their clients.

Managing a tour is, therefore, a primary job in the tourism industry. These thousands of tour companies need millions of professional tour managers. This is a challenge. Unfortunately, a majority of individuals have no vocational training to be tour managers. On many occasions, with time, tour guides elevate themselves to tour managers. Most of them learn on the job. Bigger companies do try to train their tour managers, but they are severely constrained by a shortage of professional trainers.

Today, these thousands of individuals who have chosen to be tour managers are seeking expert advice to be better professionals. A large number of skill training institutions are preparing trainees to be tour managers. A large number of vocational schools, colleges and universities have introduced courses on managing tours. However, they are all constrained by the paucity of training materials. And therefore, this work has been created for them.

Acknowledgements

As William Arthur Ward once said, 'Feeling gratitude and not expressing it is like wrapping a present and not giving it'. Any work of creativity requires a lot of patience and support of those who are around. We borrowed time that was due to them to complete this work. As we present this work to our audiences, we are bound by gratitude towards all the visible and invisible help that poured in as we were busy compiling this book, oblivious of the contributions.

Ever since I travelled to the USA three years back and took a package tour for the Niagra–Washington DC–Philadelphia–Las Vegas that was led by a Chinese tour manager, I realised the importance of a tour manager in facilitating a vacation. I also learned to appreciate the difference between a tour guide and a tour manager. I strongly felt that it was important to introduce this profession to youngsters as a career option by highlighting in detail how a tour manager works, what roles and responsibilities he holds, and the challenges he faces while handling groups.

When I returned from my trip, I started searching for a detailed book on this and to my surprise, I could not find any. This became food for thought, and I decided to write on this subject. The idea was solidified when I took an extensive tour of Europe and the UK. This time, I observed and imbibed as much as I could, with the sole purpose of collating the information for my book. Then on, there was no looking back.

As they say, nothing happens if God does not make it happen. Therefore, first and foremost, I would like to express my heartfelt gratitude towards the Almighty for all the strength, knowledge and abilities that He bestowed upon me to write this book. I could feel His blessings at every step of this journey.

In all humility, I would also like to thank my co-author, mentor and friend Professor Nimit Chowdhary for inspiring me to write this book and introducing me to the author within me. Without his push and invaluable guidance, this book would have remained a distant dream. He gave me the freedom to experiment with my ideas, for which I am eternally grateful to him.

The most important person in my life who made me believe in myself and remained a rock-like support while I was writing this book is my husband Sorabh to whom I am indebted forever. Without his endless support and love, this piece of work would have remained only an idea. Having shared the best partnership in both travel and life, he helped me with valuable inputs at every step. For all the countless nights and days when I was giving all his time to this book, he stood by and never complained about my lack of attention towards him. I thank him for making me travel the world, as I was able to observe tour managers first-hand and jot down what I learned about their work and life.

In this journey of writing, my parents showed unflinching faith in me. There were times when I would get very impatient as the completion of the book seemed a distant vision. My parents asked me to stick to my conviction with passion and dedication. They kept that fire alive within me. Last but not least, I would also like to thank my elder sisters, my nieces, Atishaya and Atima, and my nephew, Vihaan, for all their unwavering love—they kept me going.

No one who achieves success does so without the help of others. The wise and confident acknowledge this help with gratitude. (Alfred North Whitehead).

Shailja Sharma

Ever since I completed my previous book *Handbook for Tour Guides*, I wanted to write a book for tour managers. However, my engagements kept me away from this. My co-author Shailja Sharma worked meticulously to lead this assignment and complete it in a timely manner. I would also like to thank my wife Professor Monika Prakash, my parents and my sons Chinmay and Anunay for the time that I stole for contributing to this book, which otherwise belonged to them. I would also like to thank my colleagues both at Jamia Millia Islamia and Indian Institute of Tourism and Travel Management. Amit Kumar and Anveshi Gupta from SAGE India deserve a special mention for their support. We would also like to thank the many inputs and insights that have helped shape this work.

Nimit Chowdhary

About the Book

This book is about how to manage a touring group on holiday. Travel companies identify tour managers to lead a group of visitors and expect them to be thorough professionals. Some good practices have evolved over time, and, to begin with, a tour manager must understand them and follow them. A tour manager is the face of the company and is simultaneously responsible to both the company and the guests for organising a relatively successful tour.

This book is an essential reading for tens of thousands of individuals who aspire to be tour managers. It is divided into five sections. Section A sets the stage by talking about what the job of a tour manager is all about, what are the expectations from a tour manager and what skills are required to be one.

Section B of the book is about the pre-tour preparations that a tour manager must make to deliver an excellent experience to the clients. Who all should he be networking with? What kind of documents should he organise for the tour and what all preparations are required? Section C of the book is all about conducting a successful tour. It details the different situations and what all the tour manager must ensure for a successful visit. These cases include receiving the group at the airport, checking them in at the hotel, facilitating visits to the attractions, managing the coach, other modes of transport and closing the tour.

Often, the tour operators who engage a tour manager to accompany the group desire that the manager double up as a tour guide at various sites where there are no site-guides available or they are too costly to be engaged. In India, there is a restriction that only a licensed guide can lead a tourist within the premises of the monument. Apart from this limiting case, the tour manager must be able to interpret the attractions and sites professionally. In India, many tour managers enrich their roles by getting trained as tour guides. Section D deals with the techniques of commentary that a tour manager must know and should be skilful.

Section E of the book is about professional wisdom. It addresses issues that will ensure success for the tour managers, such as cross-cultural sensitivities, handling demanding tourists, dealing with questions from the guests, partnering with important stakeholders and the group dynamics. The last part of the book is a compendium of real decision-making situations presented as caselets. Authors have collected these incidents from tour managers and used them for training.

About the Authors

Shailja Sharma, MBA, MTM, PhD, is a faculty with the Indian Institute of Tourism and Travel Management and Chairperson for the BBA (T&T) programme at the Noida campus of the institute. She has a total of 13 years of experience with 11 years of experience in teaching and training in tourism and 2 years of corporate experience. She has trained over 1,500 tour guides and tour leaders. She is a qualified trainer of World Federation of Tourist Guide Associations (WFTGA) from London. She has designed and delivered tour leadership programmes for travel companies. She has also delivered various tour guiding and leadership programmes for various state governments too. Besides these, she has designed and delivered various training programmes for a range of stakeholders in tourism which includes tourist information officers, senior government officials posted in state tourism departments, cab drivers, etc.

She has a PhD in tour guiding and has published research in reputed journals. She has also authored a book. She has been also associated on research projects with the Ministry of Tourism, Government of India (MOT-GOI), and Indian Council of Social Science Research (ICSSR). She has travelled extensively across five continents around the world to earn an insight into tour management and leadership.

Nimit Chowdhary, BE (Mech.), MBA, PhD, is a full professor and heads the Department of Tourism, Hotel, Hospitality and Heritage Studies of Jamia Millia Islamia. He was earlier with the Indian Institute of Tourism and Travel Management. He has more than 24 years of teaching and research experience. He has also taught as a full professor at Instituto Tecnológico y de Estudios Superiores de Monterrey, Mexico (2001); Shaoxing University, China (2005); and Mizoram University (2007). He has also taught as a visitor at the University of Girona, Spain; University of Gotland, Sweden; Global Entrepreneurship Acad., Slovenia; Indian Institute of Management, Indore; ABV-India Institute of Information Technology and Management, Gwalior; Indian Institute of Quality Management, Jaipur; Entrepreneurship Development Institute of India, Ahmadabad, and many other places.

He has trained over 2,500 guides and tour leaders. He has designed several training programmes to be rolled out all over India. He has travelled extensively within the sub-continent to deliver these training programmes, has carried out research for various agencies such as UGC, ICSSR, All India Council for Technical Education (AICTE) and MoT-GoI worth around ₹5 million, and has also sourced/designed/coordinated/delivered trainings and consultancies worth around ₹45 million.

He is a recipient of many prestigious awards and fellowships in and outside of India such as the AICTE Career Award for Young Teachers; SIDA Fellowship, Sweden; Guest Scholarship, Sweden; Linnaeus Palme Exchange Programme Grants, Sweden; PIMG Research Excellence Award, Gwalior; and Scholars' Grant (EMTM), Erasmus Mundus, Europe among others.

He is a referred researcher in the field of tour leadership and has published on the subject in many international journals. He has supervised doctoral level researchers on tour leadership. He has authored eight books and more than hundred papers.

SECTION A

JOB OF A TOUR MANAGER

The first section of the book is about the building blocks for a tour leader's profession for novice learners. It shall help in establishing a connection of the readers with the job of a tour manager. The section would give an overview to the readers about understanding the concept, need and significance of a tour manager in the tourism industry. It would also help the readers identify the differences between a tour guide and a tour manager, introduce the readers to the various roles of a tour manager that he is expected to perform, help the readers to understand and appreciate the strategic role of tour leaders in delivering a positive tourism experience to the guests and introduce the learners to the various aspects of this profession that shall give them a balanced opinion about the pros and cons of this job. After being exposed to the concept, importance and salient features of this profession, the learners would get an in-depth insight of the competencies and skills required for this job. In a nutshell, this section shall expose the students to a new career option in the tourism industry: The tour manager's job. After reading Section A, the learners would know the following:

1. Who is a tour manager and what is his role in the tourism industry?
2. What are the common aspects of tour managing as a profession?
3. What is the requisite skill set that a person may acquire to become a successful tour leader?

So let us all get started on to the journey of learning about managing a tour as a profession. Happy learning!

1

Being a Tour Manager

LEARNING OBJECTIVES

- Who is a tour manager?
- Why do companies and tourists hire the services of tour managers?
- What are their general roles?

Shivaay was leading a group of 20 Spanish guests. It was raining heavily and the group was proceeding towards Delhi after a stopover at Kosikalan near Mathura for tea and snacks. Everyone was relaxing in the coach and enjoying the weather. After the bus started its journey towards Delhi, about halfway there, the tour manager realised that Shyam, the pilot of the coach, was not able to put proper brakes while driving the coach. On enquiring from Shyam, he realised that the brakes were not working properly. They did not know exactly what to do. Both of them were scared and were contemplating how to deal with the situation that had gone beyond their control.

Holidaying is trending. In the modern-day era, travelling has become an essential part of peoples' lifestyle. As a result, the tourism industry is growing exponentially across the world. Given the limited time that a visitor has to make sense of the place, he would like to be assisted by a professional. This professional, besides taking care of the routine logistics of the tour, also helps the guests understand the place. This professional is the tour manager. A tour manager has been designated by different names in various parts of the world. He may be addressed differently as a tour leader, tour conductor, tour director or tour escort in different travel companies. In this book, we will use the term tour manager to refer to all of these.

INTRODUCTION

Travelling has undergone an enormous change. Tourism is evolving; it has not remained passive anymore. The modern-day tourists are not just confined to visiting and seeing a destination. They want to live in that destination. The new tourism is about cultural immersion. It is more about gaining first-hand authentic experiences at a destination from a local's perspective. It may be in the form of experiencing local life at the destination by walking along the local streets, venturing to the local markets, trying the regional cuisines, staying with the host community, cooking food with them, singing and dancing with them, or participating in their local events and festivals.

While choosing to travel to a destination, the traveller has two choices: either he travels alone or goes in group package tours that have fixed departures. Many tourists across the world, especially families and old-aged tourists, prefer to travel in group package tours and not on their own. There are many reasons for going on package tours. One of the significant advantages of going in groups is that these trips are more economical as there are group deals for the tourists. Also, with more people around, the tourist feels safer. The first-time travellers who may have an itch to travel alone prefer to go in groups as they may feel more secure in the presence of others. Another significant advantage of going in group packages is that the guests do not have to waste their time in planning their trip and then struggle to make travel arrangement at every point. Group departures are hassle-free for the tourist as everything from preparation to execution is the headache of the travel company. Camaraderie may also be another reason for going in groups, as for many, travelling is an opportunity for socialisation. Sometimes, moving in group packages also gives lifetime friends.

Besides these reasons, the primary reason for travelling in group package tours is getting the complimentary services of a person who can make a lot of difference to a trip with his presence. This key person is the tour manager. He may be considered as free of cost (FOC) from the guest's perspective as the tour operators/travel agents gives complimentary services of a tour manager to the tourists booking a package tour with the travel company. However, from the company's perspective the tour manager's costing is inbuilt in the overall group costing of a package tour. Many hotels may give deals to travel agents/tour operators by giving a complimentary stay to the tour manager along with the complimentary meals for the duration of his stay along with other guests on group bookings. Earlier airlines also used to give deals on group bookings on which the tour manager would fly free of cost though this practice has been discontinued by most of the airlines now.

It is important to clarify here that it is not necessary that tour managers only handle groups. They may be required to take up Free Independent Traveller (FIT) assignments. Many FIT tourists who may be travelling on customised packaged tours may also hire the services of a tour manager. These kinds of tourists may make their arrangements through a travel company that may depute their tour managers to take up the individual assignments. The particular assignment may just be a day tour or a tour for multiple days. In day tours, the tour manager may pick up his guest at the airport and help him check in at the hotel. He may then take him around the city sometimes, maybe for food walks, heritage walks, shopping walks and so on. He may also hire the services of a local guide while visiting monuments.

It is worth mentioning here that he is not a 'tour guide'. A tour guide is different from a tour manager.

A tour guide is a person who is hired at a destination or at an attraction for a limited duration of time. He may be recruited by the tour operator for half-day or full-day sightseeing tours. Therefore, his role is site-specific as he interprets a site for his guests on guided tours or takes them around the city for sightseeing, unlike a tour manager who remains with his guests all the time on the trip.

Guides are a specialist for the attractions at a destination. They are responsible for painting the picture of a destination or attraction that they make their guests visit. There are different types of guides: monument guides, full-time guides, part-time guides, linguistic guides, etc. One significant difference is that in many countries, like in India, a tour guide requires a licence to operate.

Then, the question is, who is a tour manager? Unlike tour guides, the scope of responsibilities of a tour manager is quite multifaceted. Now let us delve into the meaning and role of a tour manager.

WHO IS A TOUR MANAGER?

In simple words, a tour manager guides the group of holidaymakers from the beginning till the end to on various domestic and international trips. He is responsible for the overall administration of the group during the tour. He travels with them at every point of the trip, that is, at the airport, hotel, restaurants, sightseeing attractions, local markets and on different modes of transportation such as coaches, airlines, trains, cruises, ferries, gondolas and so on. In other words, he helps in the real-time execution of an itinerary planned by the company that he works for.

A tour manager accompanies his guests throughout the tour and helps them discover and explore the places being visited. Gradually, the tourists start living a destination through the eyes of the tour manager. For this reason, tour managers are also referred to as the 'brand ambassadors of a destination' as they promote and sell the destinations to their guests.

A tour manager does not need a licence to operate. He may be associated with various travel companies at the same time or work in the capacity of a freelancer.

IMPORTANCE OF A TOUR MANAGER

A tour manager plays a very strategic role for a travel company. He is the face of the company and runs the entire show on the tour. He is the front-line staff of a company who directly interacts with the tourists and delivers the travel promises that the company has made to its guests. He is a vital link between the company and his guests. He is responsible for the 'moments of truth'. Being the representative of his company, a tour manager has the onus of carrying the reputation of the company. His conduct with his guests can decide the future business of his company to a great extent. If the guests return happy, they may like to travel with the same company in the future. Guests may also spread a positive word of mouth to others which may mean business for the tour operator/travel agent.

From a company's perspective, a tour manager is like the glue which keeps the group of guests together. Besides this, he facilitates the company's guests with their travel arrangements and assists them in making decisions during the tour. The objective of hiring tour managers for travel companies is to ensure that guests have a holiday of their lifetime with the services of a tour manager available for the guests throughout the tour. Through the services provided by the tour manager on the tour to his guests, the company ensures that everything on the trip goes pleasant and trouble free for the guests as well as the company.

For the guests, a tour manager plays a crucial role on the tour. They look forward to his directions for doing things. For them, a tour manager is a torchlight who lights the way for them. Now let us have a detailed discussion as to why tourists prefer to hire the services of a tour manager during their holiday.

A HASSLE-FREE HOLIDAY

Some tourists are not comfortable venturing on their own. They do not favour wasting their precious time hunting for places, hotels, local restaurants and local markets. They do not want to bother themselves at every point, struggling to figure out which sites to see, where to eat, where to shop, where to stay and so on. Therefore, guided or escorted vacations are taken by such guests to have a hassle-free holiday as they have a person, that is, the tour manager, who manages the whole show for them. The logistics may have been pre-arranged by the operations department of the company. However, a tour manager ensures that there is no difference between the cup and the lip, that is, what has been precisely promised to the client initially while booking the tour is actually delivered during the trip. This will allow the guests to just sit back and relax during their vacation, and not unnecessarily get bothered in fixing arrangements for their travel.

LOCAL EXPERTISE

Guidebooks may not always be great help for the guests. Sometimes, tourists want to know and explore the destination better. For that, the services of a knowledgeable tour manager, who has the local expertise, are required.

SAFETY AND SECURITY

There is always a fear of the unknown when the tourist travels to a destination for the first time. The tourist needs a person who can help him conquer that fear. A tour manager bridges the gap between the known and the unknown. The fear of being lost in a strange place is the driving force for tourists to take the services of a tour manager.

ACCESS TO HOST COMMUNITY

The tourist is often interested to know about the local life at the destination. Beyond gazing, they are genuinely interested in 'feeling' the life at that destination. However, they may not have direct access to the local community. A tour manager is a link who connects the tourists to the life of locals. He introduces the guests to the experience at the destination and helps them unfold new perspectives of a destination.

PLEASURE OF BEING TAKEN CARE OF

A tour manager is the caretaker of his guests. He takes care of every need of his guests throughout the trip. Therefore, the tourists feel more comfortable and secure in the presence of a tour manager. They know that they are safe in the hands of an experienced person who can protect them from any difficulty that they may face on the tour.

ROLES OF A TOUR MANAGER

Based on the earlier discussion, a tour manager has certain roles to play that are discussed in brief here.

LEADER

A tour manager leads his group at every point. He guides and directs his guests. He never leaves them alone. He also takes decisions for them.

FACILITATOR

A tour manager is basically the facilitator at a destination who ensures that travel arrangements go smooth and are as enjoyable as possible for his clients. He makes the stay of tourists at a destination more comfortable and hassle-free with his presence.

CARETAKER

It is the responsibility of a tour manager to take care of the safety of his guests. As a caretaker, he may ask his guests to look after their belongings. He also ensures that the guests are taken to all places, they are provided food on time, they get adequate rest during the tour and their individual requests, if any, are met on the trip.

COMPANION

A tour manager acts as a fellow companion of his guests during the trip. The only difference is that the guests have high expectations from this mate unlike from other fellow tourists on the tour. The tour manager acts as a friend and a philosopher for his group. Like a friend, he accommodates his guests' wishes in every way he can.

TRAVEL CONSULTANT

A tour manager acts as the local consultant for a destination. He provides an insight into a destination that the guest is visiting. He advises his guests what activities to undertake at the destination during their free time, what special events to attend, what to see around, what to experience, what to eat and what to shop. He is the local guy!

LIAISON

A tour manager acts as a liaison officer amongst all service providers. The tour manager may liaison between the following:

- The company and the guests
- The local community and the guests
- The local service providers and the guests

PRESENTER

A tour manager provides instructions to his group members at every point in the destination. He helps in building a connection to the place with his guests. He provides commentary at destinations, and instructs his guests about the dos and don'ts at a destination. He must present exciting facts of a destination in the most informative, engaging and professional way.

ORGANISER

A tour manager organises everything during the tour as per the timetable given to him. He ensures that every point as promised in the itinerary is covered. Though the things may have been pre-arranged by the company, a tour manager coordinates and reconfirms with the local service providers to organise the travel arrangements on time. He ensures that rooms are ready for his guests, guests are served meals on time, they are taken to places around, they are taken for activities and so on. He knows the art of organising time minute by minute as he has to adhere to the itinerary strictly.

MODERATOR (OF EXPECTATIONS)

A tour manager must be able to handle the expectations of his guests gracefully. He should not shirk from his responsibilities. Instead, he must try to deliver more than expected so that the tourists go back home happy. He must understand the needs and wants of his guests, and clearly inform them about what he can and cannot do for them as per the guidelines of his company.

ENTERTAINER

A tour manager should also take care of the entertainment of his guests. He should make the vacations of his guests more exciting with his presence. For the entertainment of his guests, he may organise games or recommend activities that they may like to pursue during their spare time, for example, adventure activities, nightlife, shopping and so on, at a destination.

ACCOUNTANT

A tour manager must be good with numbers. He may anticipate the expenditures that he may have to incur on the trip and accordingly plan the money required during the tour. He may carry cash or keep debit/credit cards with him for making the payments towards services and optional activities organised during the trip. He must also keep his documentation updated, that is, have a proper record of all the bills and receipts received during the trip for the services taken for the clients. These bills and receipts are required to be submitted later to the travel company on the completion of the tour.

TROUBLESHOOTER/GRIEVANCE HANDLER

For the guests, a tour manager acts as a single window clearance system to all their problems. A tour manager is a troubleshooter for the guests on the tour who takes away all their worries by giving them solutions for the difficulties they may come across. For every grievance, they approach a tour manager. Seemingly, for many guests, a tour manager is a crucial psychological support.

SALESPERSON

A tour manager may act as a salesperson for his company as he may promote the other related travel products of his company such as related tours or other domestic and international packages through brochures and relevant literature. He may also be selling the optional excursions on a tour to his guests that may not have been included in the package.

CRISIS MANAGER

A tour manager may have to deal with unforeseen circumstances. He should, therefore, be prepared to deal with any kind of emergency situation that may come on the tour.

SUMMARY

For travellers to an unfamiliar place, a tour manager is a crucial omnipresent support made available to them by the tour company throughout the trip. He is the one who organises everything on a tour at the right time and at the right place. To be able to do this, a tour manager has to don different hats: leader, facilitator, caretaker, companion, presenter of the place, organiser, liaison officer, moderator, accountant, consultant, entertainer, troubleshooter, crisis manager and so on.

Activity 1 Visit an attraction

Visit an attraction of your choice in your city. Try to figure out a group of tourists who are being led by a tour manager. Ask any five tourists in the group individually the advantage of hiring a tour manager. If possible, record videos or take pictures with the guests. Now prepare a presentation of 10 minutes to be given in the classroom on the advantages of hiring a tour manager from the tourists' perspective based on the interaction you had with them. You may also document the same in the form of a report and submit it to the teacher.

Activity 2 **Interview top management**

Divide yourself into groups of five each. However, the composition may vary depending upon the strength of the class. Each group may plan a visit to three travel companies in their vicinity that organise group package tours for vacationers. Try to meet the top management of the companies and understand the roles of a tour manager through the information you get straight from the horse's mouth. Ask them the modus operandi of hiring these tour managers and the challenges faced by the company staff while dealing with tour managers. Also, try to identify if the tour managers are invited as freelancers based on contracts or the companies send the employees as tour managers during group tours. You may also try to understand the kinds of specialised tours and destination tours organised by these companies.

POSSIBLE SOLUTIONS TO THE OPENING VIGNETTE

- As the coach was moving fast, they did not have much time to take a decision. Immediately, both of them decided that the only way to stop the vehicle was to hit the co-pilot side of the coach with the median at an angle to break the speed and eventually stop the vehicle. This action of hitting the median to stop the coach will not only reduce the hitting impact on the coach but also result in minimum injuries to the passengers on board. Taking anything head on to stop the coach would definitely result in more serious injuries or maybe casualties.
- Shivaay immediately apprised his group about the situation and prepared his guests to be mentally prepared to hit the divider that may give them minor bruises instead of facing a major accident while on the road that may even kill them.
- He however asked his guests not to panic and to maintain their cool.
- Immediately, on being hit, first aid was provided by Shivaay to his guests.
- However, the real catch was that the group had a flight to catch early morning at 2 AM.
- Shivaay immediately called his company and apprised them of the situation. However, the company expressed its inability to arrange for an alternative coach at such a short notice, especially it being a Sunday night and also when there was hardly any time for the group to reach Delhi and catch their flight.
- To play safe, Shivaay explained the whole situation to his group members and the pilot of the coach, Shyam. He apprised them that the alternative coach may not be able to reach within the stipulated time and his guests might end up missing their international flights.
- Nobody wanted to miss on their flights. Ultimately, everyone mutually agreed to continue on the same coach till Delhi taking a risk. However, Shyam ensured safety of everyone and said that he would drive very slowly till they reached the hotel. He ensured his full support to Shivaay and everyone.
- Shivaay also reassured his guests about their safety and said that the safety of his guests was his top priority.
- The scary journey came to an end as everyone was driven safely to the hotel.

- Eventually, another coach was arranged in the hotel that transported the guests from the hotel to the airport. All were finally able to reach the airport on time.

Lessons Learned

- A tour manager must be able to take on-the-spot decisions.
- From the given situation, it is clear that sometimes a calculated risk has to be taken to avoid a bigger catastrophe.
- However, a tour manager must carry out a risk assessment prior to taking a risky decision. In such unfavourable conditions, a tour manager must be prompt to analyse the situation and act accordingly. His right and corrective action in such situations can save the life of his guests.

2

What Is a Tour Manager's Job?

LEARNING OBJECTIVES

- What is the life of a tour manager's profession?
- What are typical aspects of this job that one must consider before opting for this as a profession?

Ayush was sitting with his guest after the dinner in the hotel at Jaisalmer. This time he was dealing with a group of American clients. While Ayush was chit chatting with his guests, one of the hotel staff rushed hurriedly to Ayush and informed him that Siya, one of the female guest of the group, was running and screaming nude in the swimming pool area of the hotel.

Every profession has some strings attached to it. As every coin has two sides, the job of a tour manager also has both pros and cons. While opting for this profession as a career, one must be very clear at the very outset as to what is the nature of this job and whether one can meet its requirements or not.

Let us have an elaborate discussion on each of the salient characteristics of this profession that are discussed in brief here.

FREELANCING

A tour manager's job may be described as a freelancing job. A tour manager may associate himself with different travel companies and work on a contractual basis with them. Alternatively, he may commit to a particular company. He may work for international corporations, domestic companies or special interest tour operators.

Besides working for travel companies, he may also take up individual assignments for the tourism authorities like handling a group of delegates or FITs depending on his personal rapport with the tourism authorities.

A tour manager may also be self-employed. Nowadays, this is the new trend. Many new start-ups/travel apps have been started by young travel enthusiasts who have a hang of destinations. These tour managers organise private tours for the groups on their own without being associated with any company. They may themselves liaison with all the local suppliers of a destination and offer independent tour packages to the travellers. When the travellers book their travel arrangements with the tour manager, he may lead the group through the destinations. The package may be offered for short haul destinations or multiple destinations.

SPECIALISATION

While choosing to join this profession, a tour manager may opt to work for outbound, inbound or domestic tour operators/travel agents. If he wants to serve his countrymen within his country, he may work for a domestic travel company. If he has an interest in other cultures and likes interacting with foreigners, he may become an inbound manager and contribute to the tourism in his country's economy. If he has a lure for travelling overseas with his nationals, he may choose to become an outbound tour manager.

Likewise, he may also choose his area of specialisation in which he wants to lead the groups. He may become a tour manager for leisure tours, business tours, nature-based tours, food tours, heritage tours, wine tours, wildlife tours, mountain excursions, museum tours or any other special interest tours.

YOU ARE YOUR OWN BOSS!

Every tour operator/travel company has its own regulatory framework within which a tour manager must operate. There would always be a code of conduct set by the company that a tour manager is expected to follow. Every travel company would also have reporting relationships where the tour manager must report to and follow the set protocol of the organisation he works for.

A tour manager is expected to follow the fixed itinerary assigned to him by the company. In case of any the unforeseen situations, a tour manager may have to take decisions that he must report to his company, and he may also seek their opinion before proceeding for any corrective action when required.

In spite of all the precincts mentioned above that constrain a tour manager's movement, he still enjoys autonomy in his job to a reasonable extent. Compared to any other profession, where one has to work under close supervision, this role promises least intervention by the company unless and until it is really required. This profession allows a tour manager to be on his own. No one is continuously poking in his job or keeping track of him. He does not have to work under any constant supervision or under someone. He does not have to seek any continuous guidance or instructions from anyone, or report continuously about his every move to anyone. He does not have someone bossing him at the top of his head as his boss may be miles away, which is a tremendous psychological relief. Therefore, this profession gives him enough autonomy.

While on a tour, he is expected to manage things on his own. He is supposed to make decisions, find solutions and deal with situations on his own unless he really sees himself stuck and needs the assistance of his company staff.

With the passage of time, when he becomes a senior tour manager, his negotiation power may increase. He may be able to dictate his terms and working conditions to an extent to the company he works for. This may be a significant advantage in this profession.

THRILLING JOB

A tour manager can have some of the most intense, exciting, risky and remote experiences of his life in his job. Every day can be a bundle of joy for him. Every day has something new to offer! Welcome to an Indiana Jones Adventure! You may be on a jungle safari or tasting the sumptuous local delicacy of a country on a cultural tour; visiting the snow-capped mountains of Switzerland or hiking the hills; visiting a vineyard in Melbourne or going on a gondola ride at Venice; watching a whale show at SeaWorld, Los Angeles or going for a cruise with your group members! That is how life would be for you—thrilling and exciting!

SEASONAL JOB

The seasonality of this occupation may be considered as both an advantage and a disadvantage. A tour manager's job is entirely dependent upon the number of people travelling to a destination. The peak season for any tour manager is when there is a maximum number of tourists visiting that destination. Generally, the peak season of a destination is when the weather is congenial for the tourists to travel to that destination. Many destinations that enjoy pleasant temperatures year round have tourist footfalls throughout the year. However, even if the temperature of a destination is not welcoming, many destinations still position and sell themselves as year round destinations by associating themselves with different tourism products during different seasons of the year.

Taking India as an example, the season for inbound tourists (foreigners) is generally from October to March when the outdoor temperature is congenial for tourists. Hence, October to March is the super busy time for inbound tour managers in India when they may have to take up back-to-back trips due to the massive tourist traffic in the country.

However, some foreign tourists also visit India during summers. The main reason for foreigners visiting India during summers is that it is an off-season time for the tourists. Therefore, the rates of the packages are quite cheap, which may be affordable for backpackers who wish to visit India besides seeing the summers as they may not experience it in their country due to the kind of topography that exists there. However, inbound tour managers may report less volume of work during summers as compared to the season time.

As compared to inbound tourism, domestic tourism in India is around the year. Notably, during summers, from May to July, when children have summer breaks, many Indian families plan their trips mostly to hill stations of India to evade the scorching heat. Therefore, a tour manager may have work around the year if he is working as a domestic tour manager. Similarly, business tours at local locations take place throughout the year, which is a perennial source of business for the tour managers working for MICE domestic tour operators.

However, it may be mentioned here that many inbound managers who wish to work throughout the year may also work for domestic tour operators during their lean inbound tourist season.

Therefore, a tour manager may work for only 6 months while some may choose to work for 7–9 months, and still some may work round the year depending on their personal choice and willingness to work.

The good part about the seasonality is that a tour manager has to work only for a limited period of time. In other words, he has months of leisure time. He is, therefore, mentally relaxed to pursue other things during his free time. During the off season, he may choose just to sit back home and spend quality time with his family or pursue another job for some time. Alternatively, he may pursue any of his passions or may else choose to go on a vacation.

FLEXIBILITY

A tour manager has the liberty to decide when he wants to work. Though he is constrained by the peak season of work, still this job allows him enough flexibility to determine the work timings. Since the tour manager enters into a contract with different companies, he has the choice to choose when he wishes to work. When he feels unwell or overstressed, he may decline the assignments. This liberty empowers him. There are hardly any such professions where you can afford to choose your work timings. However, the disadvantage is that if you are not working, you are losing on money.

LUCRATIVE JOB

Being a tour manager, one can make a fortune. A smart tour manager may make money at every point. This profession is gratifying as far as the salaries and perks are concerned. There may be multiple sources of earnings.

A tour manager gets paid on a daily basis for the number of days he operates a tour. He receives the daily wages, also referred to as a tour manager's allowance, that may vary from company to company and work experience that he has in the field of leading. As a general practice, senior tour managers are paid better as compared to freshers. Besides the tour manager's allowance, he earns a significant portion of his income from commissions. He may charge a commission at different points of the tour. Generally, the tour managers have a fixed commission structure with the local suppliers that they are in touch with that the company may not have arranged. A tour manager may have a commission at local restaurants where he takes his guests for eating. He may have commissions with various other suppliers where he may offer his guests optional activities or excursions. While taking a group for activities such as hot air balloon rides in Jaisalmer, river rafting or any other water sports, a boat ride in Varanasi, an elephant ride at a fort in Jaipur, a prayer ceremony in Badrinath in India, a casino in Las Vegas or a show, for example, the Lido show in Paris, tour managers may have a fixed percentage of commission on every activity that they offer to tourists.

A significant portion of a tour manager's income comes from the shopping done by his guests at the shops he may take his guests to. Commissions are a vicious racket of the tourism industry. In some countries, by law or by practise, this practice of commissions is despised. However, in many parts of the world, this is still a common practice.

A tour manager during the tour may take his guests shopping as this is one of the most desirable activities asked by the guests. In some cases, a tour manager may leave them for shopping in the local markets and ask them to meet him after a specific time. In such cases, the guests shop on their own, and the tour manager does not earn any commission. However, he may recommend certain shops to his guests if he does not go with his guests inside the store. In such cases, he may or may not have a prior fixed percentage of commissions on the shopping done by his guests. Alternatively, a tour manager may take his guests to the shops either fixed by his company or by him where he has a set commission structure on the amount of shopping done by his guests. The shopping commission may again vary from country to country and person to person. It may go up to 40–45 per cent in some countries, which is quite a considerable amount for a tour manager. However, he may have to share his commission with a local tour guide and the tour driver who have comparatively fewer shares compared to the tour manager. In other cases where the shops have been fixed by the company, the commission may be shared with the company too.

Besides these sources, a tour manager may make money through gratuities too. In many countries, it is a common practice to give tips to the tour manager. Some guests may be very generous in giving tips if they are happy with the services offered by the tour manager, which may mean a lot of income for the tour manager.

Besides the monetary rewards, a tour manager may get many fringe benefits from the company he works for. He may get mobile phones or mobile bill reimbursements, laptops, a daily allowance, bonuses, uniforms and so on depending on the policy of the company he is working for. Everything from travelling, boarding and lodging to excursions and entrance to various attractions during the tour is complimentary for the tour manager. Many travel companies also offer discounted travel to the tour managers as an incentive for different domestic and international destinations that can be a big motivation for them to travel on vacations.

TRAVELLING JOB

A tour managers' job is not a desk job where one's whole day is spent in front of the desktop from nine to five. It is a field job. A tour manager's job involves extensive travelling. It is more about staying outdoors and exploring the world. The tour manager lives a large part of his work life with a suitcase and a rucksack moving from one place to another.

While people spend a fortune on travel, the tour manager gets to travel the world on the company's money, that is, FOC. The whole trip is underwritten by the travel company that hires him.

NO OFFICE

A tour manager has no office. The world is his office as he is continuously on the move. He only has to visit his company's office when the company calls him for a new assignment, a meeting, training, informal catch-ups, a new product launch or for settlement of bills.

Since he is not working in a regular office environment and is mostly out on tours due to the nature of his job, he does not have to meet any colleagues except during the occasions mentioned earlier. Therefore, he does not have time for office politics. It saves his precious mind and time from the negative energies. Needless to say, he must still maintain cordial relations with his colleagues.

GLAMOUR

The job of a tour manager may appear very glamorous from the outside. This role promises extensive travel that may also include overseas trips depending upon the kind of tours one chooses to conduct. Mostly, the tour manager has the privilege of travelling in the best of the airlines or the other modes of transportation. They stay in some of the best hotels and other accommodations, and have some of the most exceptional dining experiences at the best restaurants. They also get to see best of the attractions around the world and watch some of the best shows at the destinations. It sounds glamorous to visit the most spectacular landscapes and man-made structures!

LONG HOURS

Before opting for this profession, one must understand that this is not like any other regular nine-to-five job. This job demands a lot of one's time and energy. One may have to remain on duty for long hours. A tour manager sometimes has to work 24×7, that is, round the clock during the trip. A tour manager, when on duty, does not have any weekends to relax. He is even required to work on weekends. In fact, when the whole world is enjoying their vacations, for example, Christmas and New Year holidays, that may be the peak season of his work. Though travelling is the best part of this profession, the same travel can become an exhausting activity too for the tour manager if he has the pressure of handling back-to-back tours without appropriate breaks in between. A tour manager must also keep a check on his physical fitness to keep up with the hectic routine of this job.

MUNDANE

A tour manager's job may get mundane after a while. He may be travelling to the same destination again and again, and repeating the same itinerary. This may get personally very boring for the tour manager. Travel may look lucrative; however, frequently travelling to the same destination may be dull and dreary.

MEETING PEOPLE

One of the most exciting parts of this profession is getting an opportunity to meet new people. On different journeys, a tour manager comes across hundreds of various kinds and types of tourists. He gets an opportunity to understand new cultures of different countries from a close range. This is a rare opportunity of its sorts.

SERVICE-ORIENTED JOB

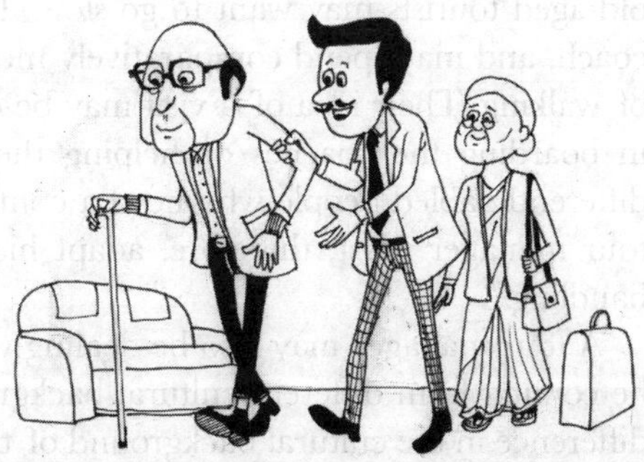

The tourism industry is a service industry. A tour manager's job is to serve the people. While opting for this profession, one must know that he is choosing a service-based career where he must have the spirit of helping others.

STRESSFUL JOB

The job of a tour manager is very demanding and taxing. Sometimes, this task can become nerve wrecking for the tour manager. A tour manager is always under continuous pressure to meet deadlines. His job is time bound. He must do everything on time and ensure that the trip is moving in a time-bound manner. In other words, a tour manager has to follow the set timetable given to him by his company. He is under continuous pressure to complete the day's itinerary. The tour manager cannot afford to sit back and relax at any point in time during the tour. He cannot have the luxury of delaying things. He must ensure that he does not skip any thing mentioned in the itinerary. Otherwise the guests may complain about him.

CHALLENGING

A tour manager must be ready for unexpected situations. The job poses challenges as a tour manager is leading a group of people for whom it is an unknown territory and many of whom may not be prepared to handle these unanticipated situations. The group is vulnerable. It is a tour manager's responsibility and skill to bail out the group and himself from these awkward situations. Circumstances may vary. So does the expectations. Let us elaborate.

DIFFERENT PEOPLE

A tour manager may be dealing with different kinds of groups every time. A group may vary regarding age, gender, interests, nationality or religion. A group of students may want thrill and excitement. In that case, the tour manager may have to play the role of a teacher for the students. He may have to lead them to various fun-filled activities with subtle control. Whereas, a group of old-aged tourists may want to go slow. They may take the time to eat and to get down from the coach, and may spend comparatively more time at the attractions as they might have a slow pace of walking. Their idea of a visit may be different. He may also have to assist the old-aged tourists in boarding the coaches or helping them with their luggage. There may also be a group of differently-abled people who need a continuous assistance of the tour manager during the trip. A tour manager must, therefore, adapt his behaviour according to the profile of the guests he is handling.

A tour manager may also be dealing with travellers from various parts of the world. They may be coming from different cultural backgrounds. Sometimes, a challenge is thrown because of the difference in the cultural background of the visitors. There may be a mixed group. It is not easy for the tour manager to cope with people from different cultures at the same time. Therefore, it becomes very challenging for the tour manager to carry everyone in the same direction despite their distinct cultural differences. However, this can be exciting for him as well.

Sometimes the tour manager may have to deal with demanding tourists. Some tourists may always be in a grumbling and cranky mode, while some may be laughing for no reasons. A tour manager must be able to deal with such people.

VARIETY OF SITUATIONS

Sometimes there may be situations beyond the control of the tour manager. It may be in the rain, scorching heat or chilling winter that he needs to operate the given itinerary outdoors. A tour manager may have to lead his group in 45 degree temperature or on a bewitching snowy day. Sometimes, due to natural calamities at a destination, the itinerary cannot be completed as promised. For example, in the case of sudden floods at a destination, a cruise cannot be offered, while the same had been promised to the client. However, a tour manager must organise a substitute for his client so that the guest does not feel that he has not got value for his money.

There may be some bizarre situations. A client may lose his passport or may get food poisoned on the tour. Yet another client may miss out on his flight. A tour manager has to make all the necessary arrangements in such situations. Sometimes a tour manager may himself not be in the best of health. He may be quiet ill. He may still have to carry the tour. In all such situations, a tour manager must face the inevitable realities with a bold face and without getting anxious.

VARIETY OF EXPECTATIONS

When the tourists travel on escorted vacations, they have a high level of expectations from the tour manager. In fact, everyone in the group might have a different expectation from the tour manager. Therefore, for the tour manager, it is not easy to please everyone. As they say 'one may please some people all of the time and all people some of the time, but one cannot please all people all of the time'. Also, not only is the tour manager expected to handle the expectations of tourists but he also has to coordinate with other suppliers during the tour and keep his office informed as well. Therefore, a tour manager is under continuous pressure to manage the expectations of multiple stakeholders at the same time. This may put him under considerable pressure.

ON A RADAR

A tour manager is always under a continuous scanner of his guests. All eyes are continually on the tour manager. People may frame strong opinions about him. They would always be judgemental about him. The tour manager is accountable to his guests all the time. This constant 'under-observation' might cause considerable stress to him.

MULTITASKING

A tour managers' job demands him to manage multiple things at the same time. He may be required to do the coordination, liaison and take care of his guests at the same while also managing to answer their questions besides keeping his office in the loop. This makes his job challenging too!

All these situations reflect how challenging this profession is.

AWAY FROM HOME

The most challenging part of a tour manager's job is to stay away from his family. A tour manager has a difficult family time. He has to sacrifice his family life to be on duty. The call of his duty is his first priority. He may have to remain away from his family for months. The commitment to the client stands supreme when he is on duty. When his family needs him, he may not be there to support them during his duty time. He may also miss out on important family occasions that may fall during the tour. As a result, his family life may suffer.

SOCIAL LIFE

The life of a tour manager is not a bed of roses. It has thorns too. A tour manager cannot afford to have a very active social life. There are times when he is away for months and not in touch with his relatives and friends. Long-term relationships are not easy to maintain. Sometimes, out of sight may mean out of mind. He may not be able to show up on social gatherings, such as birthdays, anniversaries, weddings and so on of his near and dear ones, as he may be on tours during that time. He may not be able to 'fit in' as a result of lost contacts for a long time. As a result, his social life may go for a toss. Therefore, striking a balance between the personal and professional life can be personally very challenging for a tour manager.

BABYSITTER JOB

A tour manager's role is that of a babysitter. Like the babysitter, who takes care of and nurtures the baby with the utmost attention, a tour manager must look after every need of his guests. He must feed them, bring them to different places and assist them in every possible way that he can.

SUMMARY

A tour manager is a journey mentor of the tour. The job of a tour manager offers a world of opportunities. However, it is worth mentioning here that it is also not a cakewalk. It has its own share of highs and lows. Though this profession promises goodies such as money, glamour, extensive travelling, thrill, flexibility, autonomy, meeting new people and a decent lifestyle, it can get very taxing and demanding for the tour manager. One must not forget to appreciate the hard work and dedication of this person who goes in making a tour successful for his guests.

Activity 1 Interview three tour managers

Interview any three tour managers from three different travel companies. Prepare a set of questions in the form of a questionnaire. You may also use open-ended questions to solicit maximum possible information. Ask the tour managers what kind of challenges they face in this profession? What are the advantages and disadvantages of being in this profession? You may document the same in your own words and submit a report of the interviews taken along with the visiting cards of the tour managers. Through the three interviews taken, you may highlight the common features of the profession observed in all the interviews along with any special feature spoken by an interviewee about the profession.

Activity 2 **Why do you want to be a tour manager?**

Divide the class into groups of four–five members each and give 15 minutes to each group for a group discussion on the reasons as to why they want to become a tour manager? Also highlight the apprehensions that the group members may feel being in this profession. Now take a chart and divide it into two columns highlighting the mentioned points. Take another 15 minutes to jot down the points on the chart. Make the chart as attractive as possible. This may be followed by a 10 minutes presentation of the chart followed by a question-answer round from the audience where the group may try to defend its members.

POSSIBLE SOLUTIONS TO THE OPENING VIGNETTE

- On learning about the situation, Ayush immediately asked the hotel staff to arrange for female hotel staff to control the lady since, if he had interfered personally, Siya could have filed a molestation case against Ayush. Therefore, Ayush decided to play safe.
- Immediately, the hotel staff rushed to the swimming pool and took her out of the pool, patted her dry and covered her with a blanket. They assessed that she was not behaving normally.
- The same was informed to Ayush. On learning this, Ayush immediately thought of seeking the doctor's advice. The doctor came and diagnosed her. The doctor confirmed that lady was suffering from mental imbalance and therefore gave her immediate medication that was needed at that point of time.
- However, to safeguard himself, Ayush took a letter signed by every individual in the group that they were the witnesses of the incident.
- Ayush also apprised his company later about the whole incident.
- Ayush decided to continue with the itinerary. However, he made it a point to give special attention to Siya so as to prevent any further incidents in the future.

Lessons Learned

- A tour manager's profession is very challenging. A tour manager may not know what challenges he may have to face next.
- Gender sensitisation for a tour manager is a must. While dealing with women travellers, a tour manager should be extra cautious.

3

Skill Sets for a Tour Manager

LEARNING OBJECTIVES

- What are the qualities that a tour manager must possess?
- What makes a good tour manager?

The year was 2014. Kiev, a 22-year-old boy from England, was on a trip to India along with other members of a group. He, along with the group, was travelling in the state of Uttar Pradesh in India. More specifically the group was travelling from Lucknow to Shravasti, which is an almost five-hour drive. Abhay was their tour manager.

Everything was normal. The coach was moving and half of the members were in deep slumber. Suddenly, the winds started moving forcefully. The whole city was badly hit by the storm Hud-hud. After contacting his other colleagues who were also travelling in the same area, he got to know that almost all roads to the city were blocked due to fallen trees. Though there was a fear of the weather in the mind of Abhay, he still did not show it to his guests and tried to maintain his cool and take care of his guests while on their way to Shravasti.

On assessing the situation, Abhay decided to stop the coach and park it in an open safe area where there would be less effect of the storm. As the coach was approaching a safe place, suddenly, Kiev got up from his seat and rushed to the front door, perhaps to have a better gaze of the storm. Before Abhay could just make sense of what Kiev was trying to do, suddenly a tree fell on the rear-view mirror of the coach and then on Kiev's left shoulder, and he was severely injured. Kiev and everyone else were shocked. Kiev started shouting and crying due to the sudden pain, and, as his entire left part of the body got numb, he could not move. Everybody panicked too! Abhay had a crisis situation at hand. But he had skills to handle that.

Every profession requires a specific set of skills, knowledge and abilities (SKAs) to perform that job effectively and efficiently. Some capabilities may be inherent in a person, while some skills and knowledge may be acquired over a passage of time as the individual becomes more and more experienced in his job.

Tour leading is not a rocket science. Simply put, it is the ability of a person to accompany his guests on the tour and take care of their requirements. Though it may sound effortless, leading and attending the guests could be difficult as the tour manager may have to deal with different people and uncertain situations that may become very challenging for him.

Let us now have a detailed discussion on each of the required SKAs needed to become a successful tour manager.

SKILLS

Skills may be the qualities that may be acquired through right training and practice. The more a tour manager practises, the more skilful he becomes. We have listed down some of skills that a tour manager may learn and develop practising this profession is as follows.

TRAVELLING

A tour manager must have a bug for travelling. Travelling must excite him. Most of the time, the tour manager would be on his toes moving from one place to another. There are instances when a tour manager who is accompanying a group returns home, and, within a few hours, he must start again for the next group. Therefore, a tour manager must have a passion for travelling.

LEADERSHIP QUALITY

Right from the beginning of the tour, a tour manager becomes the cynosure of everyone's eye. Every guest looks to him for directions and guidance during the trip. Therefore, as a leader, a tour manager should be able to guide his guests by giving them proper instructions at every point. He should always be in control of his group.

GOOD STORYTELLER

A tour manager must love his city/country. He must be able to present his country in the best light. He should be very passionate about showcasing the culture and heritage of his country by reciting exciting stories and anecdotes in the most engaging way. His love for his city/country should be reflected in his tone and his choice of words.

ORATOR

A tour manager gets paid for speaking. He must, therefore, be an excellent public speaker. He must be able to address his guests with conviction and confidence. There must be clarity in his thoughts and his tone. He must know what he is talking about, and must make sense at all times.

TONE

A tour manager must keep a check on his tone. He must be clear, audible and not too fast or too slow in his pace. He must speak loudly and clearly. He must not also sound rude or impolite.

SEASONED PROFESSIONAL

A tour manager must have a professional approach. He must not get personal with his clients. He must remain dignified at all the times and conduct himself properly and with grace.

RESPONSIBLE

A tour manager must act responsibly towards his duty. He must behave responsibly towards his guests, his company, his suppliers, the government, the local community, the environment and the destination. He must understand that he has a crucial role to play in promoting a destination. He must also sensitise his guests towards the climate of the destination.

INTERPERSONAL SKILLS

A tour manager must be people person. His job involves extensive interaction with the client. He, therefore, must like meeting new people and get along with people. He must be genuinely interested in interacting with new people. He must have excellent interpersonal or PR (public relations) skills to strike a good rapport with his guests. He must be polite and courteous in his approach towards his guests and the local vendors.

COMMUNICATION SKILLS

A tour manager must have the right skills to communicate with his clients, the company and local suppliers. He must be fluent in the language and must use a good choice of words. He should have the clarity of thought and be able to communicate the same to his guests in the clearest and most audible way.

LISTENING SKILLS

Listening wins more friends than speaking. A tour manager must, therefore, have excellent listening skills. He should not only be a good speaker but a good listener too. He may have to listen to endless complaints and questions of his clients on the tour. He must, therefore, develop the patience to listen.

MANAGEMENT SKILLS

Managing guests is an art. It is essential for a tour manager to be good at managing things and people. A tour manager must be able to manage different people and different situations at the same time.

DECISION-MAKING SKILLS

A tour manager must have a rational and a calculative approach for taking decisions that he might have to make during the tour. His choices can have an enormous impact on the group. Sometimes, one decision can save the life of his guests. A tour manager must, therefore, weigh the pros and cons of alternatives available to him, and accordingly take the right decision in the light of the circumstances and to the best of his knowledge. He may at times also seek the opinion of his clients for arriving at individual decisions that may require the cooperation of his guests.

For example, a route might be closed for a particular attraction. Now the tour manager may have two choices. He may take an alternative route to reach the same attraction or cover another attraction meanwhile on the way to save time. Therefore, a tour manager must evaluate the given alternatives and then act accordingly.

TIME MANAGEMENT

Managing time is an art. A tour manager must be good at this art. A tour manager must be able to utilise his every minute judiciously. He must ensure that everything is covered as per the timetable given to him in the itinerary. Even if he is running behind his schedule due to any reason, he must try to catch up with the itinerary set for the day. Prior planning for the day and keeping the guests informed in advance always help to manage time more efficiently. To achieve what is planned in the itinerary and be on time, he must also coordinate with various suppliers (e.g., the local transporter, restaurant or others) and concerned persons (museum staff, tour guides or others) before departing for the tour.

PUNCTUAL

A tour manager must understand the value of time. He must respect time. He must always reach before his guests. He should always be punctual while on duty.

MULTILINGUAL

A tour manager must be able to speak the language of his guests as well as have command over his own language. Knowing more than one language increases the scope of his job. Therefore, a tour manager must be conversant in more than one language. Things become much more comfortable for him when he travels to another country and speaks the language of the local inhabitants.

CROSS-CULTURE COMPETENCE

A tour manager must not only have the knowledge of his own country's culture but should also learn about the other cultures of different countries and regions. This skill can be acquired after taking some tours. Before taking up any group, a tour manager must learn about the nationalities of his guests and must do enough research about their cultures. He must know how people of different nationalities and cultures behave. A tour manager must thoroughly learn about the local sensitivities of his guests' culture and take every care not to make any gestures that might offend his guests. He must be able to handle cross-cultural differences in a graceful way.

GENDER SENSITISATION

A tour manager must understand the difference in handling different genders. He should be able to differentiate the needs of one gender from another. The requirements of lady clients may be different from those of male clients. Sometimes he may be leading a group of lesbians, gays or transgenders. Therefore, he must respect every guest and be sensitive towards their needs.

KNOWLEDGE

It is said that 'knowledge is power'. The right knowledge empowers a tour manager as he feels more confident to handle the queries raised by the clients on the tour. For the guests, the tour manager is a living Google search engine who has all the answers to their questions. Therefore, it is significant for a tour manager to acquire the right knowledge in the areas mentioned here.

KNOWLEDGE OF A DESTINATION

A tour manager must keep himself updated and gather all the possible facts and figures about the history, geography, politics, culture, tourist attractions and other tourism products of a destination before he departs for the tour. He must know the social mores, culture, traditions, values, folklore, dances, fairs and festivals, religious practices, norms and regulations, and lifestyle of the locals at the destination being visited. The knowledge of a tour manager can make up for all the deficiencies during the trip.

TECHNICAL KNOW-HOW OF THE TOUR

A tour manager must prepare himself at every front. Before venturing into this profession, a tour he must gain insight into the operational aspects of managing a tour. Many things come with practise and experience only. However, a tour manager must gain knowledge as to how the tours operate and what are the various working relationships and linkages in the tourism industry. He must try to understand the intricacies and technical know-how of his job. He must gather information about the various formalities to be done before and during the trip that may include the following.

- Formalities for pre-tour preparations
- Departure and arrival formalities at airports
- Hotel formalities
- Instructions to be given at attractions
- Learning map reading
- How to deal with emergency situations
- How to handle difficult guests

Knowing the operational aspects of his job adds to his confidence.

TRICKS OF THE TRADE

Just like any other profession, even this profession has a set of tricks that a tour manager must learn to be successful in his job. A tour manager must understand the overall functioning of his job.

AWARENESS

A tour manager must be mindful of the environment around him. He must keep his eyes and ears open all the time. Before and even during the tour, he must keep himself abreast of the latest happenings in and around the destination being visited. He must know the sequence of events happening around. These help him to make informed decisions and to keep his clients informed.

ABILITIES

Abilities are the innate qualities or behaviours that exist within a person. A list of abilities to be a good tour manager is provided here.

SERVICE ORIENTED

Tourism industry is service oriented. As they say, 'Service, service, everywhere: Everyone wants to be served, but no one wants to serve'. Thus, a service-oriented approach is one of the most essential requisites to be in this profession. A tour manager must have a service attitude. He must know how to serve and take care of his guests.

DYNAMIC AND ENTHUSIASTIC

A tour manager must have a vibrant and a vivacious personality. He should always be charged and full of energy so that others try to follow him. He must exhibit high levels of energy and enthusiasm while on duty.

OUTGOING

A tour manager must be outgoing by nature. He should be a great conversationalist. He must be able to connect with his guests and break the ice within the group by striking engaging conversations with his guests so that they feel more comfortable. He must be bold and should not shy away from people or situations. In other words, he should be the 'show stopper' of his group.

PLEASING PERSONALITY

Having a pleasant personality is like the icing on the cake for a tour manager. He must be well groomed and well-dressed before presenting himself in front of the tourists. Presentation matters a lot. He must also keep a check on his body language.

It is said that 'first impressions are vital'; therefore, tourists' frame an opinion of a tour manager by seeing how he carries himself. The way a tour manager dresses and presents himself speaks a lot about him. He must work on his personal hygiene too. He must remain neat and tidy, and smell good. A tour manager must not look enervated. Instead, he should carry himself smartly and be well-dressed at all times while meeting his guests.

SOCIAL PERCEPTIVENESS

A tour manager must have the ability to understand his guests' perspective. In some situations, especially during an emergency situation such as the loss of one's passport or luggage, a client may behave unusually. A the tour manager should not get agitated on someone's behaviour; rather, he must put himself in the shoes of his guests and try to empathise with them. Instead of framing a low opinion about his guests, a tour manager must seek to understand as to why his guests are behaving in such a manner. He must develop social perceptiveness.

ENGAGING

A tour manager must be very charming in his approach. He must find out new ways to engage his guests in different ways. He may engage his guests' by asking them questions, taking up questions, encouraging discussions and talks, involving them in games, movies and songs and so on.

TACTFUL

A tour manager may have to act diplomatically at times. He must be able to handle people and situations tactfully. He must have the knack of handling problems with wit and smartness.

CONFIDENCE

A tour manager must have faith in himself. Overconfidence is wrong, but belief in oneself is always right.

HUMILITY

A tour manager must be humble in his approach. Arrogance breeds enemies, not friends. Therefore, a tour manager must have a down-to-earth-approach. He should always be approachable to the guests.

GOOD OBSERVER

A tour manager must have an eye for detail. He must observe things very minutely. Nothing should escape his eyes.

POSITIVE APPROACH

Everyone has problems. The only people in the world who do not have problems are the ones who are buried in cemeteries. Everyone else has issues. Likewise, during a tour, a tour manager may have to deal with issues at every step. He might have to deal with stressful situations and endless grievances of his guests on the tour. To deal with such difficulties, he must have a positive outlook towards things. He must know how to troubleshoot problems. He must always see positive in negative and pull his guests through the issues.

PROACTIVE

A tour manager must have a nose for sensing the problems which might come his way. He must anticipate contingency situations that he might have to deal with, and he must develop an action plan in his mind as to how to handle these cases. Likewise, he must anticipate questions from his guests.

FRIENDLY

A tour manager must be amicable in his approach. He must be able to get along with his guests. However, he should not get overfriendly with his guests that they do not even listen to him.

ASSERTIVE

A tour manager must be able to put across his point assertively. He should not dictate his guests; however, he may ensure that his guests take his things seriously. He must be assertive in his approach.

FLEXIBILITY

Flexibility is the name of the game. A tour manager must be flexible in his approach. Flexibility here does not mean letting the things go off. It means that the tour manager must be accommodating at times when the situation demands him to be. In other words, he must be able to adapt himself to circumstances. He should not be rigid and conservative in his approach.

A tour manager must be able to get along with situations and people.

CALM AND POISED

A tour manager should be like a swan. A swan on water stays calm from the outside, but beneath the water, it is continuously paddling and struggling. Similarly, a tour manager on facing difficult situations should act calm from outside though there may be a storm inside him.

A tour manager may be trapped in crisis situations at times. Sometimes certain tours go seamlessly without any problems; whereas, in some tours, one may have to deal with unforeseen circumstances. However, a tour manager must be prepared for such contingency situations. There might be a fire broken out in the coach, a guest might die during the tour, there might be an argument between the group members or a medical emergency may happen. A tour manager must not panic in such situations. On the contrary, he must maintain his calm and handle the crisis in a poised manner. He should not get hyper, and should control his emotions in front of the guests.

HONEST

A tour manager must be honest in his dealings. He must have an ethical behaviour towards his duty. He must not lie to his guests. In case things have not been arranged for any reason or there is a delay in operating the itinerary due to any reason, a tour manager must openly communicate to his guests about the shortcomings and be honest to them. If he does not know the answer to a particular question, he should honestly confess his ignorance on the matter. He must restrain himself from fabricating any false stories to his guests. People like honest people!

UNPREJUDICED

A tour manager must be impartial in his approach. For him, every guest is important. He must treat everyone equally irrespective of any cultural background to which his guest may belong to.

GOOD MEMORY

A tour manager must have a sharp memory. He may have to keep track of various things that he has to do during the tour. Sometimes, he may also become a storyteller of his destination for which he may be required to learn the facts and figures related to his city/country by heart. Therefore, he must have a good memory.

HUMOUR

A tour manager must have a good sense of humour. He may amuse his guests in different ways by cracking jokes or adding humour while giving commentary. He must be able to bring a smile on the face of his guests by entertaining them in different ways.

PATIENCE

A tour manager must have loads of patience to deal with his guests. He might be dealing with different guests every time who may react to things differently. However, he must not respond. Instead, he should handle the situation calmly. He must not get ruffled when his guests ask him questions.

PHYSICAL STAMINA

A tour manager's job is very hectic and strenuous. A tour manager he has to accompany the group for days together. Sometimes he may have to do back-to-back tours. His physique should endure regular travelling.

SUMMARY

The tour manager is a critical part of the tour. He is an exemplary figure on the tour for his guests. It takes a lot to be a tour manager. Embodying the right traits and qualities to become an ideal tour manager may take a lifetime. However, to be a seasoned professional tour manager, one must continuously work on his skills and never get complacent with himself. He must train himself further and improve upon his grey areas to give a seamless and effortless travel experience to his guests with his presence.

Activity 1 **Self-assessment**

Spend 10 minutes with yourself and identify qualities that you have in yourself that makes you fit to choose this profession. What qualities you do not see in yourself as a tour manager? What will you do to develop those qualities? Share your views with the class.

Activity 2 **Review**

This activity is more appropriate for a small set-up of class. The class may be divided into group of two members each. Based on the earlier interaction that happened in the classroom, each member may be encouraged to review the qualities of the other member. The strengths and weaknesses of the member being reviewed may be conveyed to him. However, this discussion must be conducted in a healthy way that does not disparage the other group member.

In the cases where the members are not familiar with each other, the same activity may be conducted in a slightly different way. The two members may learn about each other's strengths and weaknesses. During presentation in the classroom, the two candidates may share each other's strengths and weaknesses with the other classmates.

POSSIBLE SOLUTIONS TO THE OPENING VIGNETTE

- Abhay immediately rushed for the first aid in the coach and applied the ointment on Kiev's shoulder.
- He also tried to empathise with him and reassured him that he would be taken to the nearest hospital once the situation gets better.
- Meanwhile, he also contacted his company and apprised them of the situation to keep them in the loop as they were lagging behind the scheduled arrival.
- He asked everyone on board to stay calm and to cooperate with him and wait for the situation to get normal.

Lessons Learned

- A tour manager must be able to take on-the-spot decisions as and when the situation arises.
- For the safety of the guests, he must brief his guests on the necessary guidelines that the guest may follow while in the coach.
- A tour manager must also be vigilant towards his guests while on the coach. He must keep an eye on his guests and be watchful of their moments.

SECTION B

PRE-TOUR PREPARATION

Section B of the book is an attempt by the authors to orient the readers about the preparations that are required to be made by a tour manager before he starts the tour.

This section would clarify the various aspects that have to be borne in mind by the tour manager before proceeding for the tour. It is a stepwise guide to the different documentation and homework required to be done by the tour manager while taking an assignment.

It establishes the importance of thoroughly going through the practical details of going through a group file that has been handed over to the tour manager by his company. It also reinstates the importance of acquiring knowledge of the destinations that a tour manager has to take his group to. He must familiarise himself thoroughly with the essential details of a destination so that he may be able to deal with the questions raised by his guests more confidently.

Liaising with service providers is another task that has to be performed by a tour manager before taking a group for leading. A separate chapter has been dedicated to this that discusses the various service providers with whom a tour manager should establish a connection before starting the tour.

Carrying the necessary documents is another essential aspect for a tour manager that must be taken seriously. This document may be referred to as a tour leader file or tour manager's file.

After going through this section, learners would have a clear understanding of the following pre-tour preparations that a tour manager must initiate when he is given a tour:

1. What are the things to understand about a group while going through a group file?
2. What aspects of a destination should be mastered over?
3. Why is it essential to connect with the local suppliers before taking a tour, and who are the local suppliers with whom a tour manager should establish contact before the start of the trip?
4. What does a tour manager's file contain?

So let us kick start with this section on pre-tour preparations!

Happy learning!

4

Pre-tour Preparation for a Group File

LEARNING OBJECTIVES

- What are the steps that a tour manager must follow when he is given an assignment?
- What information must he gather about his group members before he departs for the tour?

Ajay was leading a group of 10 tourists who were from different parts of India. They were all travelling to Kashmir. After having visited Srinagar, the group was all set to visit Gulmarg, known for its spectacular landscapes and also as the highest golf course of the world. It was the month of February and the weather was chilly and harsh. Everybody was excited in the coach while moving from Srinagar to Gulmarg—singing, dancing and enjoying themselves. On reaching Gulmarg, at a height of approximately 2,700 metres above sea level, a client named Rachna started feeling uneasy. Rachna started getting breathless. Ajay realised that she was travelling alone and there was no one from her family or friends on the tour with her. On realising that it could be a case of altitude sickness, Ajay enquired if she had any past medical history. To his shock, she replied that she was asthmatic and was not carrying any inhaler with her on the tour.

Conducting a smooth and a hassle-free tour is the prime responsibility of a tour manager. Every tour manager wishes that his guests return happily with smiles. However, to achieve these smiles, a tour manager has to ensure that everything goes as promised in the itinerary and as communicated to the guests. For that, a tour manager must do his homework well. A lot goes into the preparation of a tour. Preparation by the tour manager may be at different levels before the start of tour. These may include the following.

- Pre-tour preparation of a group file
- Pre-tour preparation for the destination
- Pre-tour liaising with service providers
- Pre-tour preparation for himself
- Pre-tour preparation for an airport
- Pre-tour preparation for a hotel
- Pre-tour preparation for sightseeing attractions

A detailed discussion on each of the preparations to be done by the tour manager before the start of a tour has been done separately in the subsequent chapters. In this chapter, we shall have a general discussion on the other preparations required to be done by the tour manager before departing for a tour. We shall have a discussion on the preparations to be done for a group file by the tour manager before the departure of the group.

INTRODUCTION

A tour manager may work as a freelancer for a tour operator/travel agent. He may choose to work for one company or for different companies. Generally, when a tour is confirmed, the tour operator/travel agent apprises the tour manager about the assignment that he may be required to undertake. A tour manager may be informed a month before or even earlier about the schedule of the group arrivals. There may also be times when last-minute information is given to the tour manager about a group assignment on account of another tour manager not turning up due to an emergency situation that requires an immediate replacement. However, such circumstances are quite rare. Generally, the tour managers are given the schedules well on time. Usually, rosters that reflect the tours assigned to a particular tour manager are rolled out quite ahead of time.

Now the real work of a tour manager starts when he is given the schedules of his assignment. On being informed about the assigned dates of group arrival, he may begin doing his preliminary research about the group and the itinerary that he is expected to deliver.

It is essential for a tour manager to thoroughly go through the group file that he has been assigned with. The tour operator/travel agent may give him a paper file which contains the necessary details of the clients as well as the itinerary to be followed. However, many companies in today's scenario have converted themselves into paperless offices as they use technical interfaces for dealing with tour managers. These tour operators/travel agents have online portals where every tour manager is given a particular login id. When he enters the login ID, he may have access to the details of the tours on which he has been booked for. Every trip may be given an ID that may be separate from other trip IDs. On clicking on a particular ID link, a tour manager can have a full view of the details of the tour that he has been booked on.

A tour manager may prepare himself on two fronts. He may gather all the necessary information about the trip as well learn about the profile of the group. Following is a detailed discussion on each of these.

TRIP DETAILS

Before taking up an assignment, a tour manager must have a complete idea of the whereabouts of the trip. He may learn about the details about the trip that includes the elements mentioned in the subsequent subsections.

TRIP CODE

A company may operate multiple tours. Sometimes, there may be simultaneous departures. A trip may be assigned a particular code by the tour operator/travel agent to identify and differentiate it from other trips/packages being offered by the company. A tour manager must know his trip code, and, after logging in the online portal, he may view the detailed profile of his clients after entering the trip code.

DATES OF OPERATION

A tour manager must know the exact dates of operation of the group assigned to him. He should be well aware of the departure and arrival dates of the group.

DESTINATIONS BEING COVERED

A tour manager must adequately scan through the file and know the destinations that are included in the itinerary. He must initiate his learning about these destinations.

PACKAGE DETAILS

Different guests may book different holiday packages that may vary in terms of prices. Services may vary accordingly. Therefore, a tour manager must know the package that his guests have been booked in. He should have a detailed knowledge of the 'services' that have been promised to the clients in the itinerary.

Generally, a tour package has inclusions, exclusions and extras. Usually, a package includes land arrangements that may be the accommodation, meals, local sightseeings, transfers, entry fees and so on. It is essential for a tour manager to know the services have been included in the package tour and the services which are chargeable. Generally, chargeable exclusions may consist of gratuities, porterage charges, items of personal nature such as making personal calls from the hotel or giving clothes for laundry and so on. Also, the 'extras' may be optional tours or excursions such as adventure tours or a visit to amusement parks that are chargeable. Therefore, a tour manager must keep track of the services promised, services that are excluded from the package tour and services that may be given on payment basis to the guests during the trip.

TRAVEL TIPS FOR TOUR MANAGER

Besides the aforementioned, a tour manager may be given some handy tips by the tour operator that he must abide by. It may include the guidelines, such as promoting responsible travel, not forcing the clients to shop from particular shops or forcing them to indulge in optional activities and so on, within which a tour manager must operate. The companies may share its manual with the tour manager that may have the details of the code of conduct that he is expected to follow during the tour.

GROUP PROFILE

A tour manager may gather the following information about his group's profile.

GUEST LIST

A guest list contains the list of clients' names who have been booked on a particular tour. Through the guest list, the tour manager gets an idea as to how many clients have been booked with him on a particular trip. In case he has the contact details of the clients, he may also establish a connection with them before they leave their city/country to join him on the tour.

AGE

People of different ages may require different treatment. Youngsters will need to be treated differently from elders. It is, therefore, necessary for a tour manager to know the exact composition of the number of children, teenagers, middle-aged and old-aged guests in the group.

GENDER COMPOSITION

A tour manager must also know the exact sex ratio of the group. He should know the number of males and females travelling with him on the tour.

PURPOSE OF TRAVEL

A group may be travelling to a destination for different purposes. The purpose of a group visiting a destination may vary from just visiting pilgrimage sites or heritage sites. Some groups may have come to experience the countryside, while others may have come for adventure. Still some others may have come to a place seeking for special interest tours such as photo tours, cookery tours, winery tours and so on. Therefore, clarity of purpose of the group is essential for a tour manager. This helps him plan things according to the interests of his guests.

GUEST PROFILE

A tour manager may have a broad idea of the profile of these visitors. Having an idea about the occupation of the guests may be helpful for the tour manager. Dealing with a group of doctors will be different from dealing with students or dealing with businessmen. Learning something about the profession of the guests helps a tour manager to have a topic of common discussion with his guests that may impress them too.

NATIONALITY OF GROUP

A tour manager may have a group of guests from a particular nationality or a mixed group from different nationalities. Everyone may have diverse cultural backgrounds. Even if the tour manager is handling only a specific nationality, the people may be from different regions of that country, and their culture may also vary drastically (e.g., India).

However, by and large, most of the traits of a particular nationality are similar. Knowing the nationality of guests in advance helps a tour manager to gain insights into the culture and lifestyle of such guests. He may be better placed to handle the cross-cultural differences in a graceful way if he has read about their local sensitivities well in advance before his group arrives.

RELIGIOSITY

Religion could be a sensitive issue that needs to be addressed very carefully by the tour manager. A tour manager must handle the religious sentiments of his guests carefully. Questions and comments about any religion should be avoided. Religion also decides the meal preferences of guests to an extent. For example, tourists from an Islamic community will not eat pork. Likewise, Hindus from India may not wish to eat beef. Therefore, before starting the tour, a tour manager must have a prior knowledge of the religion of his guests.

SPECIAL REQUEST

Many clients may have special requirements during the tour. Guests may be categorised as follows:

- VIPs such as bureaucrats, celebrities and so on
- Senior citizens
- People with special abilities
- Parents with toddlers
- Diabetic patients
- Vegans
- Jains (followers of Jainism religion in India who do not even eat garlic and onion)

A tour manager must understand the need of such guests and try to ensure that their needs are catered to.

MEAL PREFERENCE

The file may also contain details of the meal preferences of the guests. It is important for the tour manager to know about the meal requirement of his guests as he may have to communicate the same to airlines, hotels and restaurants before ordering the food for his guests.

LIKINGS/PREFERENCES OF THE GROUP

A tour manager must have an idea of the likings of his group. In general, he may form a perception based on their age and profile. For example, youngsters may be interested in adventure, while middle-aged and senior citizens might be interested in passive sightseeing. By going through the details of the group members, a tour manager may be able to assess the general pulse of his group members. However this may not always hold true.

LANGUAGE

A tour manager must know the language that his group members speak. In a group of guests from different nationalities, it is always advisable for a tour manager to communicate in English that is mostly understood by all across the globe. However, while handling a group of particular nationality, for example, Chinese, he may be required to speak Mandarin, their local language, if he knows the language. There would always be some group members who might not be comfortable with the language spoken by the tour manager. However, based on the language understood by the majority of guests, the tour manager should decide the language in which he will converse with the group.

SPECIAL DATES

A tour manager must confirm with his company if any birthdays and anniversaries of his group members are falling during the trip. These small occasions are moments of celebration, cohesion and merrymaking. A small gesture from the tour managers' side such as arranging for a cake and flowers goes a long way in creating a lasting impression of him and his company. These special celebrations on the tour remain forever in the hearts of the other guests as well.

MISCELLANEOUS INFORMATION

The file may have other miscellaneous information regarding the clients that may include the passport details of clients (in case of inbound/outbound tours), travel insurance details, any special remarks in case a client has taken any deviation and so on. A tour manager must also go through this miscellaneous information meticulously.

SUMMARY

In short, a tour manager is expected to thoroughly scan the group details before he departs with his group. Going through the details minutely makes the tour manager better equipped to handle the group more effectively and efficiently. He should not leave things to chance and must display utmost professionalism in dealing with his company and his guests. The group assignments are opportunities for business for him that he must not turn down due to his sheer negligence or lack of knowledge. Every assignment should be given equal importance, whether the composition of the group is small or large, whether it is for fewer days or more days, or whether it is an inbound assignment, outbound or domestic assignment. He put his heart and soul in the given task of handling the group. He must review every group file with utmost care.

Activity 1 **Email a hotel**

Write an email to a hotel confirming the hotel arrangements for your group. Also, prepare a rooming list of 15 pax booked in your tour and send the same as an attachment along with the meal preferences and special requests of the guests, if any.

Activity 2 **Roleplay**

Prepare a set-up of an office of a travel company. You have been appointed as the tour manager on behalf of the company. You visit the office and are given a group assignment of 35 pax to handle. Now, during the course of interaction with the office staff, what questions would you ask related to the group assignment? Do a mock practice of the same.

POSSIBLE SOLUTIONS TO THE OPENING VIGNETTE

- Ajay immediately took charge of the situation and asked her to take long deep breaths.
- Meanwhile, he arranged for hot coffee for her to drink as caffeinated drinks help to provide some relief.
- He tried to pacify Rachna and calm her with his words.
- He immediately informed his company about the situation.
- He also rushed his client to the nearby hospital and got her treatment started.
- Meanwhile, he asked his group to enjoy the activities arranged for them at Gulmarg.
- He also asked his company to arrange another person for Rachna who would look after her till she was fit enough to return.
- Meanwhile, Ajay proceeded for the tour with other group members.

Lessons Learned

- On being given a group assignment, as part of the pre-tour preparations, try to learn about the clients as much as possible.
- Always check the medical history of the guests, especially before visiting places at high altitude or which might be strenuous for the guests.
- Brief your guests about the risks associated while visiting a place, such as altitude sickness and sea sickness.

5

Familiarisation with a Destination

LEARNING OBJECTIVES

- What is the role of a tour manager in selling a destination?
- What are the areas of familiarisation that a tour manager should gain knowledge on before leading a tour at a destination?

Mary, a 60-year-old woman, was on a solo trip to India for 20 days. She was travelling from Chile to India to see and understand the culture of India. After visiting New Delhi, the capital of the country, she proceeded to Pushkar, a small town in Rajasthan, to attend the Pushkar Fair. She had planned to be there for 12 days. Having an interest in learning about the religions of India, she desired to attend the ceremonial aarti (a Hindu religious ritual of worship) at Pushkar.

On reaching Pushkar, the very first day she decided to attend the aarti at Brahma ghat in the evening. She went there with Rahul, the tour manager. As she was the only woman, the tour manager was leading the way. Suddenly, she slipped from the stairs and hurt herself badly. She broke into tears as the pain was immense and she felt as if she had broken her backbone. However, Rahul knew what was to be done.

A destination is at the pivot of the tourism industry. The traveller's whole experience revolves around a destination. When a tour manager is given an assignment of leading the group, he may be given an itinerary in which he has to cover only one destination, or sometimes multiple destinations are to be included as per the plan.

A destination may be a city, state or country. A tour manager may be asked to lead the group of tourists in different towns either in his own country or at international destinations.

A destination may be defined as a place of interest for the tourist typically known for its inherent or exhibited natural or cultural value, historical significance, natural or built beauty, and offering leisure, adventure and amusement.

From a tourist's perspective, a destination is the main subject of interest. When a tourist visits a destination that may be on his bucket list, he may wish to learn as much as possible about that destination during his stay. Moreover, if he is travelling to that destination for the first time, his interest may be even more. He may be inquisitive to know each and every aspect of the destination.

INTRODUCTION

A tour manager is a marketer, storyteller and spokesperson of a destination. He is the local expert of the destination. For a destination, a tour manager is the brand ambassador who gives a deeper insight of the history, geography, culture and life of a destination to its guests. In other words, through his more profound understanding of a destination, he introduces the local experience of a place to his guests.

Being on group tours, the tourist expects a tour manager to know everything about the destination that he is taking his guests to. For the guests, a tour manager is an encyclopaedia who can answer every question posed by them about the destination being visited. To satisfy the expectations of his guests and avoid feeling embarrassed, it is essential for a tour manager to be thoroughly familiarised with a destination he is travelling to with his guests. A knowledgeable and learned tour manager invites respect from his guests besides personally feeling more confident and relaxed.

Many travel companies organise familiarisation (FAM) trips trips for its tour managers so that they may get real and authentic information about the airport, hotel properties, attractions, amenities and so on at the destination. Travelling before taking a group assignment to these destinations allows the tour manager to have a hands-on experience of the destination and gain more confidence in leading the groups to the destinations. Many amateur tour managers who are venturing into this profession may also be sent as trainees along with their seniors to learn and acquire knowledge about a destination.

The earlier discussion is apparently indicative of the fact that a tour manager must thoroughly gear up himself about a destination before he takes a tour to that destination.

Now let us delve deep into each of the areas of a destination that a tour manager must have knowledge of before leading groups.

KNOWLEDGE OF WEATHER

A tour manager must have an idea of the forecast of weather of the destinations to be visited during the tour. Generally, as the clients are smart enough these days, they themselves find out the weather forecast through the Internet. Still, there are a large number of tourists who don't know how to use the Internet and are entirely dependent on the tour manager or the travel company they have booked their tour with. In many such cases, when the tour manager departs with his group from his city for another city or a country, he may have a meeting with his guests (pre-departure meeting) in the company or the hotel where he may inform his guests about the weather. Many travel companies also mention the weather details in their itineraries.

It is relevant for the guests to ask about the weather as the clothing which they have to carry shall depend on the weather of that place. It is advisable for the tour manager to have the weather forecast for the entire duration of the trip as he may suggest his guests to carry the things that they may require on the tour according to the weather. For example, in case showers are expected, he may ask his guests to keep rain gear or an umbrella with them in advance. During sunny weather, he may ask the guests to keep umbrellas and sunscreen lotions. Likewise, in winters, he may ask his guests to keep enough woollen clothing with them.

KNOWLEDGE OF TOPOGRAPHY, DEMOGRAPHY, HISTORY, GEOGRAPHY, MYTHOLOGY AND POLITICAL DYNAMICS

Every destination has its own demography. A tour manager must know about the basic facts of a destination such as its total population, religion, the occupation of people, languages spoken etc. He must also be aware of the topography, geography and local history of that destination. He must even have information about the political dynamics of the destination being visited such as the government set-up, the policies, the role of government in the city and so on. This knowledge helps him to keep his guests engaged during long journeys besides satisfying their inquisitiveness. Besides this, he must know the mythology of a place. This may hold truer for a country like India where people worship many gods and goddesses.

KNOWLEDGE OF INTERESTING FACTS

Every destination has a unique selling proposition (USP). In other words, every destination has something unique about it which sets it apart from other destinations. A tour manager must be well versed with the interesting facts about the destination being visited so that he may keep his guests engaged and maintain interest in his commentary by sharing specific startling facts and figures about that destination. Besides this, he may sound more knowledgeable to his guests and therefore command more respect from them. For example, the state of Kerala in India (God's own Country) is known for its lush greenery, backwaters, houseboats and culture. Likewise, Rishikesh in Uttarakhand, India is known as the Yoga Capital of the world. Similarly, while visiting Paris, a tour manager may introduce Paris to his guests as the Fashion Capital of the world.

KNOWLEDGE OF LOCAL'S LIFESTYLE

Many tourists have a natural inquisitiveness to know about the local culture of a destination. These tourists are eager to learn how these local inhabitants spend their daily lives, what they do during their free time, what is their livelihood and so on. A tour manager is a gateway to the life of locals at a destination. Through his understanding of the living cultures of a destination, he may be able to give a 'local feel' to his guests. He is also expected to have a thorough understanding of the local sensitivities that he may ask his guests to observe at a destination.

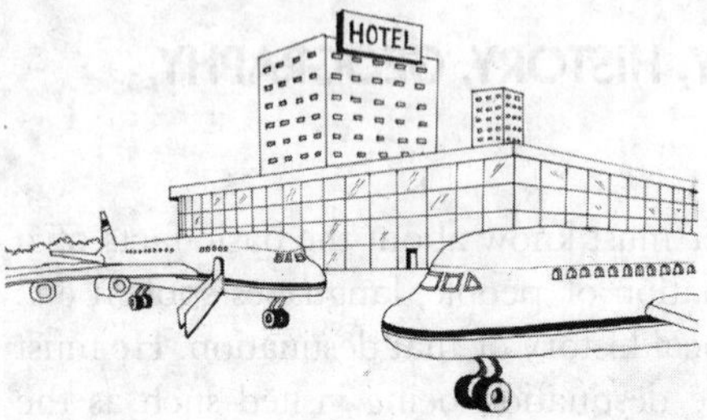

KNOWLEDGE OF SUPERSTRUCTURE

A tour manager must have a fair idea of the necessary superstructure available at a destination. He should know the number of airports (both domestic and international), railway stations, highways, hotels, convention centres, shopping malls and so on available at a destination besides the man-made attractions.

KNOWLEDGE OF AMENITIES

A tour manager must be aware of amenities at a destination. He must be mindful of the nearby ATM machines, foreign exchange counters, police stations, supermarkets, banks, ambulance facilities, Wi-Fi facilities, etc. available at the destination.

KNOWLEDGE OF POINTS OF INTEREST (PLACES TO SEE AROUND)

An itinerary may contain some sightseeing attractions. From a tour managers' perspective, it is important to have an exhaustive knowledge of each attraction before he actually travels with his group. A tour manager must know the importance of attraction, its unique features, its history, its dos and don'ts, and so on. On being given an itinerary, a tour manager may start preparing and gathering the following information about the attractions to be covered as per the itinerary:

- Approximate distance and time to reach the attraction from the hotel
- Estimated time and distances between the attractions planned for the day

- Stopovers that may be taken in case of long distances (generally, it is advisable to take rest breaks after every one to two hours in case of long journeys)
- Best routes (regarding time and traffic) for reaching an attraction
- Meeting point at the attraction
- Briefing point at the attraction
- Parking areas in or around the attraction
- Entry fee for the attraction
- Camera/video policy of the attraction
- Facilities at the attraction such as restrooms/refreshment facilities/Wi-Fi facilities
- Visiting hours of the attraction
- Closing days of the attraction

KNOWLEDGE OF ACTIVITIES

Every destination offers some promising activities for its guests. These activities are sometimes the major attractions for the guests besides other sightseeing attractions at a destination. The activities at a destination may be adventure-related, shopping, experiencing the nightlife, watching local shows and going for excursion tours such as wine tours, walking tours, heritage tours and so on.

Most of the activities are generally included in the package. However, in some packages, there may be some days when the guests are asked to be on their own. Also, sometimes guests want to venture out on their own in the late evenings after the day's itinerary gets over to maximise their idle time. They may seek advice from the tour manager as to what to do, which mode of transportation to use to reach the point of activity, how to return to the hotel from the activity point and so on. Hence, a tour manager must be able to suggest to his guests the various activities that they might undertake during their free time. Therefore, he must have the prior knowledge of 'activities' at a destination.

For example, at Amsterdam in Europe, Las Vegas in North America and Goa in India, a tour manager would recommend his group members to experience the nightlife of these destinations, visiting pubs, discotheques, cafes, watching shows, playing casinos and so on during the night time.

KNOWLEDGE OF GOVERNMENT RULES

Many destinations may have government restrictions or regulations that a tour manager must be aware of. For example, in the state of Gujarat in India, alcohol is prohibited as the state has been declared as a dry state. The same information must be passed to the guests when the tour manager travels with them. Likewise, in some places, for example, in

Singapore, chewing gum is prohibited. Therefore, a tour manager must have the knowledge of all these restrictions so that he may brief his guests about the requirements before visiting that destination so that his guests do not violate any of the rules due to their sheer ignorance.

KNOWLEDGE OF IMPORTANT EVENTS

Many destinations across the world are famous for events. Some events may be of local importance, while some may have international significance. Many destinations also use these events as a tool to showcase their culture and heritage, besides using them as a marketing tool. An event may be a festival, a fair, a business event or a ceremony like celebrating the birthday of Queen Elizabeth in London and so on.

While taking up a tour, the manager must be aware of the critical events, if any, taking place at the destination on the dates of the trip. The tourists may like to participate in these events as it may be an opportunity of a lifetime for them to attend a local festival or an event of that destination.

Even otherwise, it is essential for a tour manager to know about the dates of local events as on the day of the event, some sightseeing points may be closed or some roads may be closed. Therefore, there might be a need to divert from the known routes or make certain changes in the itinerary by the tour manager.

KNOWLEDGE OF LOCAL RESTAURANTS

Food is a significant part of the trip. Sometimes all meals may not be a part of the package tour. At times, even when all the meals may have been included in the package, many guests do not want to eat at the hotel or the restaurant pre-arranged by the company. Many guests may like to taste the local cuisine or local drinks of the destination at the local restaurants, cafes and pubs of the destination. The tour manager should be able to guide his guests to the must-visit local eating outlets and famous street food eating points, how to reach these eating points and what to try at these places.

Therefore, a tour manager must have prior knowledge of the local food outlets, and the cuisines and beverages they are famous for. A tour manager should also know the best modes of reaching these food points and even the best way of coming back to the hotel from these eating points.

KNOWLEDGE OF SUPERMARKETS

When tourists visit a destination, they may like to purchase their day-to-day requirements from nearby markets. They may want to try the local stuff such as fruits, dry fruits, drinks, spices or other things that the destination is famous for. They may also buy some day-to-day items that they may have missed while packing for the tour. Therefore, they may ask the tour manager about the whereabouts of the supermarkets nearby. Hence, to advise his guests, if the need arises, a tour manager must know the nearby supermarkets, especially around the hotel where the group is staying or also at the places where the party takes a stopover for a rest break or stops for lunch/dinner at a local restaurant.

KNOWLEDGE OF PHARMACY SHOPS/HOSPITALS

Anyone may fall ill during the tour. Some tourists might want to buy medicines for their ailments as they might not be feeling well. They may seek the help of a tour manager to learn about the nearby pharmacies/hospitals.

Therefore, a tour manager must have prior knowledge of the nearby pharmacies/hospitals at the destination in case any guests need a medical help during the trip.

KNOWLEDGE OF LOCAL PUBLIC TRANSPORTATION SYSTEM

Every destination has a public transportation system that may comprise of local buses, taxis and trains. Generally, all the local transfers are taken care by the tour company. However, sometimes the guests want to venture on their own to explore the city life. Here, they may seek the advice of the tour manager as to how to reach the places they wish to see on their own. Besides, they may otherwise also be inquisitive to learn about the public transportation system available at a destination. Hence, he must have prior knowledge of the best modes of transportation in terms of reach, time and money which the guests can use to reach from one point to another so that he can advise his guests accordingly.

A tour manager should be able to guide his guests about a number of things: which mode of transportation to use to reach a particular point; how to use that transportation system; the approximate fare for using the different modes of transportation; how to make the payments; how to recharge the travelling cards and so on. He must also familiarise himself with the map of routes of the transportation systems on which they operate. A tour manager should also acquire prior information on the distances and total time to reach the important points of interest and the hotel.

KNOWLEDGE OF LOCAL MARKETS

Shopping is one of the more exciting activities for the tourists when they visit a destination. Tourists want to take back home the best gifts from the place they visit for their friends, relatives and themselves. Every destination is known for its specific shopping items that a tourist may carry back home as a memory. These unique shopping 'must buy' things of a destination are called souvenirs.

In package tours, generally, the guests are given a specific time for shopping. When going for shopping, the tourists have many options as to what to buy and which particular shop to buy from. As the tourist might get confused, he may ask the tour manager to recommend the best places for shopping and what to shop from there as they may have a limited time of shopping. Also, the guests do not want to be duped by local shopkeepers by paying a high price for a low-quality product. Therefore, they may seek the opinion of tour manager as to what to buy, from where to buy and whether to bargain during shopping or not. However, the guests may also be aware of the commissions that the tour manager may have for the shopping done by his guests from particular shops that he may have recommended to them.

Some of the items that the tour manager suggests to his guest as a must buy from some places around the world are as follows:

- Miniatures of the Eiffel Tower from Paris, France
- Cuckoo clocks from Black Forest, Germany
- Swiss watches, bells, chocolates and different types of cheese from Switzerland
- Godiva Chocolates from Brussels, Belgium
- Crystals from Swarovski Museum, Wattens, Austria

Therefore, before travelling to the destination, a tour manager may list out the famous local shopping markets and souvenirs that he may recommend his guests to buy.

SUMMARY

Every destination carries an essence that must be put across to the tourist in the right perspective and spirit. A tour manager bears the onus of presenting a destination in the most lively and memorable manner to the tourists. He has to be such a seller of the destination that the tourists want to come back to the destination again and again. To put across the real essence of the destination and project it at is best, a tour manager must thoroughly acquaint himself with the destination at every front. He may visit the destination before the tour, talk to the destination specialists like tourism officials of the destination or merely surf on the Internet about the destination to gain maximum knowledge about the destination being visited. The bottom line is that for a successful tour, the tour manager must do the right preparation for a destination so that he is thoroughly familiar with the place. This helps setting off nervousness that allows him to deliver pleasant experiences to his guests. Right preparation can help the tour managers address random yet anticipated questions that his guests may ask about a destination.

Activity 1 The travel show

Divide the whole class into groups of seven–eight members and let them choose a destination of their choice. Alternatively, the trainer may assign them famous destinations of a country. Ask the students to organise an exciting travel talk show for their destination being aired on a television channel for a duration of about 45 minutes to 1 hour. Ensure the participation of all the group members. Be as creative as possible. You may also use props to conduct the activity. Take it as an opportunity to showcase and market your destination at its best. Seven–eight members from each group may conduct the show on the stage.

One member may become the host and the moderator of the show, who shall basically conduct the whole show. Two other members may be invited as experts of the destination. They may act as senior officials from the tourism government authorities. The other persons invited for the talk may be a food blogger, a local tour guide, a native, a tourist, a representative from the media and so on. Now, in the panel discussion, you may ask each speaker to cover the following points:

- History and USP of the destination
- Important sites and attractions of the destination including local markets
- Amenities at the destination, for example, Wi-Fi facility, if available, hospitals, foreign exchange facilities, ATMs, local police station, embassies at the destination, if any, and so on
- Important festivals of the destination
- Local lifestyle and culture of the destination that may cover the local cuisine, folklore, local dance and so on
- Local sensitivities to be observed by the tourists
- Challenges faced by the tourists
- Any suggestions to improve the destination

At the end of the discussion, the performing group is free to open the house for discussion. Ask the rest of the class to ask questions related to the destination. Declare the best group based on how successfully they have conducted the show by being creative and giving relevant content. To sustain the interest of the audience, you may also add famous commercials in between or perform a cultural dance/folklore of the destination.

To encourage real-time learning, the students may be asked to visit the destination on their own and also take interesting pictures of the destination and submit the same along with a detailed write up in the form of a written report to the teacher.

If desired, the students may also show videos of the destination being covered.

Activity 2 City talk

This activity may be practised in those classrooms that have students from different cities and states of a country. Each student may be asked to prepare a talk of 3–4 minutes where the students shall cover the various aspects of their cities including the 5A's of tourism. Ensure that the information is organised sequentially and take care of the time limits. Must tell, should tell and could tell must be taken care of. Students may be asked to learn about the current tourists arrivals in their city and share the same in the classroom. They may also share the challenges faced by the tourists in their city, if any.

POSSIBLE SOLUTIONS TO THE OPENING VIGNETTE

- The tour manager immediately tried to pacify and comfort her. He then took her to the hospital, and got her X-ray and primary treatment done.
- To get her get rid of the pain totally, he further suggested various alternative treatments such as acupressure, Ayurveda and so on. He took good care of her for 10 days until her treatment was complete.
- Eventually, on her getting fit, he also took her for the aarti that was left incomplete.
- At the end, the lady returned home with very happy memories due to the extra efforts made by the tour manager.

Lessons Learned

- A tour manager must be familiar with the destination. He must know about the nearby hospitals, doctors, pharmacies and so on at a destination in case of any exigencies.
- He must also know how to make his guests more comfortable and take care of them in case any of them requires medical attention.
- The tour manager carries an onus on his shoulders of portraying a positive image of his country. The way he treats his guests with care and attention can create a positive perception in the minds of the guests about the kind of behaviours exhibited by the nationals of the country. Thus, it is desirable for him to act as a caretaker and treat them with lot of respect and affection. This can go a long way in positioning a positive image of the country that may attract more tourists. A positive word of mouth spread by the happy tourist about the local people of a destination can bring more business to a destination.
- However, a tour manager must be cautious not to substitute as a medical expert. He/she must seek expert advice at the first instance.

6

Liaison with Local Suppliers

LEARNING OBJECTIVES

- Is it important for a tour manager to liaison with local suppliers?
- Who are the local suppliers with whom a tour manager should establish a connection with before heading for a tour?

Shravan, the tour manager of the company, was leading a group of 15 tourists who had come from Australia. There were 12 adults and 3 children in the group. The group was very happy as they were all travelling to the scenic city of the country of Nepal, that is, Kathmandu. As the group was close to the border of Nepal, the coach took a halt. There was a huge traffic jam. Even after 15 minutes, when the coach was not budging, Shravan along with the pilot got out of the coach and went to enquire about the reason for the traffic jam. He also enquired how much time it would take for the traffic jam to clear. On enquiring, he was told that a political dispute had started in Kathmandu and the local public was on a rage due to which all the border areas were sealed. Nobody was clear as to how much time it would take for the situation to get normal.

With a heavy heart, Shravan went inside the coach and updated his guests about the ongoing situation. He apprised his guests about the protest in the city and blocked access to the country. On hearing this, the group was hugely disappointed. Few minutes converted into hours, and now everybody became panicky. Children started getting cranky too as they were feeling hungry now. Shravan was distressed too!

Tour operators/travel agents offer tour packages in which various different travel components of different suppliers are bundled together as a single package. An ideal tour package may contain air/train tickets and the land arrangements that may include the accommodation component, local sightseeing, local transfers, meals, activities and other ground transportation arrangements including the services of a local guide and a tour manager. Organising these travel components for a package requires a lot of coordination with the service providers of the tourism industry.

A tour manager may be given the task of taking his guests to one destination or to multiple destinations. The more the number of destinations, the more is the volume of work for the tour manager to speak to all the local suppliers at all the destinations.

INTRODUCTION

A package tour may broadly involve two aspects—planning and execution. In a travel company, the operations department is primarily responsible for planning the tour and making back-end arrangements. However, the real implementation of a tour package is the job of a tour manager. He has to ensure that all the travel arrangements are delivered to the client as promised in the itinerary. For this a tour manager must personally liaison with the local suppliers before the commencement of the tour and during the trip. This is important for three reasons.

RECONFIRMATION OF SERVICES

First, though the travel arrangements have been already made by the tour operator/travel agent, a tour manager must speak to the service providers before the start of the tour for the reconfirmation of services. Generally, all the travel arrangements by the company are made well in advance. Sometimes, it may be months before or even a year before. Occasionally, the local supplier may be simultaneously occupied making travel arrangements for other tour operators/travel agents also. As a result, the arrival date of a group may skip from his mind. Therefore, the idea of liaison with the service providers by the tour manager is to remind the local suppliers about the arrival date of the group and also to confirm if the services have been arranged for the guests as promised to them. This timely confirmation with the local suppliers may evade many embarrassing situations the tour manager might have to face if the local supplier has not made the travel arrangement on time. He may contact them personally or email them about the expected arrival of his guests so that the suppliers are well informed in advance to welcome the group.

MAKING RESERVATIONS

Second, many travel companies may also give authority to the tour manager to make specific travel arrangements for activities such as boating, hot air ballooning, and going out to local restaurants for meals etc. For this, a tour manager may have to contact the local vendors in advance and establish a rapport with them to make advance bookings so that the guests are given services on time.

TIMELY DELIVERY OF SERVICES

Third, the liaison is quite important during the real execution of the tour. On a trip, the tour manager has to be in constant touch with the local service providers/suppliers. He is required to coordinate with these local suppliers on a daily basis and to keep them updated from time to time about the arrival of the group so that the guests do not waste their time endlessly waiting for things to happen and cause an overall delay in the decided itinerary.

Now let us have a discussion on the following local suppliers/service providers with whom the tour manager must establish prior contact to ensure the timely delivery of services.

LOCAL TRANSPORTERS

A significant amount of time of the guest is spent on the coach, travelling from one place to another. A coach is like a second home for the guest. Before the departure of the tour, it is essential for him to contact the local transporter and get the details of the coach (its make and coach number) and contact details of the driver from him. He must enquire from the local transporter about the physical condition of the coach, if everything is in order both machine-wise and hygiene-wise. He may confirm about the air conditioning, audio and video system in the coach, availability of microphone, first aid box, provision of water facilities for the guests and any other facility, if provided by the transporter. He may also confirm the pickup time and the place and may also learn about the routing to be followed during the tour.

HOTEL STAFF

A tour manager may need to establish contact with the hotel both before the departure of the group and during the arrival at the destination. He must have all the contact details of all the hotels that the group shall be staying at during the tour. On getting the assignment of the trip, he must contact the hotel staff and reconfirm the rooming list with the hotel besides confirming the meal requirements, in case the meals have been arranged in the hotel. He may also remind the hotel staff of the special requests made by the clients if any. There may be special guests in the group such as differently able guests in the group, senior citizens, vegans, VVIPs etc. who might have special requirements that must be catered to appropriately by the hotel staff. He may also use this opportunity to collect information about the hotel property. He may obtain information about the star rating of the hotel, its location and the amenities (e.g., Wi-Fi facilities, swimming pool, spa and so on) offered by the hotel. He may also inquire the hotel staff about other details such as check-in and check-out timings, types of rooms, the distance between the airport/railway station and the hotel, availability of porters etc. Though, it is worthy to mention here that the same information of the hotel property may be accessed by the tour manager through internet also.

Now during the tour, a tour manager may inform the hotel staff about his arrival at the destination once he reaches the airport/railway station. He may advise the hotel staff in advance of the estimated check-in time of the group. This allows the opportunity for the hotel to prepare the rooms for the arrival of the guests and also the meals, in case they are to be served in the hotel. This timely coordination by the tour manager can save a lot of time for the guests and create a good impression of the overall services arranged by his travel company.

LOCAL RESTAURANT STAFF

Many meals for the guests on a tour are arranged in the local restaurants at a destination by the tour operator/travel agent. Alternatively, a tour manager may be asked to arrange for local restaurants on his own. In both cases, the tour manager should establish contact with the restaurateurs before the start of the tour and during the tour. He must confirm about the number of tables inside the restaurants that can accommodate the guests. He must inform the restaurant staff about the number of guests for whom meals need to be arranged along with the menu of meal that needs to be served to the guests.

Also during the tour, before arrival at local restaurants during sightseeing, the tour manager must share his location details with the restaurant owner/staff and inform them about the estimated time of arrival of the group at the restaurant. He may call them 2 hours before so that the restaurant staff has enough time to keep the food ready to be served to the guests without wasting their time when they arrive at the restaurant. This timely coordination assists the tour manager to remain on time for the next scheduled points on the itinerary planned for the day.

A tour manager must also re-check with the restaurant staff whether the meal preferences of the guests have been taken care of. Meal requests may vary from vegetarian/non-vegetarian to vegan food, local cuisine of a place, Jain meals (followers of Jainism religion from India who don't take onion and garlic in meals), gluten-free meals etc.

AUTHORITIES AT ATTRACTIONS

For sightseeing attractions, a tour manager must liaison with the authorities, including the staff/managers. For most of the attractions, an entry fee is charged. For example, most of the monuments, museums, art galleries, theme parks, national parks and artificial landmarks charge an entry fee. Also, at times, advanced reservations may have to be done for buying tickets for watching shows at forts, hotels and so on besides just visiting them. With a large group, it becomes difficult for a tour manager to arrange for the tickets in one go, especially when the re is rush. Advanced timely coordination of the tour manager with the authorities helps him organise entry tickets in advance so that he doesn't have to waste time standing in queues or end up in a situation where there are no reservations for shows due to limited availability of seats.

Before the departure of the tour, a tour manager may seek the necessary clarifications from the attraction authorities regarding the specific norms (if any) to be followed there attraction. He may pass on the information to his guests during the briefing. For example, for watching certain shows in the hotels of Las Vegas, USA, one has to be dressed in formal clothes and shoes.

COACH DRIVER

A coach driver is one of the most essential parts of the tour as guests spend a lot of time travelling in the coach. The safety of the guests is in the hands of the tour driver. Therefore, it is essential for the tour manager to establish a rapport with the driver before departing for the destination. Before leaving for the tour, he must personally contact the driver and learn about him—his name, past driving experience, pickup point, routes and so on. The same may be required for introducing the coach driver to the guests.

LOCAL TOUR GUIDE

At points of interest, a tour manager may explain about the places. However, at other points, a detailed commentary may be required which requires the expertise of a local tour guide. For local sightseeing tours that may be for half-day or full-day, the services of a local tour guide may be hired by the travel company.

Therefore, before the start of the tour, a tour manager may connect well in time with the local tour guides who they may hire at different destinations as per the itinerary for interpreting the sites. He may speak to the local guide and exchange pleasantries with him. He may then share the group details and the details of the local attractions to be covered during the sightseeing tours. For multiple destinations to be included in the itinerary, different local guides may be contacted accordingly.

AIRPORT/AIRLINES AUTHORITIES

A tour manager may be required to liaison with the airport authorities and airlines staff as well. His personal relationship with the ground staff at the airport and at the airlines helps in assisting his guests in the frontier formalities conducted by the authorities. Sometimes, in case of loss of luggage, the personal rapport of the tour manager with the airport authorities can help his guests in tracing their lost luggage more quickly. A tour manager may also call the airlines authorities in advance to reconfirm the flight timings, airport terminal number, gate number and baggage allowances. Besides, he may speak to the airport staff to keep himself abreast of any changes/regulations that may have taken place at the airport and that need to be conveyed to the guests. Alternatively, he may have access to the website of the country's airport/airlines to gather information if required.

RAIL AUTHORITIES

Many packages include trains as a mode of transportation within a country or across countries (e.g., Eurostar that runs from London to Paris). A tour manager may, therefore, liaison with the local rail authorities. Before departing for the tour, he must check for his reservations with the railway authorities, although he may check this online too. He may also check with the authorities in advance about the updated train timetables, amenities inside the trains, any regulations to be followed inside the trains or at the train stations, security requirements and so on. Through his liaison with them, he may request the authorities to make advance reservations so the guests won't have to wait unnecessarily standing in queues. His cordial relations with the railway authorities may help him in times of exigencies too.

RIDE OPERATORS/OTHER TRANSPORTERS

A package tour may also include exclusive rides on cruises, ferries, water taxis, boats, cable cars, gondolas, horse carriages, camel safaris, elephant and yak safaris, bicycles, cycle rickshaws, jeep safaris and so on. The tour manager must have prior contact numbers of the ride operators who organise these rides.

Before arriving at the destination, he may call the organisers and make reservations with them for his group. In case the reservations have been already made by the operations department of the company, a tour manager may just call to reconfirm the group reservations with them. He must also check with them about their timings of operation, days of operation, charges and modes of payment, and the facilities available in these modes of transportation.

ACTIVITY OPERATORS

A tour package may be filled with a number of activities for the guests. The activities may range from adventure to experiencing the nightlife, shopping to visiting farms and factories and so on. Before the start of the tour, the tour manager must contact each activity operator personally and confirm the reservations for his group members. He must also reconfirm the timings of operations of the activity operators so that he may plan the itinerary accordingly. Also, there may be some rules and regulations that he needs to inform his guests before undertaking such activities. A tour manager must clarify all these rules with the activity operators so that he can pass on the right information to the guest so that they may prepare themselves accordingly. For example, at certain nightclubs, guests are allowed to enter the premises only in formals. The same must be communicated to the guests. Likewise, a visit to chocolate factory or wineries may be arranged for the guests according to their timings of operation.

SUMMARY

Building a cordial relationship with the local suppliers is an integral part of a tour manager's job. A tour manager cannot just anchor on the company for all the back-end arrangements and stay least bothered. In fact, he must personally speak to each local supplier and reconfirm the arrangements for his guests. A timely step before the start of the tour can really save the tour manager from the embarrassment that he may have to encounter in case the services have not been arranged as promised to the guests. This helps him to save face in front of the guests if things are not in order. He must also learn how to keep his suppliers in good humour so that the on-tour experience of the guests goes seamless and enjoyable.

Activity 1 Play a service provider

Divide the class into various groups. Ask each group to perform a role-play depicting the dialogue between the tour manager and each service provider reconfirming the arrangements made or required to be made for the clients. You may assign the following service providers to each group:

- Local transporter
- Pilot of the coach
- Hotelier
- Local restaurateur
- Attraction authority
- Gondola ride operator
- Hot air ballooning operator
- Local tour guide

Activity 2 Call the restaurateur

You are leading an Indian delegation of government officials in China. You are on a tour with your group in local market for shopping. After 2 hours, you have arranged for a Chinese lunch in a local Chinese restaurant for your group. Being the tour manager, you give a phone call to the local restaurateur almost 2 hours prior to the arrival of the group. Now exchange the dialogue that shall take place between you and the restaurateur.

POSSIBLE SOLUTIONS TO THE OPENING VIGNETTE

- The first thing that Shravan did was to prepare his guest mentally for the unseen situation that was beyond his control. He briefed his group members about the political protest in the country.
- He also tried to establish contact with local travel agents and known government officials to learn about the current ongoing situation in Kathmandu.
- Meanwhile, he also tried to make alternative arrangements in local hotels near the highway in case they had to spend a night at the border, if the situation would not get better.
- He also tried to establish contact with midway restaurants to arrange for food and water for the guests.
- At the same time, he kept sharing the updates that he was receiving with his guests as well as his company.
- He also asked his guests to take out extra stock of clothing from their luggage and food items if any and other necessary items that may be required by them, in case no accommodation could be arranged nearby and the guests may have to sleep in the coach at night.

- He also tried to enquire from the driver and the locals nearby about the alternative routes, if any, to reach the destination.
- To kill time and keep his guests engaged and entertained, he also organised games for them.

Lessons Learned

- A tour manager must be honest to his guest no matter whatsoever be the situation. He must inform his guests about the exact situation that he and his group may be facing.
- He must be able to prepare his guest mentally for the worst.
- He must be updated and aware of the local situations of the city he is visiting with his guests.
- He must also have knowledge of the alternative routes to the destination.
- He must also contingency plan ready with him in case any situation arises.
- He must have a liaison with all the local suppliers of tourism service providers.
- He must also have the contact details of service providers of tourism industry (e.g., travel agents, government officials, restaurants and hotels) whom he may contact for any assistance, in case of any exigency.
- The safety of guest should be the top priority for the tour manager. He must assess the risks and weigh the alternatives rationally. Accordingly, he may take a decision based on the need of the hour.
- A tour manager must not lose his cool under any circumstances. He must exhibit a lot of patience to deal with any emergency situation that he may encounter on the tour.
- He be sensitive to the needs of children or any other guests who need special care.

7

Pre-tour Documentation

LEARNING OBJECTIVES

- Why is it important for a tour manager to carry the necessary documentation on the tour?
- What are the essential documents that a tour manager must carry with him on a tour?

Parry was the tour manager working for Zubeen Travels. He was a very confident and a professional tour manager. He was known for being the most organised tour manager of the company. This time he had the assignment of leading a group of Indians to Dubai on a leisure trip. He met all his guests at the Indira Gandhi International Airport and departed for Dubai via an Emirates flight. He always used to carry hard copies of all the necessary documents that may be required on the tour. However, this time, he decided not to take hard copies of the documents as he thought that since he already had the same data on his phone that he may have access to anytime, it was not desirable to carry hard copies of the documents adding extra weight for him to carry. As it was time to eat and enjoy the in-flight catering, he put his phone in front of the seat pocket. During disembarkation of the flight, he forgot to take his phone from the seat pocket and left to claim his baggage in the baggage claim area. He then waited for his group members to assemble and then went towards the coach on being received by the local airport representative. As he reached the hotel lobby, the hotel staff asked for the hotel voucher along with the photocopies of client's passports and visa. He reached out for the phone in his pocket and realised that it was empty. He became panicky and started searching for his phone in the backpack as all the documents were in his phone. But all in vain! Hell broke on him as he realised that he had left his mobile in the seat pocket of the airplane. The hotel staff was continuously asking for the desired documents, and the guests were getting irritated as they were exhausted and wanted their rooms to be allotted at the earliest. Parry was astounded, anxious and nervous. He did not know what to do!

Conducting tours is a responsible job. Before getting on a tour, a tour manager has to do a lot of preparation. For the smooth and hassle-free conduct of the tour, proper documentation is critical. Documentation may vary from company to company and from destination to destination. However, by and large, most of the documents are the same for most of the tour operators/travel agents. It is advisable for a tour manager to complete his documentation in all aspects as prescribed by the company he works for and the destinations he is visiting.

A tour manager must take care of all the documents on the tour at all times. He cannot afford to lose them. Many travel companies give a proper file to the tour manager that includes all the necessary documentation. The file may be called as the tour manager's file.

IMPORTANCE OF CARRYING DOCUMENTS

A tour manager may be required to carry the documents for the reasons discussed in the subsequent subsections.

EVIDENCE FOR SUPPLIERS

Many suppliers demand a receipt or printed copies of confirmation of services booked by the tour operator or the tour manager as a proof against the services reserved by them. On presenting the confirmations, the suppliers may then allow access to the services.

LEGAL REQUIREMENTS

At many destinations, carrying certain documents is mandatory as a legal compliance at some destinations. For example, while visiting specific attractions, special permits are required. A tour manager must, therefore, carry these permits with him to take his guests for sightseeing at these places. Likewise, while travelling in Europe through a coach, while crossing the borders of a country, the tour manager is required to show the passports of his clients at the check post to the immigration authorities. For this, he must keep all his documentation ready in advance.

REFERENCE POINT

Generally, a tour manager has to keep track of many things. Therefore, he may not be able to memorise every detail of the itinerary and, hence, may miss out on important matters. In case the ground handling agent (GHA) misses out any service as promised by him, the tour manager may show the printed copy of confirmation of services sent by GHA to the tour operator that may act as an evidence at that time. Also, there may be special requests, deviations etc. on to be taken care of in a group which is very hard to remember for a tour manager. Having the required information in a proper file makes the tour manager feel more organised, comfortable and confident. He may refer to the file repeatedly for any clarifications that may arise in his mind. He may also go through the detailed itinerary and necessary instructions to be followed during the tour, whenever required. Therefore, proper documentation serves as a reference point for the tour manager.

TOUR MANAGER'S FILE

Now let us have an elaborate discussion on the kinds of documents that a tour manager may carry in his file before departing for a tour.

PHOTOCOPIES OF TRAVEL DOCUMENTS

While dealing with inbound/outbound departures, a tour manager must carry multiple copies of passports and visas of his clients who have been booked on the tour. The photocopies of passport and visa may be required for two reasons. First, for security reasons, the hotel authorities may ask for the passport copies of the guests who are staying in the hotel property. Second, these copies may be required if a client loses his passport. Therefore, a tour manager may keep these documents.

However, during extended trips with multiple stays at multiple hotels, a tour manager may find it difficult to take multiple sets of passport and visa copies as it may increase the weight of the baggage. In such cases, a tour manager may not carry these documents. However, he may provide the same to the hotel by taking the clients' passport at the hotel during the check-in procedure. He may request the hotel staff to make the photocopies of both passport and visa and file the same for their records. He may then return the passports to his clients.

Alternatively, he may carry the soft scanned copies of passport in a pen drive and submit the pen drive to the hotel for copying in their system.

Besides copies of the passport and visa, it is also advisable for the tour manager to carry photocopies of passengers tickets in case a passenger may forget to bring the same at the airport. A copy of the travel insurance of each client may also be carried by the tour manager in case a client loses any of his personal stuff on the tour. The same may be required by the tour manager to fix things for his client by speaking to the insurance company. Needless to say the soft copies of e-ticket and insurance may also serve as an alternative that may be carried by the client as well as the tour manager.

GUEST LIST

A tour manager must carry a detailed list of the guests booked for the holiday. The list may contain the names of the clients along with their other details such as their passport details, meal preferences, occupancy details, any special remarks (special requests raised by the client) and so on.

COMPLETE ITINERARY

A tour manager must have the entire itinerary with him that contains detailed information about the daily tour programmes. This may have the details of the important sightseeing points and activities to be covered on a day-to-day basis during the tour.

LITERATURE ABOUT THE DESTINATION

A tour manager's file may contain all the necessary and exciting facts about a destination besides information about the various attractions to be covered. The file may also include information about the hotels where the arrangements of stay have been made for the guests besides some literature about the airport as well. Though the same information may be accessed by the tour manager from his mobile using the Internet, it is always advisable for a tour manager to carry a hard copy as sometimes there may be no Internet at the destination due to poor network connectivity.

IMPORTANT MAPS

A tour manager must carry printed copies of relevant maps of the destination, its airports, hotels, important sightseeing points and so on with him. In case the guests ask the tour manager about the whereabouts of a particular location, this may be very convenient and handy for him to answer by referring to the maps. However, today most tour managers use Google maps on their smartphones to locate a place. Again, this will be subject to the Internet connectivity.

AIRLINE CONFIRMATION

A tour manager must carry with him the copy of the confirmed group PNR (passenger name record) which contains the names of all passengers along with their flight details. This may be required by the tour manager to communicate with the airlines in case a client seeks a subsequent change in his travel dates during the tour.

INDIVIDUAL PNRS

A tour manager may carry the PNRs or airlines confirmation of those clients who may be taking a deviation in the package given by the company. Such pax may be joining the group late or reaching early or also leaving early. These pax are called deviation pax for a tour operator/travel agent as they don't exactly travel as per the group. It is advisable for a tour manager to have the details of such clients as he might be required to arrange for the transfers of these deviations pax from the airport to hotel or back forth.

ROOMING LIST

A tour manager must carry with him the updated rooming list of the hotels where his guests would be staying. A rooming list contains the names of the guests against their room occupancy that the guests have been booked in. The guests may be staying on a single room basis, twin sharing basis/ triple sharing basis or double room basis, depending on their kind of requirement. It helps the tour manager to reconfirm the same with the rooming list of the hotel that may have been sent to them by the operations team of the travel company.

HOTEL VOUCHER

It is a written confirmation of the services promised by the hotel that contains the details of the client. A hotel voucher has the name of guests and the occupancy they have been booked in, along with their check-in and checkout dates and the services promised to them. A tour manager must carry with him the hotel voucher of the various hotel properties where the guests shall be staying during the tour. A hotel voucher serves as a hotel confirmation for the tour manager that he may show at the reception of the hotel while checking in with the group. It serves as documentary evidence in support of the reservations made in the hotel by the tour operator/travel agent.

AGENT CONFIRMATION

It has a detail of all the services promised by the GHA. It may include all the land arrangements pledged by the GHA. These may consist of the airport–hotel–airport transfers, accommodation, meal arrangements, local transfers, local sightseeing points, activities, services of a local guide and any other services promised by the GHA to the tour operator/travel agent. A tour manager must carry the tour confirmation receipt with him in his file to keep a check if all the services have been delivered as promised in the agent confirmation voucher.

OTHER SUPPLIERS' CONFIRMATIONS

A tour operator/travel agent may not be making all arrangements through the GHAs/suppliers of a destination. He may have made some direct bookings by directly approaching the local suppliers like local restaurants at a destination by writing emails to them or directly calling them. Alternately, he may have booked arrangements such as sightseeing, local transfers, activities and so on through a software such as GTA (Gulliver Travel Association) or any other. In such cases, a tour manager must carry the printed copies of such confirmations that may help him show these copies as proofs of reservations for the local suppliers from whom the services are being availed.

RESERVATION CONFIRMATION

A tour manager must carry the printed copies of all reservations with him. The reservations may have been made for trains, theatres and casinos, for watching shows, taking rides in cruises/gondolas/boats and so on. A copy of the reservation may be asked for by the activity operators of these destinations to avail the services.

SPECIAL PERMITS

Many destinations require a special permit for its guests. For example, in India, while visiting Nathu La pass in the state of Sikkim, guests need to have a special permit that is issued by the local authorities. The tour manager must have the right information of any additional documentation that is a legal/quasi-legal requirement of a place, and he must make prior arrangements to procure such documents well in advance.

IN-HOUSE CONTACT SHEET

A tour manager must have access to all the numbers of his company's staff, especially the ones' whom he should contact while taking any important decision for his group members during any exigency or while making any changes in the itinerary during the tour.

IMPORTANT CONTACT DETAILS AND EMERGENCY NUMBERS

A tour manager must keep a list of contact details of the important local suppliers such as the local agent, local transporter, attraction authorities, activity operators, the driver and the local tour guide. Besides these, he must have contact numbers of the hotels and local restaurants to keep them posted about the group's movement.

Besides these contact details, a tour manager must also have essential emergency numbers of the destination he is visiting that may include the contact numbers of the local police, hospitals, ambulance, fire station, embassy numbers and so on.

EXPENSE SHEET

Many travel companies give an expense sheet to the tour manager to keep track of the expenses that he may incur on the tour. A tour manager must keep updating this expense sheet daily so that he may not miss out on any transaction that may get difficult to track later.

FEEDBACK FORMS

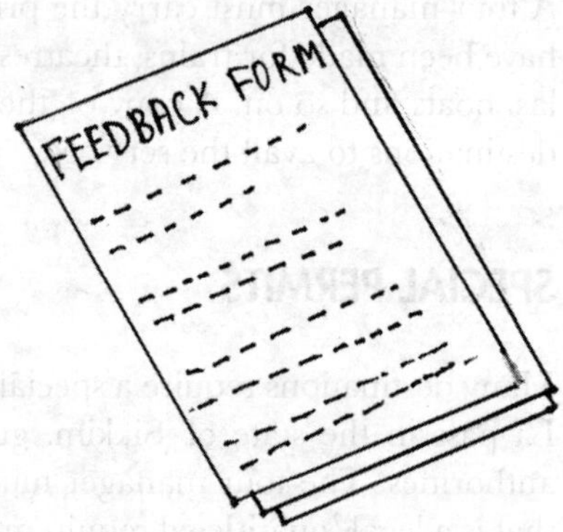

Feedbacks are significant for the overall improvement of services. A tour manager must carry the feedback forms with him on the tour so that at the completion of the tour he may distribute these forms to all his group members and know their overall experience of the trip. As everything in tourism is increasingly being technology-driven these days, printed copies of the feedback forms have been replaced by electronic format feedback where the tour manager takes the input of the clients on his tablet by asking them to rate the quality of the services availed or alternatively requesting or by asking them to post their feedbacks online.

OTHER IMPORTANT DOCUMENTATION

Many written formalities are required to be done by a tour manager on the tour while dealing with unforeseen situations. These formalities may vary from company to company. Many companies have specific prescribed forms which are to be filled by the tour manager, or he may have to get them filled from the tourist according to a situation that may come up. A tour manager must carry such essential forms such as release forms, indemnity forms, change itinerary form incidental form/ report, etc. with him on the tour as prescribed by his company.

SUMMARY

Strong documentation is the edifice of a successful tour. Every aspect of tour documentation is significant for the success of a tour. Before departing for a trip, a tour manager must mark his checklist of documents that he is expected to carry. As the saying goes, 'a stitch in time saves nine'; therefore, a tour manager must ensure that he does his homework well before departing for the tour. By doing all the necessary formalities and necessary documentation, he may be able to avoid the stress that he may have to deal with in the absence of the documents.

Activity 1 What should you carry?

Ask each group to prepare a checklist of all documents that every tour manager must carry. Now let the other group evaluate the list of documents given by the group. Declare the best group that has covered the maximum documents to be carried by the tour manager.

Activity 2 **Extempore**

Pick up any student in the class at random and ask each student to stand up and speak about a particular document for one to 1–1.5 minute. This shall help the students to clarify their concepts about the documentation required, and also improve their public speaking and offset their stage nervousness.

POSSIBLE SOLUTIONS TO THE OPENING VIGNETTE

- To manage the situation, Parry apprised the hotel staff about his situation and told them that he was not carrying any hard copies of the documents desired by the hotel staff.
- He then requested for access to a desktop/laptop with an Internet connection through which he could have access to his email to extract the hotel booking voucher and other client details.
- He realised his mistake of not carrying the hard copies of the documents and took a printout of all the documents in the hotel. He handed over the desired documents to the hotel staff.
- He also took printed copies of all other documents that may be required during the ongoing trip.
- He then thanked the hotel staff for their cooperation.
- He also bought a new phone with a new sim card to be in touch with his suppliers and group members.
- He also called in the Emirates airlines to check if his phone was available with the 'lost and found' department of the airlines.

Lessons Learned

- Always carry the hard copies of the necessary documents along with the soft copies.
- Being too dependent on technology can cost a lot of money and a lot of stress also.

8

Travel Essentials for a Tour Manager

LEARNING OBJECTIVES

- What are the things that a tour manager must carry with him on a tour?
- What can be the basis of classification for packing the travel essentials by a tour manager?

Aryan, the tour manager, was leading an incentive group of Indian businessmen to Europe. This was his first time in Europe, and he wanted to be sure that he was carrying all the travel essentials. He had already boarded the flight for Vienna when he realised that his mobile phone hardly had any battery left. He started searching for his charging cable along with the power bank in his backpack. To his dismay, he could not find any. He realised that he has forgotten to pack the same in his baggage. He became a little panicky as he realised that on reaching Vienna he would have to make urgent calls to coordinate with the local agent and the coach driver. To manage the situation, much to his embarrassment, he had to request one of his group members to borrow a power bank and charging cable for some time to charge his mobile battery. On the day they landed at Vienna, after taking rest at the hotel, Aryan had to lead his group for lunch at a local restaurant which was a 10 minutes' walk from the hotel. The coaches were not allowed inside the area. As he stepped out of the hotel along with his group, it started raining heavily. Everybody ran back to their rooms to get their umbrellas or ponchos. Aryan also rushed hurriedly to his room to get his rain poncho as they were already getting late for lunch. He was again frustrated as he realised that he had forgotten to pack the same in his baggage. He came out of his room without any rain gear. He asked his guests if any of them had an extra umbrella or a poncho. Sadly, no one had one, including the hotel staff. He was left with no option but to get wet as all guests were waiting for him. By the time he could reach the restaurant, he was drenched in the water feeling very embarrassed!

The life of a tour manager revolves around travelling. At times, the travelling may be for months, where the tour manager has to lead groups back to back. Travelling may be domestic or international.

While travelling, a tour manager should always be guided by the rule of travelling light. It is always advisable for him to carry one suitcase with a trolley that is convenient for him to carry. At the same time, he may also pack a carry-on bag with him where he keeps all the necessary items required during travel. A carry-on bag may be a backpack or a small bag with a trolley.

While navigating the globe, a tour manager must carry a number of essential items with him on a tour. A checklist of travel essentials for a tour manager before he departs for the trip is as discussed in brief here.

OFFICE-RELATED TRAVEL ESSENTIALS

These travel essentials are generally provided by the tour company on behalf of which a tour manager operates. Before a tour manager departs, the travel company hands over some items to the tour manager that may include the following.

TOUR MANAGER'S FILE

Documents are one of the most essential aspects of a tour manager's packing stuff. A tour manager has the onus of carrying all the necessary documents related to his guests during the tour. Generally, a tour manager carries a file which has all the required documentation. This file may be referred to as a tour manager's file which is handed over to him by his company. The file includes the following:

Guest List

It contains the names of the clients booked for the tour.

Detailed Itinerary

The detailed itinerary may contain the necessary literature about various destinations to be covered, their airports, hotels and sightseeing attractions, besides the complete day-wise programme of the tour.

Photocopies of Travel Documents

Showing a photo ID is mandatory at hotels during check-in for security purposes. Whether it is inbound, outbound or domestic travel, it is a requisite for the guests to submit their photo IDs in the hotel during check in for compliance with the security norms. Therefore, generally in group travel, a tour manager carries all the necessary photocopies of the documentation of guests required by the hotel. It may be any of the valid IDs of the guests. Generally, in case of foreigners, a passport is the primary ID of the guest.

However, it may be noted that if the tour manager is travelling to one destination, he may carry photocopies as he has to check in at one hotel only. However, in case the travel has been designed for different destinations, then it gets tough for the tour manager to carry multiple sets of photocopies of passports and visas for the different hotels that the group will be checking in.

It is advisable for the tour manager not to carry much baggage of photocopies with him that may increase the weight of his luggage. Therefore, when the tour manager arrives at the hotel, he may collect the photo IDs of his client (in case of foreign tourists, he may ask them to give their passports). The guests may be invited to sit in the lobby area while the hotel staff may photocopy these IDs. Eventually, on completion of the process, the guest may be handed over the passports by the tour manager or the hotel staff directly. However, taking the photocopies of the documents on a tour differs from company to company as per their policy.

Besides the copy of passport required by a hotel in compliance with the security norms, a tour manager may also carry photocopies of tickets as some guests may forget to bring their tickets at the airport. It is also advisable for a tour manager to carry photocopies of travel insurance of his clients as any client who may lose any belongings during a tour and may file for claims with the insurance company.

Passport size Photographs

A tour manager must request his guests to also carry their own passport size photographs, besides bringing his own. These pictures may be required in case a client loses his passport in another country.

Group PNR

A tour manager must carry the confirmed flight details of the passengers that he is travelling with. He may carry the group PNR issued by the airlines when he leads a group of guests in planes.

Transportation Tickets

A tour manager may carry printed copies of booked travel tickets on buses, trains, planes or any other rides reserved for the guests.

Hotel Voucher

It is a written confirmation of services promised by the hotel to the tour operator/travel agent. It contains the confirmed occupancy details of the stay of clients along with their check-in and check-out details and any services availed by them at the hotel.

Rooming List

A rooming list contains the names of the clients booked for a hotel against their occupancy in which they have been booked for. Occupancy by the guests may be on twin sharing, double sharing, triple sharing or on single room basis. A tour manager must carry the rooming list of all the hotels in which his clients have been booked for a stay at different destinations. This may help him to share the client details with the hotel staff.

Tour Service Confirmations

It contains the details of services promised by the GHA. A tour manager must carry this confirmation along with him to ensure that all services are delivered to the clients as promised in the tour confirmation voucher by the ground handler.

Reservation Confirmations

A tour may be packed with activities for which reservations may have been made in advance. A tour manager must carry a copy of such reservations, in case they have been booked in advance.

List of Deviations Pax

There would always be passengers in a group who sometimes don't travel along the group. They may join the group later or leave early or extend their stay at a particular destination. A tour manager must keep track of such passengers for whom he may be required to make arrangements for their transfers (pick and drop from airport–hotel–airport).

In-house Contact Sheet

A tour manager must have the contact list of in-house staff of the company in case he has to speak to them in times of emergency.

Important Emergency Numbers

A tour manager must keep all the important telephone numbers that he may require in case of an emergency. These may be the hotel number, local police station and ambulance number, embassy number and any other important contact numbers of a destination.

OTHER OFFICE-RELATED TRAVEL ESSENTIALS

Besides the tour manager's file that contains the aforementioned documentation, a tour manager may carry the following items handed over to him by his company:

Promotional Material

A tour manager may also carry promotional material of the company along with him on the tour. He may distribute the promotional material such as brochures, pamphlets or leaflets of the company to his guests. This material may have information of other tour packages that his company may be offering besides the general information about the profile and history of the company.

Maps

A tour manager must have all the necessary maps of a destination with him before he travels to that place. Generally, a tour manager's file may also contain printed maps of different destinations being covered during the tour. Otherwise, if the maps have not been given in the itinerary file, a tour manager may himself print the required hard copies of the maps of the destinations and attractions being covered before the start of the tour. Alternatively, at the destination, he may also seek the help of Google maps, whenever required. However, that is always subject to the connectivity of the Internet with the smartphone.

Travel Guide

Besides maps, a tour manager may carry additional guidebooks, language books and a travel guide in his carry-on baggage in case he wishes to learn more about a destination during the journey.

Cash

A tour manager must always carry enough money with him. In case he is travelling abroad, he may take the local currency of the country with him within the prescribed limit. Though these days most of the transactions have become cashless with the help of debit cards and credit cards, at certain places, cash may be required. For example, for giving tips at hotels, porterage charges at hotels, making a payment towards entry fees for visiting an attraction (at some attractions) and so on. A tour manager may also require cash for incurring any incidental expenditure in case of an emergency situation arising during the tour. Therefore, a tour manager must carry ample cash with him all the time during the tour.

Envelope

A tour manager has to keep track of all the expenditures he is making on the tour. To settle the accounts later in his company, he has to collect the receipts of all the payments made. Keeping bills in one envelope makes things more organised and streamlined for the tour manager later. He may not miss any receipts. He may, before departing for the tour, carry an envelope of his company in which he may place all the necessary receipts of the expenditures he incurs during the trip. Alternatively, he may also use the envelope for keeping the cash.

Flagstick

A tour manager may carry a flagstick with him on a tour. It is all the more important when the group size is large. At attractions, there may be a large gathering of other tourists also who may have come on their own or with escorted tours. There are chances that the group members may lose track of their tour manager. A flagstick helps the guests to identify their tour manager from a distance even in a crowd, besides keeping the group together.

Uniform

Many travel companies have a prescribed uniform for the tour managers. Generally, companies provide 2–3 pairs of the prescribed dress to a tour manager. Most companies give t-shirts/shirts and pants to the tour managers with the logo of the company embedded on them with the idea of promoting the brand of the company. Generally, uniform makes a tour manager look more professional besides helping guests to identify him more easily in a crowded place. Also, sometimes the T-shirts may be in a bright colour so that the guest may be able to locate the tour manager from a distant amid the crowd at the attraction with the heavy traffic of tourists.

Cap

Many companies also give caps to their tour managers. It acts as a shield in hot weather besides providing him a sporty look and also promoting his company.

PERSONAL TRAVEL ESSENTIALS

Besides the various essential items given by the company to the tour manager, he may carry the following personal items while on a tour:

Backpack

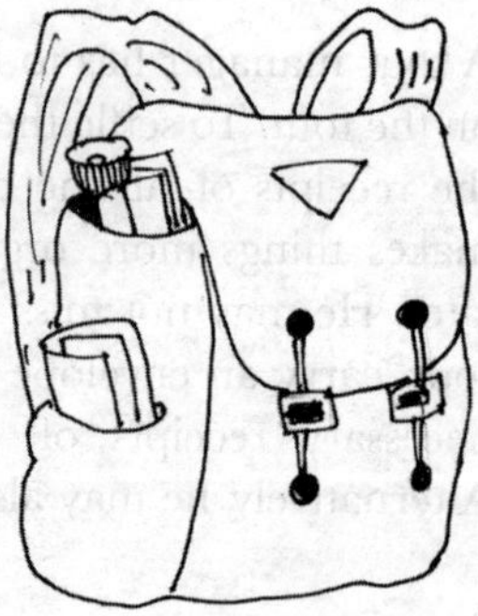

A tour manager must always take a smart backpack with him during the trip. He may keep his own essential stuff in his bag that he may require every day. It may include a power backup, charger, water bottle, any important files, notes, items of personal hygiene, deodorant, hand sanitiser and so on. This may give him hands-free mobility and real comfort. Alternatively, he may carry a duffel bag according to his own convenience.

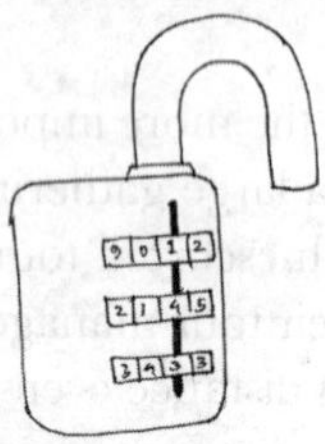

Travel Lock

Though it sounds frivolous, it is very important for a tour manager to carry a travel lock. He must lock his luggage correctly before leaving for an airport or a hotel. Even when he is travelling out with his group, he must keep his bags locked in the hotel room.

Toilet Kit

A tour manager may carry his personal items that may include a shaving kit, extra razors, shampoo, shower gel, hair gel (in case he uses), comb, toothbrush, toothpaste, mouthwash, floss, sunscreen lotion, night cream, chap stick, small mirror etc. A tour manager may carry this little travel kit with him to use it every day on the tour as many hotels may not provide toiletries. Besides these, a lady tour manager may carry all her makeup stuff and her personal hygiene items too.

Sewing Kit

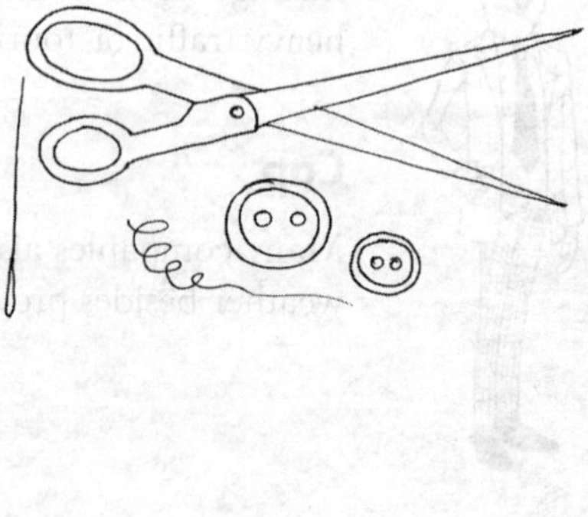

A tour manager may be in need of a sewing kit anytime. The button of his shirt may break, and he may have to stitch it. Notably, in foreign countries, this can become a task for the tour manager to buy a sewing kit as it may not be easily available or may be expensive to buy. It is therefore advisable for a tour manager to carry with him a tiny sewing kit from his place of departure that may include colourful threads besides a needle, scissors, buttons, safety pins etc.

Wet Tissues/Face Wipes

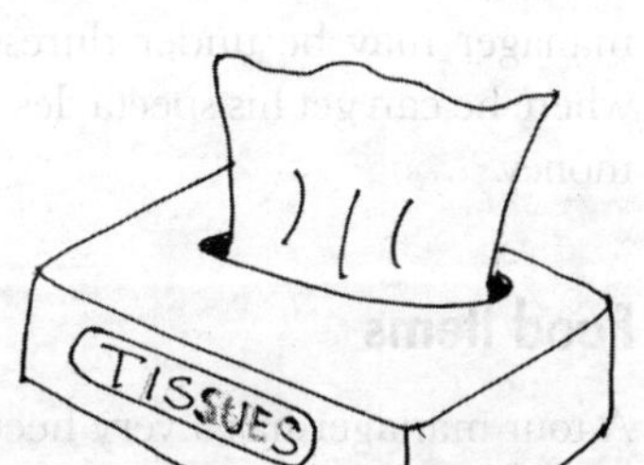

A tour manager may get weary during the long journeys on the tour. Leading the group for the whole day on a hectic day's itinerary may make him feel very tiresome. The same may be reflected on his face.

Therefore, to look and feel fresh, a tour manager must use wet tissues/face wipes on a tour. He must carry them on a trip with him.

Deodorant/Perfume

A tour manager must smell good. In hot weather, while going from one place to another, a tour manager may sweat and therefore smell foul. The tourists might feel very uncomfortable with such bad body odour.

It is, therefore, advisable for a tour manager to carry a small bottle of perfume/deodorant/cologne with him on tour. However, the fragrance of the perfume/cologne should not be very strong as many people are allergic to strong scents.

Hand Sanitiser

While travelling in a coach, the hands of a tour manager may get dirty. In case he has to eat something on a coach, he may need to clean his hands. Also, at many places, he may not get water to wash his hands. Therefore, for his personal hygiene, a tour manager must carry a sanitiser with him at all times on a tour.

Mouth Freshener

A tour manager must have a pleasant breath. When he speaks, he should not smell bad. Thus, he may carry a mouth freshener with him. If possible, he may also rinse with mouthwash, especially after meals.

Eyeglasses

In case a tour manager uses eyeglasses, he must carry an extra pair of glasses with him on the tour along with the glass case. The reason is that if the spectacles break, a tour manager may be under duress. His valuable time might go in locating an optician where he can get his spectacles repaired. Many times, this may cost significant time and money.

Food Items

A tour manager has a very hectic job. From morning till night, he may be standing for the whole day. He has to lead, walk and talk continuously. For all this, he needs a lot of energy. Therefore, it is advisable that a tour manager carry small energy packets with him. He may carry small portions of snacks with him that may include dry fruits or energy bars, wafers, cookies and so on that may give him instant energy to perform his job besides satisfying his immediate hunger pangs.

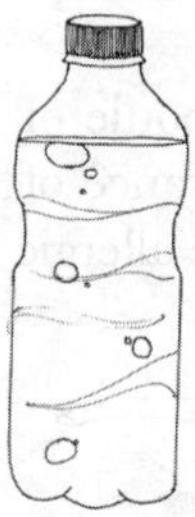

Water Bottle

A tour manager has to speak a lot. As a result, he may dry up while talking. Also, a tour manager is continuously on his toes while on his duty. He may get tired as a result and may dehydrate. Therefore, it is always advisable that a tour manager keeps on drinking water, especially when he is leading the groups in hot weather. He may buy mineral water to drink or alternatively carry collapsible water bottles which occupy less space and are easy to carry.

Travel Document Holder

While travelling abroad, a tour manager may secure all his documents such as the passport, ticket, boarding pass, debit cards, credit cards and travel insurance in a travel document holder. Besides being a more secure place, it also gives a smarter and an overall professional appearance for a tour manager.

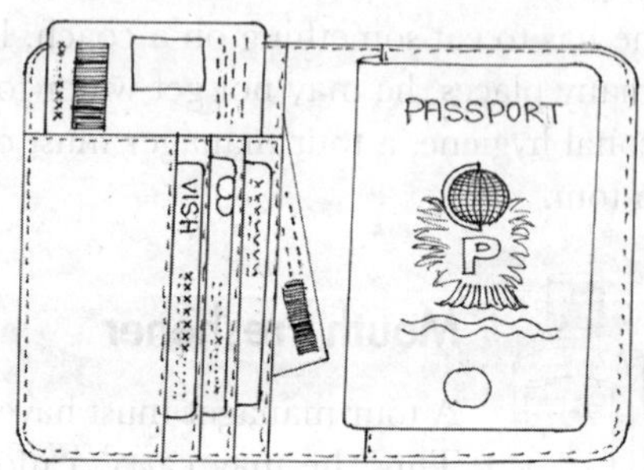

Business Card

A tour manager may carry his personal business card on a tour. He may use this card for networking with his guest and other suppliers during the trip.

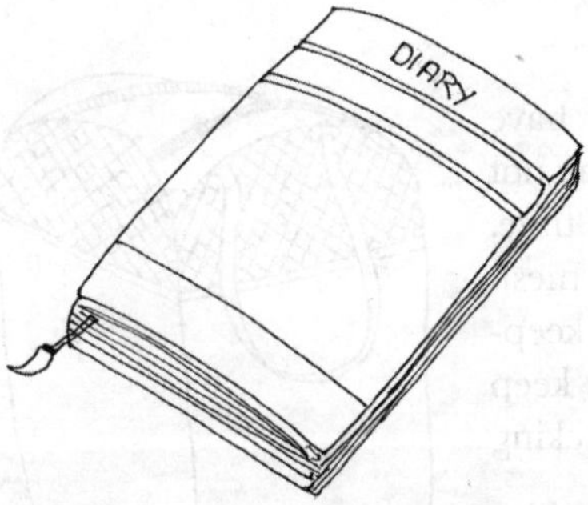

Diary

It is essential for a tour manager to make notes of certain important things which he thinks is really important on a tour. He must keep jotting down these important points in his diary which he may have to explain to his company later. Also, sometimes, for his own observation, he may be required to make notes for his own personal learning. He may carry a diary with him for the same. Alternatively, he may make notes on his phone or tablet.

Pen

A tour manager must always carry a pen with him as he may have to fill the forms at the airport/flight while embarking or disembarking besides needing the pen for making any necessary notes and writing daily tour reports.

TRAVEL COMFORTERS/FACILITATORS

These things are not essential to carry. But if a tour manager carries these items, his trip becomes more comfortable.

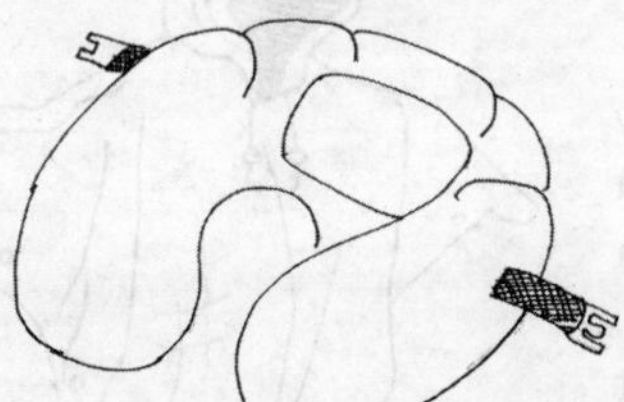

NECK/TRAVEL PILLOW

To make his travel comfortable during long flights, a tour manager may carry a neck/travel pillow with him. Though most of the international airlines also give neck/travel pillows to their passengers, he may also take his own neck/travel pillow if he doesn't get one. He may use the same in coaches too during long journeys to make himself more comfortable.

EYE BLINDERS/SLEEP MASKS

During transit flights, when there are long halts at airports, the eye blinder is a useful item for taking a nap at the airport. Though airlines also generally provide the eye blinders during long journeys, it is advisable for a tour manager to carry his own eye blinder.

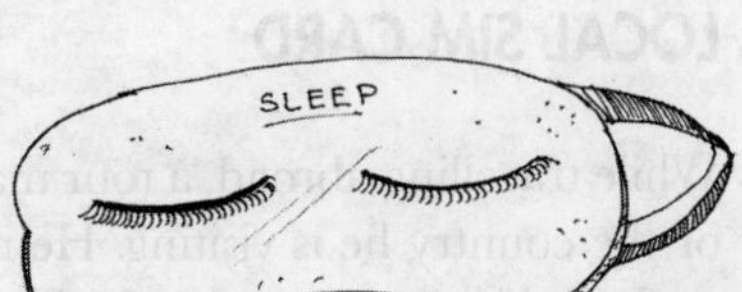

MESH OR A COLLAPSIBLE LAUNDRY BAG

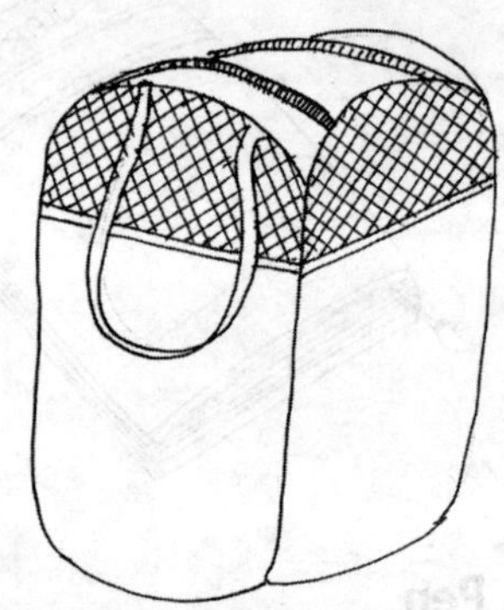

A tour manager remains on tours for a long duration. He may have back-to-back trips at times. He may have dirty clothes that he may not be able to wash on the tour at the hotels due to the scarcity of time. Therefore, he may carry a separate collapsible laundry bag or a mesh that may be placed in his suitcase as it occupies less space besides keeping the clean clothes segregated from the dirty clothes. He may keep this mesh in the hotel room to put his dirty clothes in it. On checking out of the hotel, he may pack this mesh back in his suitcase.

PACKET ORGANISERS

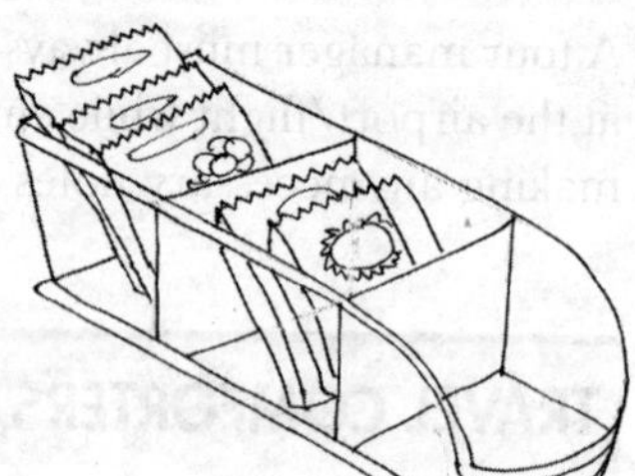

For better and more convenient packing, in the primary check-in baggage (a large suitcase), a tour manager may make use of packet organisers that help in keeping the stuff stacked in organisers. Using compression sacs, packing cubes, pouches and folders makes the packing a lot more organised by packing the things in fewer spaces with minor wrinkles on clothing. This helps a tour manager in locating his material more easily and also in keeping the things back in place quickly besides keeping the stuff clean.

RAIN PONCHO

The weather is always beyond the control of a tour manager. It may rain anytime. Therefore, a tour manager may have to operate a tour even in the rain. Thus, he may carry a raincoat or poncho with him.

It is better to carry a rain poncho instead of an umbrella as it occupies less space in packing. The hands of a tour manager also remain free as he does not have to hold anything in his hand.

LOCAL SIM CARD

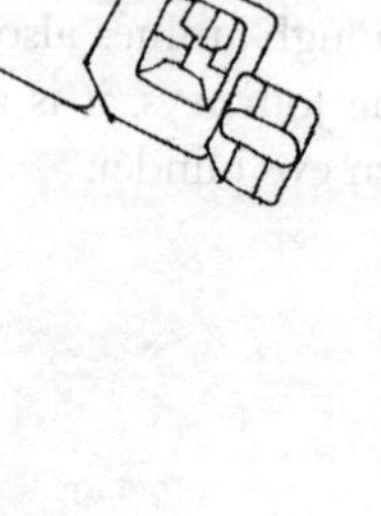

While travelling abroad, a tour manager must carry a local sim card of the country he is visiting. He must also ensure that he has a net pack for better connection and easy access on a tour.

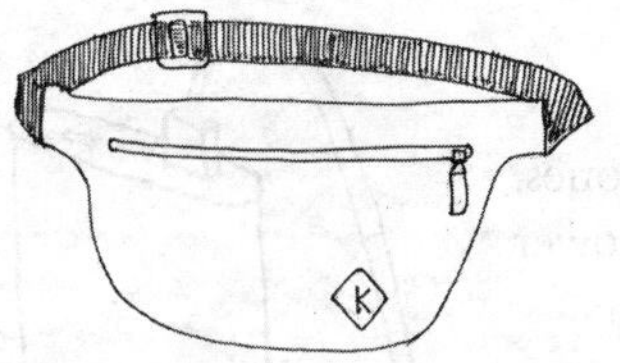

MONEY BELT

As a tour manager may be carrying quite some cash, he may, for security reasons, carry a money belt/neck wallet or an extra hidden pocket that may help him to keep his cash safe away from pickpocketers. These gears help a tour manager to place the money close to him.

ELECTRONICS

This is an era of technology. A tour manager has a high dependence on electronic items. We give you a list of electronic gadgets that he may carry with him.

SMARTPHONE

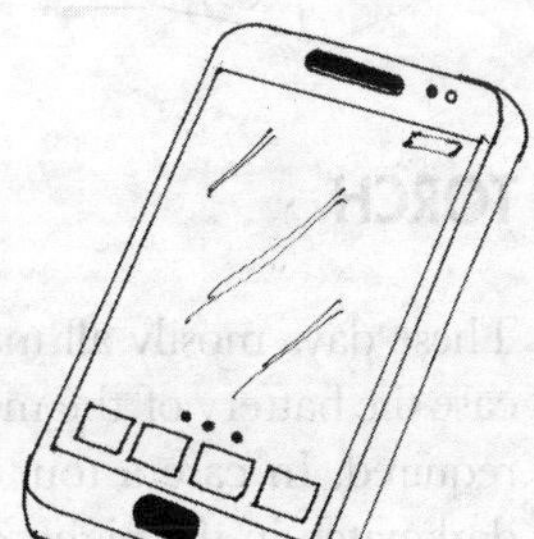

A smartphone is like oxygen for a tour manager. A tour manager may have to make essential phone calls on the tour. He may have to contact the various suppliers or make emergency calls. Also, he may have to make use of the Internet for seeking any necessary information. For travelling to different places, he may even have to keep track of the routes by using Google navigation maps. Therefore, a smartphone, not just an ordinary mobile phone, is a must for a tour manager.

ELECTRONIC ACCESSORIES

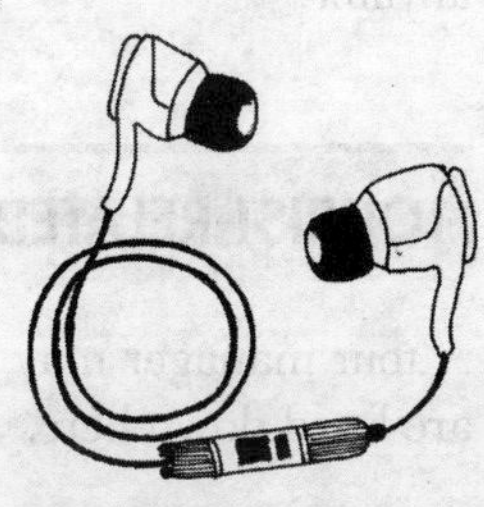

A tour manager must carry a phone charger and earphones during the tour beside a memory card for data storage. The battery of the phone is consumed quite fast as most of the liaison with the ground handling suppliers is done by the tour manager on his phone. Therefore, on getting opportunities, he may charge his phone from time to time before the battery dies. Besides, he must not forget to carry the chargers of his laptop, iPad or power backup that he may be carrying on a tour.

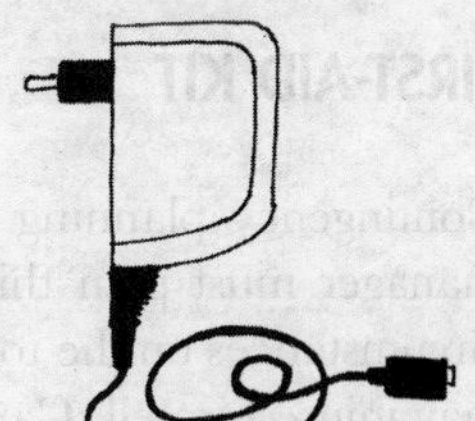

Also, a tour manager may like to listen to the music on his phone or watch a movie during a flight (all flights do not have in-flight entertainment services, especially domestic flights) or in coach while the group is sleeping during long journeys. He may carry his earphones for the same so that others are not disturbed.

Alternatively, he may also carry headphones to listen to the music to save the battery of his phone. However, it may be noted that during the daytime when he is with his guests, a tour manager must avoid using earphones as it appears to be more casual in front of guests.

BATTERY BACKUP

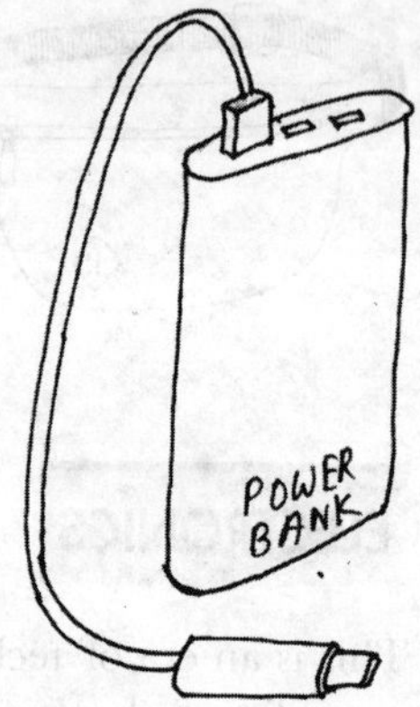

A smartphone consumes more battery as compared to other phones. Therefore, besides carrying a charger, a tour manager may take a power bank for charging his mobile on the tour.

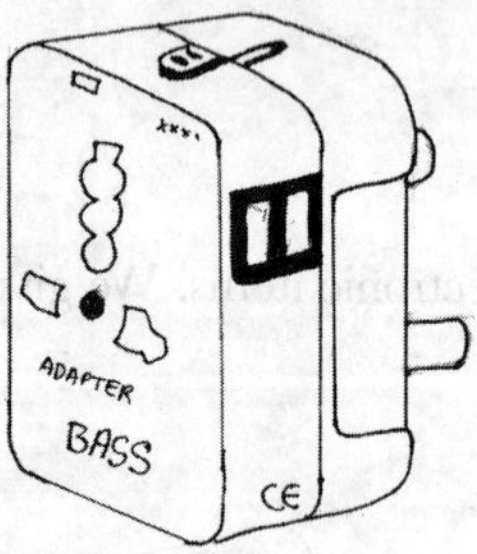

UNIVERSAL PLUG ADAPTER

When a tour manager is travelling to a foreign country, he may carry a universal plug adapter with him so that he may not find any difficulty in charging his mobile or any electronic equipment such as laptop, video camera, tablet, etc. that he may require during the trip.

TORCH

These days mostly all mobiles have an inbuilt torch. However, in case the battery of the mobile phone is discharged, a torch may be required. In case a tour manager is leading his group through a dark patch in the night, or the battery of the coach crashes down in the night, he may be required to use a torch. Therefore, a tour manager may carry a flashlight with him as it may be needed anytime.

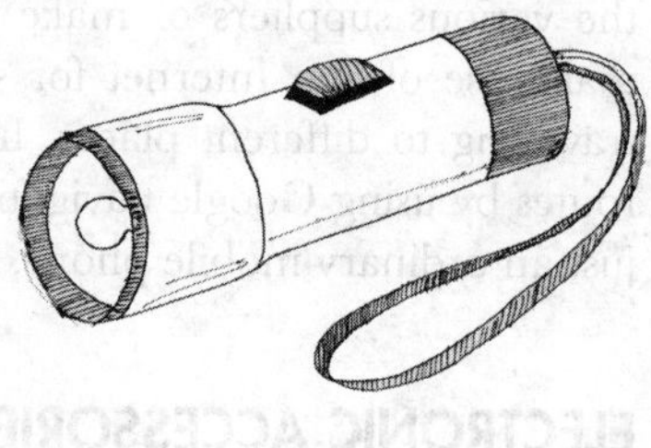

TOURIST-RELATED ESSENTIALS

A tour manager may carry specific items that may be required by the tourists on the tour. These are listed down here.

FIRST-AID KIT

Contingency planning is an essential part of the trip. A tour manager must plan things in advance to meet any unforeseen circumstances on the tour. Any client may fall sick on the tour or may injure himself. Carrying a first aid kit helps in dealing with such situations. The first aid kit generally includes a first aid manual, bandages, adhesive tapes, scissors, cotton, antiseptic solution, antiseptic wipes, antibacterial ointment, thermometer and instant cold packs. It also includes some essential medicines

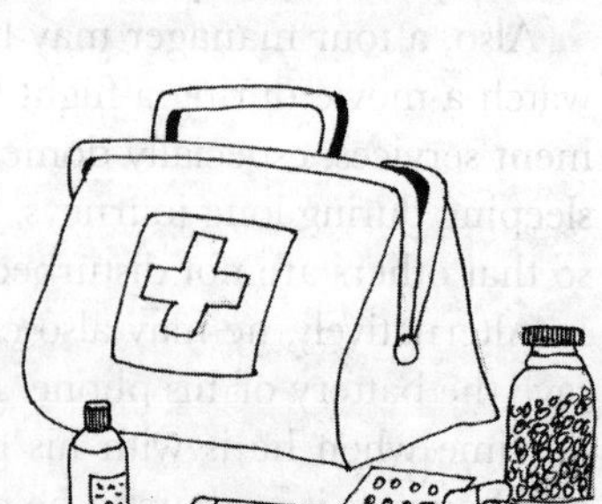

such as paracetamol, Disprin, Vicks, ibuprofen, Strepsils, motion sickness pills, altitude sickness pills, allergy medicines, sunburn relief, multivitamins, insect reliever medicine/insect repellent and so on. However, it is always advisable for a tour manager not to prescribe any medication to his client, as a client may be allergic to certain salts present in the medicine.

In case a tour manager is carrying his own medicines which are controlled drugs, he must take his doctor's prescription while on a tour.

DISPOSABLE PLASTIC BAGS

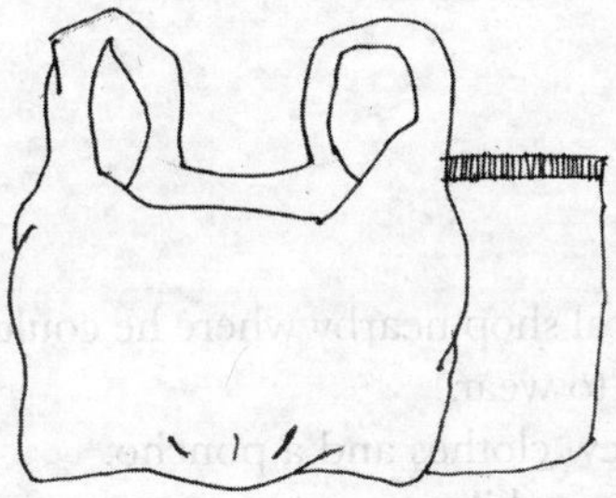

A tour manager may also carry disposable plastic bags with him on a tour. He may bring them to pack any damp item such as towel or any other personal stuff. He may also take reusable plastic bags in the coach in case any guests want to vomit or put some trash like wafer wrappers and so on in the coach.

He may also carry zip locks with him to keep any foodstuff fresh which he may be carrying for himself.

Activity 1 Paint a picture

Distribute some chits to students in the class. Ask them to draw two items each on the same chit that they must carry while travelling with a group as a tour manager. Give them 10 minutes to draw. Now collect all the chits and distribute the chits at random to different students. As a result, every student shall get a different item with him that has been drawn by other classmate. Now conduct an extempore in the class. Ask each student to speak for a minute on the picture that has been assigned to him. This will help the students to be more creative and also create a more intellectually stimulating environment.

Activity 2 Listing

Each student may prepare a list of five items that a tour manager must carry. The students may then be divided into groups and asked to club similar items to eliminate redundancy. The students may give appropriate headings for things clubbed together. The final list of travel essentials for a tour manager may be presented through a pictorial chart presentation by each group. Each group member may then explain in detail the pictorial representations of these travel essentials to be carried by a tour manager. Students may use props on the chart to make funny representations of the items to make the chart more interesting and more creative.

SUMMARY

The list of things that a tour manager may carry is very extensive. This list is handy for a tour manager while travelling to a destination as he may miss out otherwise on any essential item that may disappoint him later while searching for it. However, a tour manager must always be guided by the rule of the thumb to travel light. A tour manager must carry essential office-related documents, personal items, travel facilitators and electronic items with him. Taking the right stuff with him at the right time helps him to stay comfortable and hassle-free on the tour.

POSSIBLE SOLUTIONS TO THE OPENING VIGNETTE

- After making the group sit for lunch, Aryan enquired about a local shop nearby where he could arrange for an umbrella/poncho and also a new pair of clothes to wear.
- He then went to a close by market and spent a fortune to buy new clothes and a poncho.
- He also bought a power bank and a charging cable to charge his mobile.

Lessons Learned

- A stitch in time saves nine.
- A tour manager must always have a checklist for all the travel essentials he is expected to carry with him.
- Before leaving for the trip, a tour manager must recheck all his items in his baggage with his checklist. Otherwise, he has to unnecessarily spend a lot of time and money for buying the stuff that may cause a lot of stress to him.

SECTION C

ON-TOUR RESPONSIBILITIES OF A TOUR MANAGER

After gaining insight into the profession of a tour manager along with the pre-tour preparations that he is required to undertake on being given an assignment, it is vital for us to understand his roles and responsibilities on a tour. A tour manager plays a crucial role in providing a joyous holiday experience to his guests. He has a critical position in delivering of various exposures to his guests.

This section is an attempt by the authors to highlight the roles and responsibilities of a tour manager on a job. It starts with his role at the airport, hotel, coach, other modes of transportation and other responsibilities on a tour and ends with the closing of a trip. The section gives an in-depth analysis of a tour manager's role at different points of a trip. For the successful completion of a trip, he must be very clear about the roles expected of him at various stages of a tour. Being a companion and caretaker of his guests on a trip, the tour manager must ensure that he discharges his duties at every point with efficacy and perfection. Any miss at any point can cost him his job and also spoil the complete experience for his guests. Therefore, to do a job, it is essential for a tour manager to know what exactly is expected of him.

So, let us start with a detailed discussion on each of the roles of a tour manager at different points of a tour.

So, are you ready to learn more?

Let us start again!

9

Receiving Guests at the Airport

LEARNING OBJECTIVES

- What kind of information should be provided by the tour manager to his guests while travelling by air?
- What are the responsibilities of a tour manager at the airport?
- Is there any difference in the responsibilities of a tour manager at the airport concerning inbound, outbound and domestic travel?

India is at its best in winters. A group of NRIs from Nigeria decided to visit India on a leisure trip. They booked their arrangements through an Indian travel agent in Nigeria who had arranged for an Indian tour manager for them who would accompany them from airport at Abuja to India and back to Abuja. Neura was the tour leader of the group.

Stavya, a 10-year-old boy who was also on a visit to India from Nigeria with his mother, was excited for the holiday vacation. While they all arrived at the airport and proceeded for the check-in formalities at the airlines, it was time for Radhika, Stavya's mother, to show the ticket and passport to the airlines authorities. While Stavya was just playing with his ball, his mother was in a state of dismay! Stavya asked his mom: Why are you upset mom? Radhika said, 'Son, we are not going to India now'. Stavya started crying at the top of his voice.

Radhika was informed by the airlines that Stavya could not travel to India! He had to stay back as the passport number on the visa did not match with the passport number mentioned in the first page of Stavya's passport. The airlines stopped him and did not issue him the boarding pass. They further checked with the imgration authorities to confirm the fault in visa. It was discovered that it was a mistake on the part of the embassy. Stavya and his mother became very panicky as they did not know what to do. Radhika immediately rushed to Neura and started fuming at him. She decided to stay back in Nigeria with her son till he was issued the visa with the correct details.

Generally, a tour manager receives the tour party at the airport terminal and accompanies them after that. For the arriving guests, the airport is the first encounter with the destination. Often it is the first visit and airports being complex structures with unknown individuals manning them, the visitors may find themselves lost. The tour manager's first job is to make the guests feel comfortable. This chapter is about dealing with tourists as they arrive at the airport.

INTRODUCTION

Most of the international packages offered by the tour operator/travel agent include air travel. Many travellers may be first-time flyers who may not be aware of the airport formalities and airlines regulations. Therefore, before making such guests travel by air, it is imperative for the travel company to familiarise the guests with the various formalities and procedures to be followed at the airport. The company also need to orient the visitors about the airline's regulations so that the guests don't face any problem during the tour due to their sheer ignorance.

The tour operator/travel agent may organise a formal meeting for its clients who are going on that particular package to a foreign country to provide advance information to the guests related to the airport and airlines besides the other details on the modus operandi of the tour and the destination to be visited. This meeting may be called as a pre-departure meeting. During the meeting, the tour manager introduces himself to his guests and may share valuable information about the airport and the airlines with his guests besides the other relevant information about the trip. However, many companies may not organise pre-departure meetings. They may send this information to their guests through email or may hold the same information in the itinerary file that may be handed over to the guests personally.

In cases where the travel companies do not hold the pre-departure meetings for its clients, a tour manager may take the initiative and contact each of his guests individually. Alternatively, the company may send the required information to the guests via email along with the itinerary. The information to be shared by a tour manager with the guests may pertain to the airport and/or airlines.

COMMUNICATION BEFORE THE DEPARTURE

The tour manager may share the following information a few days before the departure of his group.

INFORMATION ABOUT AIRPORT

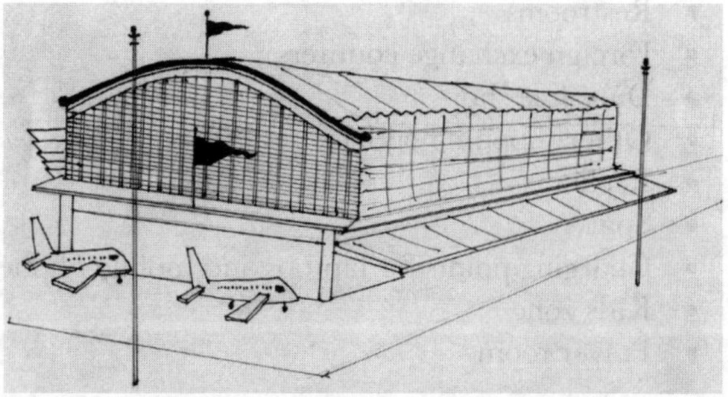

In case of international travel and during domestic travel, the terminal may be the first point of the trip from one's home. Airports are governed by different rules and regulations. A tour manager must share the following information with his guests regarding the airport during the pre-departure meeting or when he personally contacts them or sends emails to them.

Reporting Time at the Airport

A tour manager must communicate the reporting time to his guests for both international and domestic flights. Generally, in case of international flights, the visitors are advised to report 3 hours before the departure of the flight as the frontier formalities such as check-in, immigration, customs and individual screening may take quite some time. However, in the case of domestic flights, guests may report 90 minutes before the departure of the flight to complete the check-in formalities and individual screening.

Departure Terminal Number

Many airports have multiple terminals. Therefore, it is essential for the tour manager to communicate to the guests the departure terminal number from which the flight will take off.

Gate Number

There are different gates at the airport. The visitors might get confused as to which gate to enter. Therefore, a tour manager must clearly specify to his guests from where they must enter the airport which may also be the meeting point for the group members and the tour manager.

Facilities at the Airport

A tour must be aware of the services available at the airport. He must inform his guests about the facilities available at the airport. The kind of services offered may vary from airport to airport. Generally, facilities available at most of the airports include the following:

- Wi-Fi
- Restaurants
- Airport hotels

- Restrooms
- Foreign exchange counters
- Duty-free shops
- Other shopping outlets
- Recliners
- Spas
- Charging points for laptops and mobile phones
- Kids zone
- Prayer room

Frontier Formalities

In the case of international flight departures, a tour manager must explain in detail the steps to be followed by the guests at the airport before boarding the flight. He may describe in detail the various channels that the passengers have to pass through during international departure/arrivals. He may brief them about the following points in particular:

- Check-in counter of airline
- Immigration border control
- Customs clearance
- Individual screening area
- Boarding the flight

However, in case of domestic travel, the frontier formalities may be few as compared to international flights. The same may be explained by the tour manager to his guests.

List of Dutiable Items

There are specific items which are dutiable whereas certain items are non-dutiable that are declared by the government of the country. For dutiable articles, one must pass through the red channel of customs and pay the customs duty. Otherwise, one may pass through the green channel which is non-dutiable. A tour manager should have a fair understanding of the items that are dutiable, and the extent of duty one may have to pay for those things. The same must also be shared by the tour manager with his guests. This is important to communicate as many guests may just spend money shopping for expensive items such as electronic items, jewellery and so on for which they may have to pay hefty customs duty if it exceeds the permissible limit. This timely piece of advice may warn the tourists to purchase wisely keeping in mind the list of dutiable articles and the permissible limits.

Duty-free Shopping

Almost all airports in the world have duty-free shops where one can buy items at economical rates. At the airport, the tour manager may recommend his guests to purchase certain items from these duty-free stores so that they may save their money. He may also inform his guests about the free allowance permitted on duty-free shopping at the airport.

Permissible Currency Limits

A tour manager must also inform his guests on the ceiling of foreign exchange that one can take along in a foreign country. This restriction of money that one can carry with oneself while travelling abroad is called as basic travel quota.

INFORMATION ABOUT AIRLINES

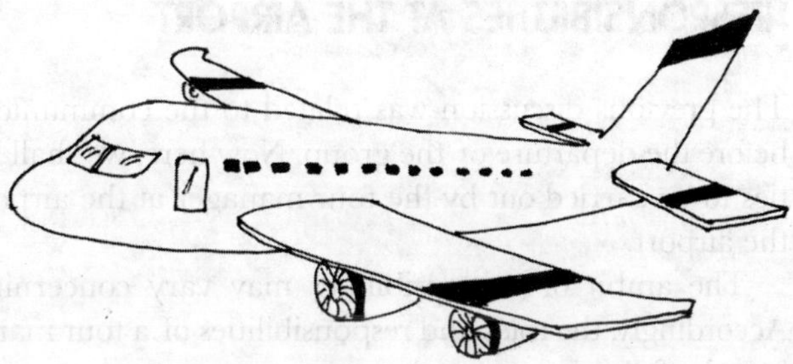

A tour manager must also communicate the following relevant information to his guests about the airlines on which they are flying.

Types of Baggage

Generally, first-time travellers are not aware of the concepts of check-in baggage and cabin baggage. Therefore, a tour manager must explain in detail the different kinds of baggage allowed in the airlines. The check-in luggage or registered baggage is the baggage that is weighed and screened through the conveyor belt at the check-in counter and, henceforth, loaded in the aircraft till the final destination. One can have access to this baggage only at one's last destination on arrival. The cabin baggage or carry-on baggage is the baggage which one carries with himself inside the aircraft. It may be a small suitcase or backpack beside a purse or laptop bag that can fit into the overhead bins.

Sharing the Baggage Allowance Rules

Every airline has a permissible limit of baggage allowance depending on the type of luggage and the class of travel. Generally, for check-in luggage, the free baggage allowance for international airlines is 20 kg for economy class, 30 kg for business class and 40 kg for first class. This may, however, vary from airline to airline. For cabin baggage, most of the airlines permit baggage weighing 5–7 kg.

However, for domestic departures in countries, airlines follow different baggage rules.

A tour manager must be aware of the baggage allowance rules of both the international and domestic airlines on which the group is flying. He must communicate the same standards to his guests well in advance so that the guests do not have to pay extra for the excess baggage during the journey. He may suggest that his guest travel light and follow the permissible limits. This piece of information may also help the guest to plan their shopping accordingly.

Besides the information mentioned above, a tour manager may share the following information in detail with his clients:

- Different classes of travel in airlines
- Items not permissible in the cabin baggage (e.g., sharp items and liquid above permissible limits)
- Prohibited items by airlines

- Facilities that are given by airlines (e.g., self-check-in kiosks, online check-in facilities, Wi-Fi services, in-flight catering, i.e., meals and beverages types, in-flight entertainment facilities, in-flight shopping and so on).

RESPONSIBILITIES AT THE AIRPORT

The previous discussion was related to the communication to be done by the tour manager days before the departure of the group. Now here, we shall have an elaborate review on the responsibilities to be carried out by the tour manager at the airport during the arrival/departure of guests at the airport.

The ambit of responsibilities may vary concerning inbound, outbound or domestic travel. Accordingly, the roles and responsibilities of a tour manager at the airport may broadly be classified into the following categories.

1. Inbound travel
2. Outbound travel
3. Domestic travel

Let us discuss each of these scenarios one by one.

INBOUND TRAVEL

In inbound travel, foreigners come to a destination from another country. The role of a tour manager is discussed in this section.

AT ARRIVAL

On arrival of the guest in his country, a tour manager has various responsibilities to discharge that are discussed in brief here.

Receive/Pick Up Guests at Arrival

Most of the travel companies arrange for pick up of guests at the airport on their arrival. Companies often use a dedicated staff who is primarily responsible for handling arrivals/departures of guests at the airport. These designated staff in travel trade may be referred to as airport reps/airport representatives or transfer assistants. They generally take care of return airport transfers (pick and drop from airport–hotel–airport) of guests.

In companies that do not hire separate airport reps/transfer assistants, picking up guests at arrivals is the duty of the tour manager. Sometimes, the guests may be coming from different countries or sometimes from the same country but from different cities. In such cases, when they are coming from different time zones, or even from same country but different cities, their arrival timings may be different. Travel companies handle these multiple arrivals by sending airport representatives accordingly. However, when most of the guests of a group are arriving at the same time, a tour manager may go to pick up his guests. This may not, however, always happen as he may meet them at the hotel directly.

However, when the tour manager goes to the airport to receive his guests, he must observe the following:

- He must be dressed up smart for the airport. He should look neat, tidy and well-groomed for welcoming the guests as the first impression of a tour manager is very important.
- To ensure that there is no last-minute confusion, he must confirm the arrival terminal number and the arrival gate from the airlines at which the group is expected to arrive.
- A tour manager must reach the airport 15–20 minutes early before the arrival/landing of his guest at the airport as punctuality is a mark of professionalism.
- On reaching the airport, he must first reconfirm the timing of flight at the display board/information screen.
- On arrival of guests, he must exchange pleasantries with his group members on receiving them.
- A tour manager must carry a placard with him mentioning the name of the company on behalf of whom he is receiving the group. Alternatively, he may have the group name/package name or the guest name on the placard for identification of tour manager by the group members.
- A tour manager must make the reception of his guests a memorable experience. He may traditionally welcome the guests (e.g., in India, generally the foreign tourists are given a warm reception with a garland of flowers and applying tilak on their forehead). Otherwise, with a broad smile on his face, he may shake hands with his guests and welcome them.

Handling VIP Guests

Sometimes, the tour manager might be required to receive the VIP guests at the airport. He must do this job very meticulously. The profile of VIP guests may vary from bureaucrats and diplomats to celebrities/industrialists and so on. With such a high profile of visitors, a tour manager must exhibit extra care at every step.

Assisting with Luggage

A tour manager may also assist his guests in baggage clearance at the airport. Many times, the visitors report a loss of baggage or damaged baggage at the airport. A tour manager should assist his guests in such situations in every possible way. He must support the guests morally at that time and help the guest file a PIR (Property Irregularity Report) with the respective airline. In case of damaged luggage reported by the guest, the tour manager should assist his guest in claiming compensation from the carriers according to the extent of damaged baggage.

Helping with Currency Exchange

Many times, the tourist does not get their currency converted into the foreign exchange in their home country. They may like to purchase the forex from the country they are visiting. In such cases, the tour manager may assist his guests in buying foreign exchange at the airport. Alternatively, he may advise his guests to buy currency from the currency counter outside in the local market depending on the rate of conversion being offered at the airport.

Assisting in Purchase of Sim Cards

In many countries, the tourists are provided complimentary sim cards in their welcome kits at the immigration counter in the airport. The idea is to facilitate the visitors in connecting with their family and friends back home.

Many airports have sales counters/vending machines of different telecom companies who sell sim cards to the tourists. In those countries where the guests are not given complimentary sim cards at the immigration counter, the visitors may feel the need to buy the local sim card to connect with their families and friends. They may ask the tour manager to assist in arranging a sim card through which they can tell their families that they have reached safely at the destination. Here, the tour manager may help the guests in the purchase of sim cards at the airport. He should suggest to his guests the various offers on sim cards available and the most suitable/cost-effective sim card of the company, and the guests should buy those according to their data/calling usage. Alternatively, he may assist them in purchasing the sim cards from the local markets.

Directing the Guests to Transport Facility

A tour manager may then facilitate the guest to the transportation arranged for them. Generally, it is a coach in which the guests are transferred from the airport to the hotel.

Handling the Luggage

A tour manager may also assist his guests in keeping their bags inside the coach, especially in case of senior citizen travellers or travellers with special abilities. Otherwise, he may ask his guest to carry their own bags depending on the country they are arriving in. In many countries, charges by porter are very high, while in some nations, porters who may help in keeping the bags on the coach are readily available.

Welcoming the Guests to the Coach/Meet and Greet

After ensuring that the luggage has been properly loaded inside the coach, the headcount of the guest is complete and the guests are comfortably seated inside the coach, the tour manager must welcome his guests on board by greeting them and introducing himself and the pilot (driver) to the guests.

Briefing About the Itinerary

After welcoming the guests in the coach, the tour manager may brief his guests about the necessary details of the day plan and then head straight to the hotel where the stay has been booked for the guests.

Adjustment of Watches

On the coach, the tour manager must also advise his guests to adjust their watches as per the time zone of the country they have arrived at. The tour manager must even ask his guests to synchronise their watch with his watch so that the guests observe the same timings at all times.

CULMINATION OF THE TOUR

Every holiday comes to an end. As all good things come to an end so does a great trip and so does the assignment of a tour manager for a particular trip. Though it may not be that easy, the tour manager bids farewell to his guests with a sense of accomplishment. Responsibilities of a tour manager at the ending of the tour are discussed in brief here.

Dropping the Guests

On the final day of the trip, after checking out the group from the hotel and assisting them in loading their luggage inside the coach, the group heads for the airport. Dropping the guests safe and sound till the airport is the responsibility of the tour manager. He must utilise this opportunity to thank his guests for all their cooperation and support extended during the trip. He may again advise his guests about the items they may buy from duty-free shops and the free allowance permitted for duty-free shopping. He may also brief his group about the various checks in formalities and other frontier formalities required to be done at the airport.

Briefing About the Tax Refunds

When tourists do shopping in a foreign country, they may get tax refunds on the shopping items. Sometimes, the visitors can claim the tax refund at the store establishment itself. However, many stores do not give tax refunds in their shops though the tourists might be eligible for it. In such cases, the visitor may claim their tax refund at the airport before their final departure from the country.

The tour manager must remind his group to take the tax refund from the airport before departing from the country. He must also correctly guide his guests about the necessary documentation such as shopping bills required to be submitted for getting the tax refund at the airport. He may even help his guest in filling the tax rebate forms at the airport.

OUTBOUND TRAVEL

Generally, in case of the outbound travel, two arrangements are possible. In one arrangement, the tour manager accompanies the group of guests from the airport to airport. In other words, he starts with the group of guests from the point of origin (his home country) and comes back to the point of origin (his own country) after having visited the other country. He remains with the group all the time.

As an alternative arrangement, the tour manager may not always fly with the group from the point of origin. The guests may have to leave their country on the own. The company may arrange a tour manager at the other country who meets the guest at the airport or at the hotel in the country.

In the first arrangement, where the tour manager departs with the group from the place of origin till the final location of arrival and comes back with them, the tour manager is expected to carry out certain responsibilities at the airport.

FACILITATING IN AIRPORT HANDLING PROCEDURES

As many travellers may be travelling for the first time internationally, they may not be aware of the frontier formalities required to be done at the airport. For them, the tour manager is a great support as he facilitates every procedure at the airport for his guests. He may assist them in group check-ins.

HELPING WITH FOREIGN EXCHANGE

Some guests may want to exchange their money for foreign currency. A tour manager may assist in facilitating his guests in exchanging the external currency at the airport with the money changers.

CHANGE OF SIM CARD

Many tourists while travelling abroad may like to buy sim cards at the airport before departing from their own country. Many telecom operators have their counters at airports for this purpose. A tour manager may assist his guests in buying an international sim card by suggesting the best suitable option according to the calling and usage of the Internet of the client.

ASSISTING WITH BAGGAGE CLEARANCE

On arriving at the destination airport, the tour manager must lead his group to the assigned conveyor belt at which the baggage is expected to come. He must ensure that all his guests have identified their luggage correctly and that they have collected all their baggage without having missed any baggage. In case of lost baggage by any guest, the tour manager must assist his guest in every possible way. He must take his guests to the respective airline counter and get PIR filed. Also, in case of any damaged property, the tour manager should assist his guest by asking the airlines to compensate the client according to the extent of baggage damaged.

COMMUNICATING DURING FLIGHT DELAYS

Flight delays are widespread due to bad weather conditions or technical glitches. These situations are beyond the tour managers' control. In such circumstances, a tour manager must keep his office staff in the loop about the delay in flight so that the team may communicate the delay to the GHA who may accordingly coordinate with the transportation department and the hotel for rescheduling their time of pick-up and check-in at the hotel in case of significant delays.

Also, in case of connecting flights, the group might not be able to catch the connecting flight due to delay in departure of the first flight. In that case, the tour manager may have to get the new flight scheduled for this group so that the group may be able to reach the destination at the earliest.

These last-minute changes may be frustrating and strenuous. However, the tour manager must maintain his calm and act very professionally in tackling these tricky situations which might crop up at any time of travel. He must also remain empathetic towards his guests as in these unexpected circumstances, as the guests are likely to react sometimes even indecorously. The tour manager must also request his guests to show patience in dealing with such cases that are beyond anyone's control.

DOMESTIC TRAVEL

Many travel companies use air transportation for domestic travel. In domestic trips, the role of a tour manager is quite limited. It may be confined to the responsibilities discussed in this section.

ASSISTING THE GUEST WITH CHECK-IN FORMALITIES

In case of domestic flights, the tour manager suggests that his guests go to the check-in counter and the individual screening area. He may also request the group members to cooperate with the airport staff.

HELPING IN LUGGAGE CLEARANCE

The tour manager may assist his guests in getting their baggage at the baggage claim area.

PROVIDING PACKED LUNCHES

Many tour operators provide packed lunches to their guests who have a long halt between their inter-connecting flights. In such case, it is the duty of a tour manager to ensure the distribution of packed lunches to his guests.

SUMMARY

Whether it is an inbound, outbound or domestic travel, the ambit of duties and responsibilities of a tour manager is very broad. His presence at the airport has an important role to play in facilitating his guests and making their travel at the airport a hassle-free experience. It is always in the interest of

Activity 1 Do you know?

Identify the international airports of the following cities:

1. Amsterdam
2. New York
3. Mumbai
4. Paris
5. Bangkok
6. London

Activity 2 Pre-departure briefing

Rising Stars has closed a booking of group of 30 employees for HSBC bank. It is an incentive group who shall be travelling to Singapore and Malaysia ex-Delhi on a 4N/5D package. The company has appointed you as the tour manager of the company who shall be leading the group.

Organise a pre-departure meeting of the group in the meeting room of the bank three days before the departure date and brief the pax about the things to take care of before the actual departure. You may cover the following points:

- Name of the airport
- Reporting time at the airport
- Meeting point at airport (departure gate and terminal number)

- Facilities at the airport
- Rules of the airlines the group has been booked in
- Check-in and cabin baggage rules
- List of restricted items in the airlines
- Information about frontier formalities
- Duty-free shopping

the tour manager to maintain a good rapport with the airline's staff, immigration officers and customs officer at the airport with whom he has to deal with on a day-to-day basis. For the successful completion of the tour, a tour manager must discharge his responsibilities before and at the airport very diligently and smartly. He must remain updated on the regulations taking place in the airline industry.

POSSIBLE SOLUTIONS TO THE OPENING VIGNETTE

- Neura immediately apologised to Radhika for all the inconvenience caused. He just empathised with Radhika and asked her to maintain her cool.
- Meanwhile, Neura informed his company about the whole incident and immediately asked his company to reapply for Stavya's visa and get the required correction done.
- He asked his company to reschedule Stavya's and his mother ticket for the day after so that they may join the group after two days.
- He further arranged for a cab that would drop Radhika and Stavya back from the airport to their residence.
- He also asked one of the staff members to speak to Ms Radhika the next day and assist her in every possible way by arranging a car for her to visit the embassy and assist her in any documentation, in case required. He also passed the number of the concerned staff to Ms Radhika.
- Meanwhile, Radhika also wrote an email to the travel company complaining about the negligence of their visa officer because of whom she could not travel to India on time. She further claimed compensation for the mental harassment she had to go through to get the things fixed till the time she flew to India for her vacation.

Lessons Learned

- Before leaving for a country, a tour manager may ask his guests to check their visa for details such as the correct spellings of the name of the guest, the passport number, the validity of the visa, the length of stay and the type of visa issued by the embassy.
- In this case, a small negligence by the visa officer of the company not only spoilt the trip of the guest but also affected the brand image of the travel company they were going with. It also created an extra financial burden on the company who later had to bear both the travellers, that is, Radhika and Stavya's hiked ticket cost as well as the transportation cost.
- It is advisable for a travel company to hand over the passport to the client only after having thoroughly checked the visa details of the client once it has been granted to the client.

10

Responsibilities at the Hotel

LEARNING OBJECTIVES

- What is the pre-tour preparation required to be done for a hotel by a tour manager before departing for a trip?
- What are the responsibilities of a tour manager at a hotel?

It was February 2015. A group of students from Britain who were on a tour to India, after having a great holiday, checked out from the hotel in Agra for their flight back to London. As the students were on the coach heading for Indira Gandhi International Airport, New Delhi, almost mid-way through the journey, Peter, a student, realised that he had forgotten his wallet and camera in the hotel room in Agra. He was taken aback. Immediately, he informed Mihir, the tour manager of the group. Being halfway there and with a flight to catch in a few hours, it was almost impossible for Mihir to take a decision to go back to Agra.

The nature of the tour manager's profession demands of him to be with his guests all the time. Whether it is inbound, outbound or domestic travel, he has a significant role to play in assisting his guests during their stay in a hotel or any other accommodation. In most of the tours, the first meeting point of a tour manager with his guests is the reception or lobby area of the hotel where the formal introduction takes place between the guests and the tour manager. From check-in to check-out of the hotel, the tour manager remains a constant companion and a caretaker of his guests. For any issue concerning the hotel, the guests may prefer to approach the tour manager first rather than the hotel staff.

INTRODUCTION

A tour manager's job, concerning a hotel, starts much before the departure of the tour. He may have to begin preparations before the commencement of the trip. Second, his responsibilities at the hotel start when the guests check into the hotel. Therefore, his duties related to the hotel may be divided into the following two categories:

1. Responsibilities before the commencement of tour
2. Responsibilities during the tour

Now let us have a detailed discussion on each of these responsibilities.

RESPONSIBILITIES BEFORE THE START OF THE TOUR

Before the departure of the tour, when a tour manager is given an assignment to handle the group of guests, he may initiate the following things regarding the hotel.

ACQUIRE RELEVANT INFORMATION

A tour manager must start gathering the relevant information about hotels he is going to stay in as per the itinerary that has been given to him. Some itineraries may have multiple hotel stays. A tour manager should, in such cases, gain knowledge regarding every kind of property his guests will be staying at. He must acquire prior information of the following:

- Hotel name and its contact details
- Location of the hotel
- Star category of the hotel
- Layout of the hotel
- Types of rooms available
- Number of rooms in the hotel
- Amenities available at the hotel
- Hotel guidelines or rules of behaviour
- Nearby places of interest or locations around the hotel
- USP of the hotel, if any

LIAISON FOR RECONFIRMATION

Before the start of the tour, a tour manager may also call the hotel staff to reconfirm the following information:

- Check-in and check-out dates of the group
- Updated rooming list
- Reconfirmation of services being offered

- Confirmation of special arrangements for guests in case of special requests placed by the guests
- Confirmation of meal preferences (vegetarian/non-vegetarian) of the guests
- Amenities available at the hotel

COMPLETE DOCUMENTATION

Documentation is another important aspect of pre-tour preparation for a hotel. Before the beginning of a tour, a tour manager may organise the following documents with him before visiting the hotel:

- Rooming list
- Hotel voucher/Hotel confirmation
- Details of hotel with its address and contact details
- Identity proofs of guests

RESPONSIBILITIES DURING THE TOUR

Broadly speaking, a tour manager has to carry out some duties during the trip at a hotel. These may be divided into two broader categories:

1. Making arrangements
2. Providing information to the guest

The detailed note of roles and responsibilities of a tour manager at a hotel or any other accommodation under these two broader functions are provided in the subsequent sections.

MAKING ARRANGEMENTS

Facilitating arrangements at a hotel is a prime responsibility of a tour manager. A tour manager must ensure that all the facilities and services as promised to a client are delivered during his stay at the hotel. He is responsible for making various arrangements at a hotel/any other accommodation.

Assisting in Check-in

On arriving at the hotel, the tour manager helps his guests to check into the hotel. Along with the hotel staff, he too facilitates in the overall allocation of rooms to his guests.

His timely intervention in the check-in procedure makes the whole process speedy and convenient for the guests. Generally, the process may take around 15–60 minutes, depending on the size of the group and availability of the hotel staff. During check-in procedure, he may request his group members to comfortably sit in the lobby area and wait for their turn. The gathering of guests around the reception area otherwise may create unnecessary confusion and hamper the front office to conduct the check-in of the guests smoothly.

A tour manager must ask his guests to cooperate while check-in is going on as it may be a time-consuming process and inevitable delays may be expected while completing the check-in formalities with the hotel staff.

Following are the steps that the tour manager may follow during the check-in procedure at a hotel:

- When the group of guests arrives at a hotel, he must confirm the rooming list with the hotel. He must ensure that the occupancy of rooms (single, twin, double or triple sharing room) is similar to what has been promised to the client, and that every client has been accommodated as per the rooming list that has been given to him by the company.
- He must also provide copies of identity proof of his clients to the hotel staff in compliance with the security measures adopted by the hotels.
- He must then assist the hotel staff in handing over the room keys/key cards to the clients.
- After handing over the room key/key card to the guests, he must be able to direct his guests to their rooms at different floors.
- The tour manager, if required, may assist his guests in opening the room through key cards for the guests who may find it difficult to understand the system of unlocking/locking though this is the prime responsibility of the hotel staff.
- In case of any issue of occupancy or room type raised by the clients during check-in, it is the responsibility of the tour manager to resolve the grievance of the guest by speaking with the hotel staff.

Ensuring That the Luggage Has Reached the Rooms

It is a great relief for the guests if the luggage arrives quickly after the check-in at their allotted rooms. This requires a lot of coordination between the driver, tour manager and the porter of the hotel. Sometimes, the driver also may unload the luggage from the coach and keep it in the lobby area. However, the tour manager must get the luggage tagged with the right room number of the guests and get it delivered timely in the visitors' room through the porter. In case, the group has to share the porterage charges during check-in and check-out, the tour manager must apprise his group in advance, before arriving at the hotel, about these expenses. In many countries, especially Southeast Asian countries like India, this might be more valid as porter services are easily available in the hotel for ensuring the delivery of luggage to the guest's room by tipping the porter as the cost of labour is affordable.

However, in case of many countries in Europe and the UK, the USA and Australia, most of the hotels expect the guests to carry the luggage on their own till the room as the hotels maintain a thin staff to do cost-cutting. In such cases, a tour manager must explicitly ask his guests to carry their own luggage from the coach to the hotel room.

Arrangement of Welcome Drinks

During check-in at the hotel, the tour manager must ensure that the guests are served the welcome drinks by the hotel staff if the same has been promised in the package inclusions to the clients while the check-in is going on.

Arrangements of the Meals

Meals are an essential part of the overall stay of the guest in the hotel. Generally, the guest staying in the hotel is either booked in a Continental Plan (a meal plan which includes only the breakfast with the room tariff) or Modified American Plan (MAP—a meal plan which includes breakfast with one major meal, i.e., lunch or dinner, with the room tariff). This is as per the package booked by him. In rare cases, the guest might be offered an American Plan (a meal plan that includes all the meals of the day along with the room tariff). Generally, the guests prefer to book their meals in the MAP, as most of the time, the group is out for sightseeing in the afternoon and the lunches may have been arranged for the guests in the local restaurants on the way to the sightseeing attractions.

Generally, the food is served in a buffet where the guests can have unlimited food from the limited items being served as per the menu of the hotel.

Many big hotels have multiple restaurants too. Sometimes the guests may be interested in eating at the restaurants inside the hotel and not in the buffet. Hence, a tour manager must be aware of restaurants available in the hotel and the cuisine for which they are famous for so that he may be able to guide his guests better in case the guests ask about the other dining options in the hotel where they are staying. He should also know the bestselling food items of these restaurants that he might recommend his guests to taste. However in such cases he may inform his guests that the food charges have to be borne by the guests themselves.

A tour manager has some responsibilities to carry out at the restaurant of the hotel. Following are the duties of a tour manager while arranging meals for his guests.

Pre-arrangement

Before the serving of meals in the hotel, a tour manager must confirm the following with the hotel staff:

- He must check for the meal timings with the hotel staff. Most of the time, he gathers information about breakfast and dinner timings from the hotel staff a day before, according to the itinerary scheduled for the day. He should also clearly communicate meals timings well in advance to his guests accordingly. He may also ensure that the meals are served on time as communicated to the clients.

- He may also check the venue where the meals are to be served in the hotel and communicate the same to his guests.
- He must see if the restaurant is clean and there are no flies/mosquitoes/other insects inside the dining area.
- He should also physically inspect the seating arrangements for his guests so that they may dine comfortably. The seating arrangement should not be so congested that it obstructs the movement of others while taking a second helping.
- He must also check the layout of the dining.
- He must remain updated on the food menus to be served to the guests as they may inquire about the food menu from the tour manager for the day.
- He may also communicate the preference of vegetarian/non-vegetarian meals of the guests to the hotel staff.
- He may also request the hotel staff to segregate the vegetarian items to be served from non-vegetarian items as some vegetarian guests are not comfortable if all the food items are placed together.
- He may also request the staff members to label the food items for the clarity of the guests.
- In case the local meals are being served, he must be aware of the ingredients used in the local dishes as some guests might inquire about the ingredients of the local dishes from the tour manager.
- He must be aware of his guest's allergies. Many guests are allergic to peanuts, eggs, dry fruits, wheat and so on. Accordingly, he may notify his guests before the start of the meal if such items are being served in the food.
- Before the commencement of the meal, may also request his guests to move in proper queues while taking their meals.
- He may also request his guests not to waste the food.
- He must also advise his guests about the restaurant guidelines, if any. Generally, in group departures, the guests are served buffet style where they can take as much food as they want. However, the tour manager must clearly communicate to his guests that if they order anything extra to eat/drink that is beyond the food items placed in the buffet, they shall have to pay extra.

Arrangements During the Meal

The tour manager must reach the restaurant 15 minutes before the guests. He must remain in the vicinity of the dining area till the guests have their meals. He should monitor the overall food arrangements at the restaurant of the hotel and be readily available for any kind of assistance if required by the guests. He must take care of the following things on reaching the restaurant of the hotel:

- Ensure that the food is ready to be served as per the time given to the guests.
- Check if the cutlery is correctly placed.
- Ensure that the meals are hot before being served. He must instruct the hotel staff to make the necessary arrangements to keep the food items hot till the time the guests are dining.
- Ensure that the food is covered adequately until the guests reach the restaurant.
- See if the food items are properly labelled.
- Ensure that both vegetarian and non-vegetarian dishes have been segregated.
- When the guests arrive at the restaurant, he must make sure that everyone is present for the food. In case some guests do not reach on time, he may ask the staff at the hotel reception to give a call in the rooms of the guests and remind them of meal timings. This is especially important during the breakfast time as many guests take time to get ready and eventually come late. Ultimately, this may lead to an unnecessary delay in the itinerary. However, the tour manager must stick to his itinerary and may request such guests to leave with him without having breakfast, if time does not permit. Alternatively, he may suggest the guest to join the group later at their own.
- Ensure that the guests are served food appropriately and also in proper quantities.
- Keep an eye on the food bowls continuously. He must ensure that the food bowls and breads being served are replenished from time to time during the dining of the guests at the hotel.
- At times, if there is less staff to serve the food in the restaurant, he might himself take the lead in serving his guests personally during the meal time.
- Ensure that the guests who have placed special requests for meals are being served accordingly.
- Ensure that no third party enters if the food has been separately placed for the group in the designated area of the restaurant.

Requesting Wake-up Calls

A tour manager must remind the hotel staff every day about the timings of a wake-up call to be given to his guests as per the itinerary decided for the day. Most of the sightseeing tours start in the morning and end in the evening. Some tours may begin very early too. Therefore, wake-up call timings may vary accordingly. This requires an everyday coordination between the tour manager and the hotel staff. Otherwise, the guests might keep holidaying sleeping for late hours, which may ultimately lead to delay in the overall itinerary for the day.

Taking Care of Special Needs of Guests

A tour manager might be dealing with people having special requirements on tour. These guests may fall under the following categories:

- Senior citizens
- Travellers with special abilities
- Women travellers
- Parents with young children
- Diabetic patients
- Travellers prone to allergies
- Jain travellers
- Vegans

In such cases, it is the duty of the tour manager to cater to the requests raised by the travellers who may require special assistance such as special equipment, extra facilities, specific food items, etc., while on tour.

Handling Hotel-related Grievances

A tour manager may have to take care of requests or complaints raised by the guests staying in the hotel. Complaints may vary such as unclean rooms in the hotel, bad quality of food being served in the hotel, lack of proper facilities in the hotel, inefficient hotel staff and so on. Some friends might want to stay together in the same room, whereas some ought to remain on the same floor. However, a good tour manager must see if the issues are genuinely sincere and resolve these matters amicably for his guests to make sure that their stay in the hotel is comfortable.

Assisting the Guests in Check-out

During check-out from the hotel, a tour manager must ensure that every client has checked out of the hotel on time by returning the room key/key card to the front office. He must also ensure that everyone has cleared their pending dues, if any, for availing any additional facilities in the hotel. He may advise his guests to settle all their due payments the night before checking out of the hotel so that there are no last moment delays during check-out in the morning that may lead to delays in the itinerary for the day.

PROVIDING INFORMATION TO THE GUEST

Every tour manager is expected to have the complete details of the hotel booked for group's stay. Providing the correct information about the hotel is a primary responsibility of a tour manager. He must share the given information with his guests in the following areas.

Orienting the Guests about Facilities

A tour manager must inform his guests about the amenities available in the hotel. He must brief his guests on the availability of the following services:

- Room service
- Gym facility
- Swimming pool
- Spas and sauna facility
- Restaurants in the hotel
- Pubs and bars, if any in the hotel
- Discotheques
- Business centre
- Wi-Fi facilities
- Complimentary activities offered by the hotel, if any, for example adventure activities
- Casino facilities, if any
- Famous shows hosted by the hotel, if any (e.g., in Las Vegas, the Bellagio hotel organises the 'Fountains of Bellagio' show every 15 minutes from 8:00 PM onwards till midnight that is complimentary for its guests)

Recommending the Points of Interest Near the Hotel

A tour manager must also introduce his guests to nearby points of interest in the vicinity of the hotel. These may be the nearby famous restaurants, shopping malls, supermarkets, local sightseeing locations, activities, ATMs or foreign exchange counters, pharmacy shops etc. around the hotel. He may suggest the same to his guests in case the guests are interested in exploring the places near the hotel on their own during their free time.

Distributing the Information Cards and City Maps

A tour manager must distribute information cards to his guest. The cards may have the necessary information such as the name of the hotel and its address, and the contact number of the hotel along with the tour managers contact number and other emergency numbers for reference of guests.

Besides, the information cards, the tour manager may also distribute city maps to his guests, as available at the hotel, that may contain the necessary information about the attractions and activities in the town in case they wish to be on their own.

Familiarising with the Layout of the Hotel

It is expected that the tour manager is well versed with the hotel layout beforehand. This becomes more imperative, especially in case of large hotels, which have more than a thousand rooms and there are chances that the guests in this hotel might feel lost. Hence, the tour manager must introduce the hotel layout to his guests. In case there is a map in the hotel lobby, it becomes easier for the tour manager to explain the layout. He must share with his guest the whereabouts of the main areas of the hotel often visited by the guests during their stay, that is, lobby, lift area, swimming pool, gym, restaurant and so on.

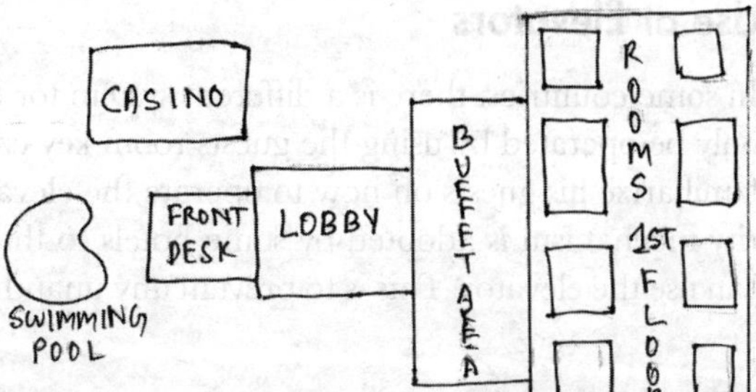

Daily Briefing

A tour manager must brief his group every day about the next day's itinerary in the hotel premises. He must remind his group about the timings of a wake-up call, breakfast timings and the meeting point of the group members at the hotel before departing for sightseeing tours for the next day. Generally, the briefing of the guests may take place at the reception area/lobby area/lounge area/dining area of the hotel.

Communicating the Guidelines of Hotel: Conduct Rules

Every hotel has specific standards of behaviour to be followed by the guests staying in that hotel. When with a group of guests at a hotel, the tour manager must communicate the basic etiquette/rules applicable to the hotel. The tour manager may advise his visitors about some of the following.

Use of Toilets

Some guests who have the habit of using wet toilets are not familiar with the system of dry toilets. For example, in the dry toilets, there is no drainage system except in the bathing area. If the water is spilled outside the bathing area while taking a bath, the water will not be drained out, and it shall enter the room that might damage the carpeted area. This may lead to penalty charges for tourists for not abiding by the rules of the hotel. Hence, it is advisable for the tour manager to always communicate the guidelines of using toilets clearly to his guests staying in that hotel.

Use of Minibar-cum-Refrigerator

In most of the hotels, there is a minibar-cum-refrigerator in which food and beverage items have been placed that are chargeable. Also, sometimes these minibar-cum-refrigerators may have sensors. Once the items are removed from their place in the minibar-cum-refrigerator, even if it has not been consumed, it is considered as consumed/sold which may add up to the price in the final billing of the guest. These things are essential for the notice of the guests and must be communicated to them before arriving at the hotel so that the guests are not shocked when settling the unwanted bills due to sheer ignorance and insufficient advice by the tour manager. Therefore, a tour manager must adequately explain the hotel guidelines for the use of minibar-cum-refrigerator.

Use of Elevators

In some countries, there is a different system for the use of elevators in the hotels. The elevators can only be operated by using the guests room key cards. Therefore, in such cases, a tour manager must familiarize his guests on how to operate the elevators to have access to their rooms easily. This security mechanism is adopted by some hotels so that only the guest who has a reservation in the hotel can use the elevator. This is to prevent any unauthorized person from entering any of the hotel floors.

Use of Television

Some of the hotels charge money for watching specific television channels. It generally happens that while surfing the TV during free time, the hotel guests might subscribe to some channels for which they might have to pay at the time of checking out from the hotel. These things might sound small, but such things are significant from a guests' perspective. Therefore, a tour manager must apprise his guests about the paid channels policy so that the guests are not shocked during check-out time when they are asked to make the payment for watching TV channels.

Drinking Water Facility

In many hotels, one or two mineral water bottles are complimentary per day for a room. However, in some hotels, mineral water bottles may not be complimentary. The tour manager in certain parts of the world, like in some countries of Europe, suggests their client to consume tap water from wash basin directly as the water is suitable for drinking. In such hotels, where the tap water is potable, the water glasses are placed inside the toilets for the guests. This timely, suggestion of the tour manager may save the extra cents for the guests.

Miscellaneous Services

A tour manager must at the very outset clarify about the extra charges that a guest might have to incur in case the guests avail the facilities in the hotel, for example, room service, laundry services, making personal phone calls and so on.

SUMMARY

To crown it all, a tour manager is the caretaker of his guests during their stay at the hotel. He takes the lead role in facilitating various arrangements at a hotel to make the overall stay of tourists a pleasant and comfortable experience. His prior knowledge of the hotel helps him in deal with guest's queries more confidently. He must meticulously and diligently understand his responsibilities and take utmost care in delivering them to make the stay of his guests a memorable experience in a hotel.

Activity 1 Visit hotels

Identify the three major hotels of your city. Visit them and learn about the category of the hotel, facilities provided, the category of rooms, hotel rules, hotel layout, distance between airport and hotel, nearby locations, markets, pharmacy shops, supermarkets and so on.

Now come back to the classroom and pick a hotel of your choice. Assume the role of a tour manager and brief your guests about the above-mentioned points that must be conveyed to them prior to arrival at a hotel.

Activity 2 Post-arrival briefing

Divide yourself into a group of four–five students. One member may assume the role of a tour manager and the other members may act as tourists. Now you are at the hotel lobby. The French group of guests has just arrived at the hotel in London. Being the tour manager of the group, enact all the responsibilities required to be performed by you during the check-in of the guest at the reception area.

POSSIBLE SOLUTIONS TO THE OPENING VIGNETTE

- Since, they were already more than halfway and they had to reach the airport on time, the coach couldn't be returned back.
- Immediately, Mihir gave a call to the hotel reception and apprised them about the whole incident. He informed the staff about the room number where Peter was staying and enquired if they had discovered any lost wallet and camera of the client. To his surprise, the camera and wallet were placed safely in the lost and found box of the hotel.
- On being reassured by the hotel that the stuff of the client was in the safe custody of the hotel, Mihir requested the hotel staff to courier the stuff to his company's address.
- In turn, he promised Peter that he shall courier the camera and wallet at his address once he receives it. In return, Peter arranged 200 pounds somehow and gave it to Mihir for bearing the expenses of courier.

- Later, in few days' time, on receiving the camera and wallet, Mihir couriered the camera and wallet of Peter at his address.
- Soon, within few days of receiving his camera and wallet, Peter's family sent an appreciation letter to the company, praising Mihir of his kind gesture. They also sent an invitation to Mihir to visit London and stay with them for a vacation.

Lessons Learned

- It always pays to be good. A tour manager may have to go an extra mile to help his clients at times. He must be ready to be a good caretaker.

11

Responsibilities at an Attraction

LEARNING OBJECTIVES

- What is an attraction? What are the different kinds of attractions?
- What are the preparations that a tour manager must do before leading his guests to an attraction?
- What are the responsibilities of a tour manager at an attraction?

Samarth was leading a group of seven Swedish clients on a local sightseeing tour in Delhi. After having made them visit Jama Masjid, he had Qutub Minar on the itinerary. As Samarth went with his group to Qutub Minar, he realized that there was a huge crowd of school girls who seemed to be on an educational tour. On seeing these tourists, the girls got excited and started approaching them in numbers.

Out of the lot, a few girls requested the tourists for a selfie with them to which his guests politely agreed. Samarth tried to take control of the situation and asked his guests to refrain from taking selfies and to stay cautious since the girls were large in numbers. But the guests did not pay any heed to Samarth's advice and kept enjoying being clicked with the school girls. Suddenly, in the heat of moment, Johnsson, one of the tourists, realised that his camera was missing. He had lost sight of it and now he was totally zapped as to what to do. With all his wit, Johnsson immediately started searching for his camera here and there. But in vain!

Sightseeing is an integral part of a traveller's experience. One of the most important motivations or the pull factors are the attractions or 'anchor tenants' at a destination that push a tourist to leave his domicile and travel to another place to see these attractions. Tourists might travel to these attractions on their own or may book a package tour through a travel agent/tour operator who may facilitate their visit to these attractions. Generally, on package tours, these attractions are clubbed and packaged as a sightseeing tour that may be for a full day or half a day. Full-day sightseeing tours include a visit to multiple attractions at a destination. However, in case of half-day sightseeing tours, the tourists might be given an option for shopping or spending time on their own after having done the sightseeing for half a day.

INTRODUCTION

A tourist attraction may refer to a place of interest where tourists visit typically for its inherent or exhibited natural or cultural value, historical significance, built beauty, offering leisure, adventure and amusement. The different categories of attractions that tourists generally visit with their suitable examples are as follows:

- **Monuments and historical places**
  - The Colosseum, Italy
  - The Taj Mahal, India
- **Forts, palaces and castles**
  - The Buckingham Palace, London, UK
  - The City Palace, Udaipur, India
- **Iconic artificial structures and buildings**
  - The Madurodam, Holland
  - The Burj Khalifa, Dubai
  - The Eiffel Tower, Paris, France
  - The London Eye, London, UK
  - The Opera House, Sydney, Australia
  - The Golden Bridge, San Francisco, USA

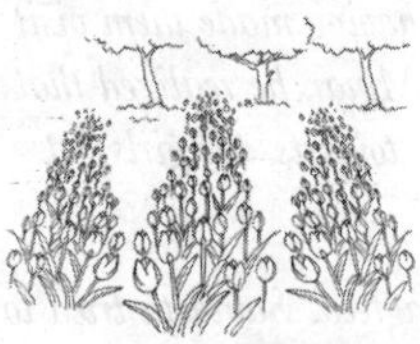

- **Botanical gardens and parks**
  - The Central Park, New York
  - The Keukenhof Tulip and Flower Gardens, Holland
  - The Royal Botanic Garden, Victoria, Melbourne, Australia
  - The Miracle Garden, Dubai
- **Museums**
  - The Louvre Museum, Paris, France
  - The Madame Tussauds Museum, London, UK
  - The Digital Museum, Amritsar, India
  - The Swarovski Crystal Museum, Austria

- **Art galleries**
  - The Metropolitan Museum of Art, New York, USA
  - The National Gallery, London, UK
  - The National Gallery of Modern Art, New Delhi, India
- **Religious shrines (temples, mosques, gurudwaras, churches and monasteries)**
  - The Sun Temple, Konark, India
  - The Lotus Temple, New Delhi, India
  - The Ajmer Sharif Dargah, Ajmer, India
  - The Golden Temple, Amritsar, India

- o The Thicksey Monastery, Ladakh, India
- o The St. Peter's Basilica Church, Vatican

- **National parks, wildlife sanctuaries, zoos and aquariums**
  - o The Yosemite National Park, USA
  - o The Serengeti National Park, Tanzania
  - o The Melbourne Zoo, Australia
  - o The Sea Life Aquarium, Sydney, Australia
- **Amusement parks and theme parks**
  - o The Disneyland, Orlando, USA
  - o The Euro Disney, Paris, France
  - o The Dreamworld, Gold Coast, Australia
  - o Ferrari World, Abu Dhabi, UAE
  - o The Universal Studios, Los Angeles, USA
  - o The Chokhi Dhani, Jaipur, India
- **Natural sites such as mountains, hills and deserts**
  - o The Mt. Titlis, Lucerne, in Switzerland
  - o The Tro aux Cerfs Volcano, Mauritius
  - o The Great Barrier Reef, Australia
  - o The Thar Desert, Jaisalmer

- **Water bodies (lakes, waterfalls, beaches and rivers)**
  - o The Lake Michigan, USA
  - o The Pangong Tso Lake, Ladakh
  - o The Manly Beach, Sydney
  - o The Rhine Falls-Europe
  - o The Niagra Falls, USA
  - o The Ganges River in Haridwar and Varanasi

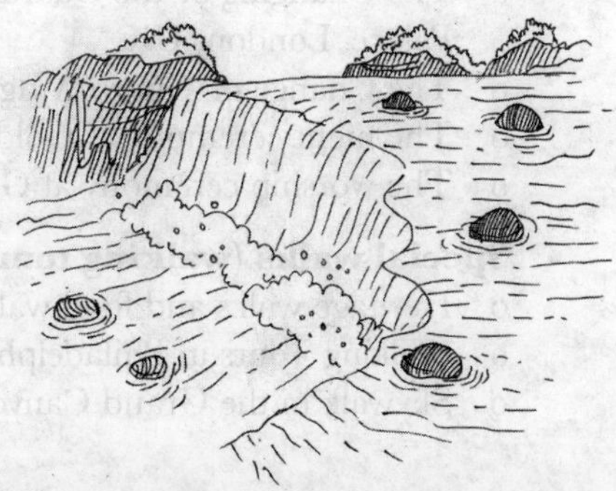

- **Famous shows**
  - o The Acrobatic Show, Shanghai, China
  - o The Lido Show, Paris, France
  - o The Ka Show in Las Vegas, USA
- **Events such as fairs, festivals and sports events**
  - o The Tomorrowland, Belgium
  - o The Pushkar Fair, Rajasthan, India
  - o The La Tomatina Festival, Spain
  - o The IPL, India
- **Activities**
  - o The nightlife in Las Vegas, USA
  - o Gambling in casinos

- o Rides at amusement parks
- o Shopping (Shopping festival in Dubai)
- o Boat tours (boat tours in Varanasi, India)
- o Food walks (Kamla Market, New Delhi)
- o Water sports and adventure activities (e.g., water activities at islands like Mauritius, and sand dune Bashing at Dubai)

- **Study tours and factory visits**
  - o Visit to cheese and shoes factories in Amsterdam, Holland for watching cheese making
  - o Moreno Glass Factory, Venice, Italy, for viewing glass manufacturing
  - o Cuckoo clocks demonstration, Black Forest, Germany, for seeing demo of cuckoo clocks
  - o Sula Vineyards, Nasik, India/Napa Valley Vineyards, San Francisco, USA, for understanding how wine is manufactured
  - o Glenburg Tea Estate, Darjeeling, India, for learning how tea is made

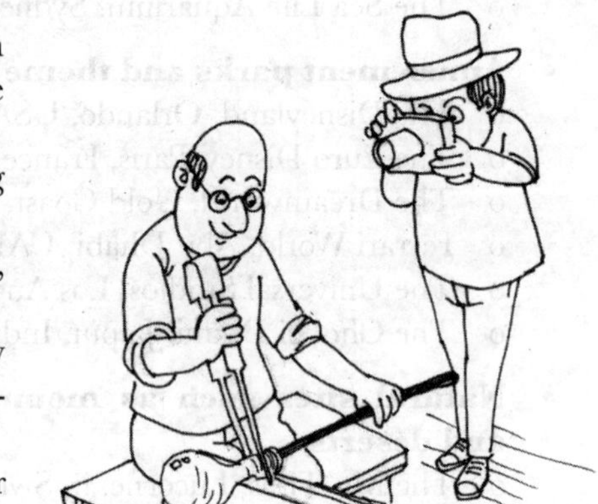

- **Special ceremonies**
  - o The Changing of the Guard, The Buckingham Palace, London, UK
  - o The Change of Guard, Wagah Border, Amritsar, India
  - o The night ceremony at Golden Temple, Amritsar, India
  - o The worship ceremony at Ganga Ghat, Varanasi, India
- **Special walks (walking tours and heritage walks)**
  - o Heritage walks and food walks in Chandni Chowk, New Delhi, India
  - o Walking Tours in Philadelphia, USA, and Rome, Italy
  - o Skywalk in the Grand Canyon, USA

WHY TRAVEL WITH A TOUR MANAGER TO ATTRACTIONS?

Travel to an attraction on a package tour is facilitated by the tour manager. The following are the advantages of travelling with a tour manager at an attraction:

- The presence of a tour manager at the attractions makes the tourists feel more comfortable as there is someone in an unknown place who takes care of them and acts as a companion to his guests.
- The tour manager acts as a spokesperson for the attraction who introduces the guests to an attraction. Through his knowledge of the attraction, he may help to interpret the

context of the attraction to his guests that may make more sense to the guests. Given the expertise of the tour manager, the tourists can gain a better perspective of the attractions.
- The presence of a tour manager at the attractions also saves time of the guests as he may focus only on important things to be shown in the attraction within the stipulated time.
- He also educates the guests about the rules and regulations to be followed at an attraction that may help them to conduct themselves in a better way at the attraction.
- He may also apprise his guests about the facilities available at an attraction.

RESPONSIBILITIES OF A TOUR MANAGER AT AN ATTRACTION

A tour manager has many roles, duties and responsibilities to perform at an attraction. The tour managers' role at attractions can broadly be divided into the following categories:

- Before visiting an attraction
- At the attraction

BEFORE VISITING AN ATTRACTION

Every attraction has certain important aspects which need to be communicated to the guests. For delivering those elements to the guests, a tour manager must thoroughly gather all the necessary information and facts about the attraction being visited by the guests. Therefore, before visiting any attraction, a tour manager must brush up his knowledge thoroughly so that he may be able to confidently deliver the necessary points to be shared with his guests at the attraction.

A tour manager must be aware of various aspects before visiting an attraction.

Visiting Hours of the Attraction

Every attraction has fixed hours of visitation. A tour manager must be aware of the visiting hours so that he may plan his itinerary according to the hours of visitation and may not miss on the attraction.

Days Closed for the Attraction

Some attractions may be closed on particular days. Besides specific days, an attraction may also be closed on account of certain public holidays. An attraction may also be closed on account of security reasons due to some event taking place at the attraction. For example, on the eve of Queen Elizabeth's birthday, many attractions such as the Buckingham Palace and nearby monuments and streets may be sealed for the security reasons. Also during the 'Changing of Guards Ceremony' at the Buckingham Palace, there may be limited access for public, and the timings of the ceremony may also be revamped accordingly. Likewise, most of the museums in India are closed on Mondays.

The famous Taj Mahal in India is closed on Fridays. It can be very disappointing for the guests if their visits are planned on the closing days. Thus, the tour manager must keep himself updated with such information before the commencement of the tour.

Entry Ticket, If Any

Many attractions may charge an entry ticket. A tour manager must be aware if an entry fee is required. A tour manager must also know the price of entry ticket in case the entry is chargeable.

Also during the peak seasons, when there is a massive rush of tourists, a tour manager may buy entry tickets in advance so that his guests do not have to waste their time at the attraction waiting for the tour manager to buy tickets. For example, due to massive rush in summers in France, it is advisable for a tour manager to buy the entry tickets in advance for visiting the top story of Eiffel Tower. Otherwise, the guests may be stranded for hours while the tour manager struggles to buy tickets among the heavy rush.

Making Reservations in Advance

At many attractions, it is advisable to make advanced reservations for access to the attraction/ watching shows to avoid any delays in the scheduled itinerary. This is important, especially during the peak seasons when there are hordes of tourists visiting an attraction at the same time that may lead to non-availability of reservations for the guests. For example, for watching the popular Lido show in Paris in summers or the Light and Sound Show in Cellular Jail, Andaman and Nicobar Islands, India, the tour manager may have to make reservations for his group in advance to avoid the guests standing in queues. He may also ensure that he gets all the seats reserved together so that all the group members may be seated around the tour manager.

Arranging Travel Documentation

Some attractions require documentation and permits for a visit. A tour manager must be aware of such requirements, if any, for visiting such attractions. He must arrange for the necessary documentation before the arrival at the attraction so that the guests may not have to waste their time waiting for the permits. For example, to visit the Nicobar Islands in India, foreigners as well as domestic tourists are required to show permits at checkposts before travelling there. Therefore, a tour manager must arrange these necessary documents well in advance, especially during peak seasons when there are queues of tourists waiting to get the permits.

Photography and Videography Policy

At many attractions, taking photographs and videography is not permissible due to security reasons and religious beliefs. At some attractions, it is allowed but with some charges. At some attractions, it may be free. Therefore, a tour manager must be aware of the policy of attraction regarding photography and videography so that he may be able to communicate the same to his guests.

Facilities at an Attraction

Tourist attractions may have some facilities to make the visit comfortable. Generally, the facilities at an attraction may include the following:

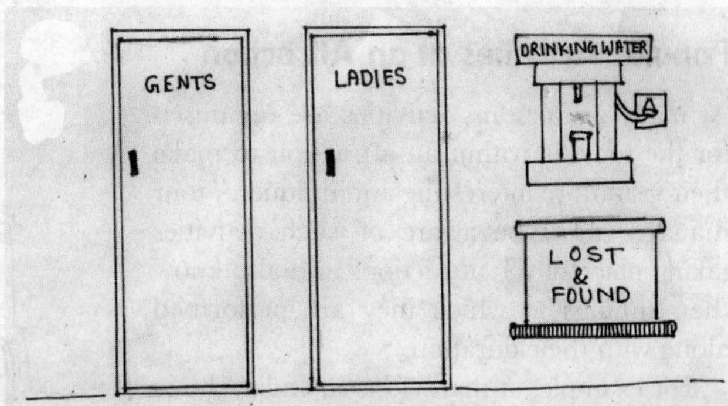

- Public conveniences such as washroom facilities, drinking water and so on
- Eating outlets and restaurants
- Shopping arcades
- Wi-Fi facilities
- Lockers
- Lost and found box
- Facilities for people with special requirements such as hearing aids, ramps, wheelchairs and so on
- Availability of audio-guided devices at an attraction, etc.
- Medical facilities, if required

A tour manager must be aware of such facilities at an attraction, and he must communicate about the availability of such facilities to his guests.

Gathering Knowledge About the Points of Interest at an Attraction

Every attraction has some stoppages that are the top visual priorities. A tour manager must stop at these locations and give an explanation to his guests that they may find very unique and exciting to learn. Therefore, it is essential for him to have prior knowledge of such points of interest at the attraction before he starts the tour. For example, while visiting the Grand Canyon in Arizona, USA, that is famous for its deep gorges, rock formations and ridges, a tour manager must suggest to his guests the following points of interests that they may like to do:

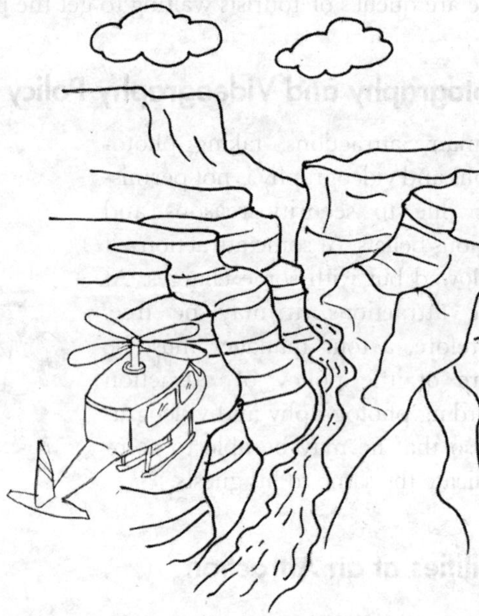

- Helicopter tours
- Visit to Grand Canyon Village
- Walk to the Bright Angel Trail and Rim Trail
- Raft at Colorado River

Popular Activities at an Attraction

At many attractions, activities are organised for the tourists within an attraction to make their visit more interesting and unique. A tour manager must be aware of such activities taking place at the attractions and also know their timings at which they are performed along with their duration.

For example, at many forts in India, shows are organised for the guests which highlight the legacy of these forts. The Light and Sound Show at Red Fort, New Delhi, and the Laser show and 7D show at Guru Gobindgarh Fort, Amritsar, are some of the excellent examples of the activities at these forts that help in sustaining the interest of the tourists besides just visiting these forts for passive sightseeing. Many other activities such as horse rides, camel rides, traditional dance performances and local street food are showcased for the tourists at Guru Gobindgarh Fort to familiarise the guests with the rich culture of Punjab and make the visit more exciting and engaging. Likewise, tourists are taken for elephant rides at Amber Fort, Jaipur, followed by a visit to Hathigaon (Elephants' village) where the guests can ride, paint, feed and bath the elephants, which are exciting activities.

Things to Carry

A tour manager must share information about the things that a guest may take or may not take at an attraction. However, it must be borne in mind that the things to carry would depend upon the attraction being visited. In general, the tour manager may advise his guests to carry the following items at an attraction:

- Umbrella
- Water bottle
- Sunglasses
- Hats or cap
- Sunscreen lotion

Also, at many attractions, many things are not allowed. Therefore, the tour manager must inform his guests about the things that may not be permissible inside the attraction. For example, in some temples such as Akshardham Temple, New Delhi, India, one can't carry electronic items, food items and leather items like purses inside the temple. However, such places may have locker facilities which the tour manager should be aware of. Accordingly, he may advise his guests to deposit their belongings in lockers. Likewise, in Disneyland, USA, visitors are not permitted to take selfie sticks with them.

Knowledge of Dos and Don'ts at an Attraction

Every attraction has its own set of rules and regulations that a tourist must abide by. It is expected of a tour manager to have a thorough knowledge of these norms of the attraction that the tour manager is taking his group to. It is crucial for a tour manager to explicitly specify these rules and regulations to his guests so that his guests may not be unnecessary stopped from entering these attractions or unnecessarily harassed due to ignorance of the rules they might violate unintentionally.

AT AN ATTRACTION

We have just identified the things that a tour manager must know before visiting an attraction. Now let us have a final discussion on the responsibilities of a tour manager at an attraction.

Following is the list of duties that a tour manager is expected to perform at an attraction.

Purchase and Distribution of Entry Tickets

Generally, most of the attractions such as historical sites, artificial structures, forts, national parks, botanical gardens, museums, galleries, theme parks and so on have an entry ticket to be paid by the tourists.

In case of escorted tours, the tour manager purchases these entry tickets at the attraction and pays the entry fee on behalf of the tourists.

He then distributes these tickets to his group members to gain entry inside the attraction.

Distribution of Map of the Attraction

One of the most important things that a tour manager is expected to do at an attraction is to search for the maps of the attraction, if any, that are available at the information counter of the attraction and distribute the same to his group members.

These maps are significant from a tourist's perspective as these contain the complete layout of the attraction along with directions and facilities available at the attraction.

For example, the map of Disneyland theme park in Los Angeles, USA, is available at the information counters which may be collected by the tour manager to distribute the same to his guests. The Disneyland map may contain the following information for the visitors:

- Layout
- Information about amusement rides, that is, timings and the venues
- Information about restaurants and eating outlets
- Information about shopping arcades
- Other facilities available such as washrooms, lockers and etc. along with their locations
- Show timings

This may be useful for the tourists to plan their stops during their visit to the park and utilise their stipulated time at the attraction in the most productive way.

Ensuring the Compliance of Group Members in Proper Queues

During peak seasons, most attractions are flooded with hordes of tourists. While visiting these attractions, a tour manager must ensure that the group members are all lined up together and that they stand in proper queues before entering the gates of the attraction. Maintaining discipline of the group is a very challenging task for the tour manager.

Visitors Briefing

A tour manager must brief the following things to his group members while visiting an attraction.

Cooperating with Security Check

Before visiting an attraction, a tour manager must instruct his group about the necessary security checks which the group might have to go through at an attraction. It may be the individual screening, that is, passing through the metal detector gates or getting their hand baggage screened through X-ray machines. He must request his group members to cooperate with the security staff at an attraction.

Communicating the Meeting Point and Total Time to be Spent

Generally, when the tour manager is leading the group, many group members may stroll and may not be able to catch up with the tour manager. Also, when the tour manager is talking about the attraction, many guests may not be interested in his commentary and get busy with other group members clicking their pictures. Also, some guests might stop at certain shopping points, whereas some might stop to eat something. As a result, the guests may lose track of the tour manager and, therefore, might get lost.

It might also happen at times that the tour manager stays at the entry point in the attraction and ask his group members to go and visit the attraction on their own. Notably, in theme parks, the tour manager might not go inside the theme park with the group and prefer to stay at the entry point. Also, an attraction may have multiple exits that may confuse the tourists.

Therefore, before the group disperses in different directions, a tour manager at the entry point of attraction must clearly convey the meeting point to his guests in case they wish to be on their own at the attraction. He must also explicitly specify the total time that the group shall spend at the attraction. In fact, the tour manager may ask his group members to match their watches with him so that there are no unnecessary delays in the departure for the next attraction.

Communicating About Facilities at an Attraction

Every attraction has certain facilities available to make the visits comfortable. A tour manager must be aware of such facilities available at an attraction. He must also brief his guests about the various facilities available at the attraction.

He must give clear directions to the guest of the washroom facilities, drinking water facilities, restaurants at the attraction, Wi-Fi facilities, locker facilities, lost and found box, and shopping points if any, at the attraction.

Communicating the Dos and Don'ts at an Attraction

Briefing about the code of conduct at an attraction is essential as there may be specific rules for every attraction. For example, in case of mountain excursions/beaches/holy shrines, a tour manager needs to mentally prepare his group to follow the specific protocol at such places before visiting them. Some prior preparations may be required on the part of the tourists.

In case of a group of tourists going for a mountain excursion, a tour manager may give the following briefing to his group members:

- Eat light before travelling
- Wear warm clothes
- Wear comfortable sports shoes that are not slippery
- Take camphor and keep smelling it as it might help in dealing with less oxygen in the air
- Carry medicines
- Keep hydrated at all times

Also, while visiting the holy shrines, a tour manager must clearly instruct his guests to observe specific rules and regulations practised in these sacred places. For example, while visiting St. Peter's Basilica Church in Vatican, the guests are advised to cover their arms and knees before entering the Church. Therefore, the tour manager must advise his guests not to wear sleeveless dress or shorts while visiting the church. Likewise, while visiting a gurudwara, the place of worship for the Sikh community, visitors must keep their head covered to give respect to their religious beliefs.

Also, while visiting amusement parks, the tour manager suggests that his group members take care of their safety by wearing safety belts during rides, and that they may not take selfie sticks inside the theme park where it is not permissible.

At many places, the tourists might have to walk a lot. Thus, a tour manager must advise his guests to prefer wearing sports shoes and not heels which might hurt their feet eventually. In case, he has some elderly guests in his group, he may suggest that they rest often or relax at pre-decided points and take a breather in case they are not comfortable walking further to cover the whole distance at the attraction.

Therefore, every attraction shall have its own set of instructions that the tour manager must communicate and convey to his guests to abide by.

Commentary at the Points of Interest

Every attraction has certain stoppages or points of interest that demand an explanation by the tour manager. Thus, on entering an attraction, a tour manager must be aware of such points of interest where the tourists might want to stop and learn about the importance of such locations. He must adequately brief his guests about the various points of interest. However, he might not be required to have minutest details of the points when he is being accompanied by a local tour guide. Though when he is travelling alone with the group, he must be very thorough with the main attraction points of interest and must be able to explain in detail these points at the attraction being visited.

For example, while visiting theme parks such as Disneyland or Sea World in Los Angeles, a tour manager must brief his group about the exciting rides and the various shows that they must not miss while visiting these attractions.

Likewise, while visiting the Madame Tussauds Museum in London, he may suggest that his guest take the exciting 'Spirit of London Taxi Ride' besides appreciating the wax statues of famous celebrities.

Keeping the Group Together

The primary issue that a tour manager faces while conducting a visit to attractions is of keeping the group together. It is the most challenging job for a tour manager as guests have a tendency of forming subgroups. These subgroups of tourists may start moving in different directions losing sight of the tour manager. These guests might not be interested in the commentary and may like to move freely on their own inside the attraction, clicking pictures and exploring the attraction. As a result, the tour manager may be unable to trace such group members who don't go along with him from one point to another point inside the attraction. This might ultimately lead to unnecessary delays during the departure.

It is essential for a tour manager to understand that he cannot afford to be a strict disciplinarian as he is dealing with those people who are in a holiday mood and not school kids. Thus, striking a balance between discipline and fun is the key to keeping the group together at an attraction.

To deal with such situation, where all the guests are likely to disperse in different directions, a tour manager may suggest to his group members during the briefing at the attraction, the meeting point and meeting time of the group where they all might meet in case they wish to be on their own or in case they lose sight of the tour manager.

Recommending the Points of Photography

A tour manager is supposed to be an expert of an attraction as he might have visited the same attraction a number of times before. Thus, it is understood that he is already aware of the best scenic points and best places from where the best photographs may be clicked. Therefore, a tour manager must be able to recommend various angles and points of photography to his guests from where the best pictures may be captured by his guests. Acting as a travel photographer consultant may delight his guests and may create a lasting impression in their minds.

Distribution of Packed Lunches

Many package tours operate on the American Plan where all the meals including breakfast, lunch, and dinner are arranged by the travel company for its guests along with the hotel stay. At some attractions in the itinerary, generally on full-day excursions or on long journeys in coaches or trains, the company offers packed lunches to its guests. The idea of serving packed meals is that the timings of the lunch should not be disturbed while travelling. Also, at some places, there is a shortage of good local restaurants where the company recommends packed lunches from its fixed caterers.

Therefore, it is the responsibility of the tour manager to coordinate with the caterer for delivering the meals on time. He should then distribute these lunches to his guests on the coach/train or at the attraction before they disperse in different directions.

Maintaining Discipline

It is the job of the tour manager to maintain the overall discipline of his group members at the attraction. Generally, at most of the attraction points, one would see a number of other tourists also who may be coming on their own or in a group. Therefore, he must ensure that his group members do not misbehave at the attraction and spoil the fun of other tourists while visiting the attraction. The guests must behave and maintain the dignity of the place being visited.

Sticking to the Itinerary

The most significant challenge for a tour manager's job is to stick to the itinerary given by the company. In package tours, guests have been promised a day packaged with famous sightseeing attractions and a number of other activities that must take place on the same day as designed.

A tour manager is always under continuous pressure to cover all the attractions as promised in the itinerary. Managing the time is the most challenging part of the tour manager's job.

This becomes more challenging as sometimes the weather and traffic may not be in his favour. Also, there might be last minute delays on the part of guests due to their spending more time than permitted at a particular attraction or spending more time at shopping arcades. Some guests might reach late for breakfast, and there might be a delay from the start of the tour.

This ultimately leaves less time for the other attraction and makes the itinerary difficult for the tour manager to operate and this puts him under immense pressure.

No matter whatever the situation, a tour manager must remain strict on time and must communicate clearly to his guests that he shall not let the whole group suffer for a bunch of stragglers. He must by any means stick to his itinerary for the day.

Selling Optional Tours

Many travel companies offer optional tours within the package tour to the guests. The idea to keep them as an 'optional tour' is that all guests might not be interested in taking such tours or might not want to spend so much of money on these optional tours. The company also wants to keep the cost of the package low. Therefore, it might give certain attractions as an 'optional' for the guests. Mostly optional tours cover day excursions (e.g., the Grand Canyon optional tour while taking a package for Las Vegas), activities (adventure activities like water sports at Islands), famous shows of destinations (watching an opera at the Sydney Opera House) or visits to theme parks (Sentosa Island Water Cove Adventure Park). The payment for the optional tours is generally collected by the tour manager at the destination itself. Optional tours operate only when there are a minimum number of tourists who are willing to go for that option.

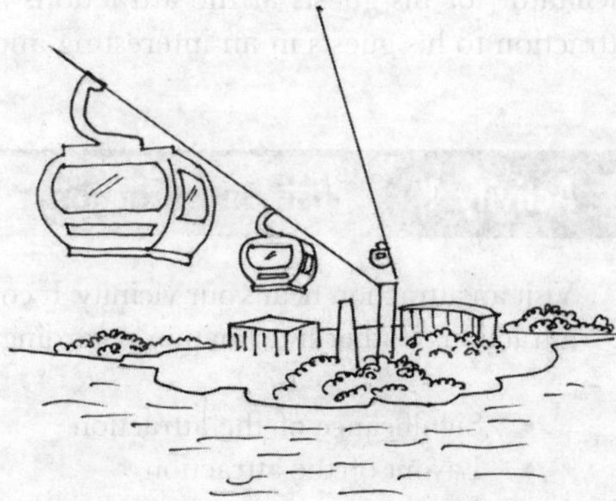

Thus, it is the task of the tour manager to educate his guests about the advantages of taking optional tours as these tours are lifetime opportunities. The guests might not come back to the same destination again. Thus, the tour manager must be able to sell these optional tours to his guests as moments that shall never come back again, and he must collect the payment on behalf of his company for such excursions.

Answering Queries

While visiting attractions, many guests have a question in their mind about that attraction. They may show more inquisitiveness to learn more about the facts about the attraction. It is the job of the tour manager to clarify all the doubts of his group members regarding the attraction by taking all their questions.

Taking Care of the Safety and Security of Guests

At all times, during the trip, a tour manager is responsible for the safety and security of his guests. He is the local guardian and caretaker of his guests. It is the job of the tour manager to warn his guests again theft, uneven terrains, dangerous areas and so on. Thus, at every attraction, he repeat the necessary safety measures to be taken by tourists relevant to that attraction.

For example, at specific attractions which are very crowded such as amusement parks, religious shrines or monuments and so on, the tour manager suggests that his group members take care of their personal belongings such as their luggage, purses, passports, mobile and so on as there are chances of them being stolen. In general, he also issues instructions to his group members to mind their steps in uneven terrain. He also suggests that his group members remain aware of touts and beggars. He may even ask the parents not to lose sight of their children. For example, at Eiffel

Tower, the parents are advised to keep their children along with them as the tower has a sky-high height.

SUMMARY

The list and gamut of responsibilities of a tour manager at an attraction are exhaustive. However, he must do his job very meticulously and must ensure that he does not miss out on any critical instructions. He must adequately brief his group before visiting an attraction. He must act as a facilitator for his guests at the attractions being visited. He must communicate the essence of an attraction to his guests in an interesting and engaging manner.

Activity 1 Visit an attraction

Visit an attraction near your vicinity. It could be a monument, museum, theme park or any other attraction. Gather information regarding the following aspects of the attraction:

- Significance of the attraction
- Layout of the attraction
- Important points to be covered at the attraction
- Visiting hours of the attraction
- Closing days, if any
- Entry fee, if any
- Camera policy and video policy for the attraction
- Washroom and restaurant whereabouts
- Rules to be followed at an attraction
- Things to carry

Activity 2 Role play

Divide your class into groups of four–five students. Ask each group to select an attraction of their own choice. To maintain interest in the activity, every group may take a different attraction. The following attractions may be covered by each group of the class:

- A botanical garden
- A theme park
- A temple
- A historical monument
- A museum

Let each group perform a roleplay of 15–20 minutes in which every member of the group may get an opportunity to become a tour manager and the other members may act as tourists. Let every member stand in front of the group as a tour manager and brief the rest of the members about the various points to be communicated to the group members before visiting an attraction. The rest of the class may watch the activity and ask questions, if any, from the group members.

POSSIBLE SOLUTIONS TO THE OPENING VIGNETTE

- Samarth tried to pacify his guest and empathise with him.
- He also took the lead of searching his guests' camera with him at every nook and corner of the place.
- He also asked the girls if they had seen his camera.
- On not finding the camera, Samarth went with Johnsson to the local police station and helped him file an FIR regarding the missing camera. However, in spite of Samarth's best efforts, the camera could not be traced.

Lessons Learned

- Ask your guests to remain cautious and alert at all times.
- Before visiting an attraction, the tour manager must brief his guests about the possible scenarios that may happen at an attraction and how to deal with them.
- He may also brief his guests about the mishappenings or incidents that may have occurred previously with other groups.
- He must also ask his guests to take care of their personal belongings all the time and to keep checking their bags from time to time.

12

Responsibilities on the Coach

LEARNING OBJECTIVES

- What is the responsibility of a tour manager on a coach during the tour?
- What are the things that should be borne in mind by the tour manager while dealing with guests on the coach?

The coach was not heading anywhere. Ali, the pilot, had taken the keys and got down from the bus. Raj, the tour leader, was requesting him to continue with the tour, but in vain.

It was a group of tourists from USA who were on a tour of Uttarakhand, the hill state of northern India. The party started from Delhi, and they were to travel on a coach for four days. Raj was a seasoned tour leader and a destination expert for Uttarakhand. He was asked by the company to accompany this group of 17 young boys and girls. The group was sure that they will leave no chance to enjoy this exotic trip to India. It all started well on a high note. The group sang and pranked as they drove. Whenever the group found interesting things on their way, they would get down from the bus to experience the same and click a few photographs.

They had already stopped four times including a scheduled stop in the last five hours, and they were already two hours behind the schedule. Realising the delay, Raj asked Ali to drive straight to the next stoppage without halting at non-scheduled stopovers. Having politely being told that they cannot break in between as they need to go as per the itinerary, the group kept on insisting and started requesting the pilot directly. Ali refused to entertain their request and this annoyed the guests. A heated argument ensued, and Ali stopped the bus at a shoulder.

Raj tried to intervene to avoid the heated arguments between Ali and the group. He requested the group not to talk directly to the pilot. However, he did not succeed. The arguments turned into a brawl and became uglier when Ali responded by shouting at one of the tourists, and, in turn, the tourist got so offended that he punched him hard on face. Ali got down of the bus and refused to drive forward.

Raj was caught in an embarrassing situation. He apologised on behalf of the tourist. Ali insisted that the tourist who hit him should come and apologise. The tourist refused to oblige.

The coach may be referred to as a 'second home' for the guests on group tours as much of the time on a trip is spent on travelling from one place to another. Moving from one point of interest to another point of interest is generally done through a coach. Travelling through a coach may be from:

- One attraction to another attraction in the same city (also called as local transfers on seat in coach [SIC] basis)
- A destination to another destination (it may be interstate, i.e., from one state to another state; intercity, from one city to another city; or sometimes, from one country to another country [e.g., Europe])

During this travel, which is generally extendable up to multiple days, a tour manager accompanies his group on the coach from the beginning until the end.

INTRODUCTION

On the coach, a tour manager has a number of tasks, duties and responsibilities to take care of. Now let us have a detailed discussion on each of the responsibilities that he is expected to carry out on the coach.

NOSE COUNT OF GUESTS

This is the first thing that a tour manager is expected to do on the coach. After the guests board the coach, he must do the nose count of his guest inside the coach. In other words, he must count the total number of passengers who have boarded the coach according to the guest list provided to him by the company. This nose count/headcount is very important for him as missing out on even one passenger may create an embarrassing situation for the tour manager and bring a bad name to both the company as well as him.

WELCOMING THE GROUP ON COACH

When meeting the group for the first time, a tour manager must welcome all his guests formally on the coach. He may do this by greeting the guest in different languages according to nationalities of the group members he is handling. This helps in creating an overall good impression of the tour manager in front of his guests. After greeting the guests, he must formally thank his guests on behalf of his company for having chosen his company to travel with. Then, he must introduce himself to the guests and share his prior work experience and his contact details with them.

INTRODUCING THE PILOT AND CO-PILOT

One important person on the coach is the driver who is also called the pilot of the coach or the coach captain. The tour manager must introduce the pilot to the guests. He must handle the pilot's introduction in a very dignified way by honouring him as the most important person on the coach before his guests. He must share the name of the pilot and also give an overview of his driving experience to his guests along with his contact details. In case of an assistant in the coach, the tour manager must also introduce the assistant, called as the co-pilot, to his guests.

SYNCHRONISING WATCHES

The first thing that a tour manager must do on meeting the group on the coach is to request the group members to match their watches with him. This is very important as everyone may come back in the coach after rest breaks according to the timings in their watches, which may be 5–10 minutes later than the actual time. Therefore, to avoid any such delays in the departures and to stick to the scheduled itinerary, he must ask his group members to synchronize their watches with the watch of the tour manager.

SEEKING COOPERATION

The tour manager must at the very outset ask his group members to extend cooperation in every possible way so that the trip can be a joyful experience for everyone. He may request his guests to extend their cooperation by demonstrating respect for fellow tourists and being on time as punctuality is the key to a successful tour. He must also request his guests to cooperate in two situations that are beyond his control. These two uncertain cases are the traffic and the weather that may be encountered by the group any time, and that may lead to the delays in the scheduled itinerary. The idea of seeking cooperation from guests on these fronts is to prepare the guests mentally so that they do not grumble later during the unforeseen situations.

FAMILIARISATION WITH THE COACH

As the guests spend a lot of their time travelling on the coach, a tour manager must familiarise his guests with the coach. He should tell the guests about the 'make' of the coach, the coach number and the colour of the coach. This is very important as in case the guests get lost in an attraction, they can go back to the coach on their own where it has been parked and, hence, join the group again.

He must also orient his guests to the emergency exits, emergency doors, fire extinguishers and first aid box inside the coach in case they encounter any unforeseen situations.

COMMUNICATING THE FOOD AND BEVERAGE POLICY

Different countries follow different rules as far as the food and beverage policy is concerned inside the coaches. In some countries, eating and drinking inside the coach is permitted, while in some countries eating and drinking is not permissible.

Many guests like to eat snacks and drink inside the coach. However, in many coaches, snacks and beverages are not permitted. The idea is that after eating snacks and cold beverages, the guest may throw the packs inside the coach and spill the garbage around. Also, when someone brings tea/coffee/cold drink inside the coach, it may spill, thereby making the coach dirty. Therefore, he must request his guests not to bring drinks or eatables inside, in case the same is not allowed inside the coach.

AVAILABILITY OF DRINKING WATER BOTTLES

In many coaches, the company keeps a stack of mineral water bottles for its guests that may or may not be chargeable. The idea is to make the travel of guests comfortable and hassle-free as they may have to buy bottles from outside, when thirsty. As a result, the coach driver may also have to take frequent stops to allow the passengers' time to buy a water bottle for them. This may lead to unnecessary delays as a result. Therefore, to avoid such situations and to make the travel of the passengers more convenient, many travel companies stack water bottles on the coach for their guests. In case, such a facility is available inside the coach, a tour manager during the beginning of the tour, must clearly inform his guests about the availability of drinking water.

COMMUNICATING ABOUT THE SMOKING AND DRINKING POLICY

In most of the coaches, smoking and drinking are not permissible. The tour managers, at the beginning of the coach ride, should share with the group, the policy regarding smoking and drinking on the coach.

MAINTAINING THE VEHICLE HYGIENE

Generally, one coach is booked for a particular group of guests, and it remains with the group all through from the beginning till the end of the tour. Keeping the coach clean, therefore, becomes very essential. In most of the countries, there is no assistance for cleaning coaches during the trip. Thus, at the beginning of the trip itself, a tour manager must clearly specify and communicate to his guests about the importance of keeping the coach clean. The guests may be warned that in case they fail to keep the coach clean, they might have to clean the coach themselves only. Therefore, at the onset of the tour, he must inform his guests not to litter inside the coach or spit inside the coach. He may request his guests to keep garbage bags with them and keep collecting the litter. On reaching a site, the guests may dispose of those garbage bags in the dustbins placed there. Alternatively, many coaches have dustbins placed inside them where the guests can throw the wrappers, bottles or other litter when the coach is moving. In case there is a facility of dustbin inside the coach, the tour manager must point out to this available facility and request that his guests to make use of it instead of throwing the garbage here and there.

SHARING INFORMATION ABOUT WASHROOM USAGE

Nowadays, most of the coaches have an inbuilt lavatory at the back of the coach. Generally, a tour manager discourages the use of toilets inside the coach except in case of desperate situations. The reason behind not using these toilets inside the coach is that it causes a foul smell which is annoying for those sitting at the back of coach near the lavatory. Also, enough rest breaks after every 1.5–2 hours are planned in between the long journeys where one can use these public conveniences. Also, when getting down from the coach during the rest breaks, use of public conveniences at these places sometimes may be chargeable. In such cases, where there is a charge for use of public restrooms, he may advise his guests to keep loose change or coins for using the public toilets.

DELIVERING COMMENTARY ABOUT THE DESTINATION

The commentary is an integral part of tour manager's job on the coach. While the coach is moving, a tour manager may initiate a talk about the destination being visited. He must share with his guests the necessary information, interesting facts, the history, geography, politics, culture and life of people at the destination being visited. While moving on the coach and passing by the important landmarks, a tour manager must point out attractions that the he considers are important for the guests to know.

However, the commentary should not be very long, and it should not happen that the tour manager keeps blabbering nonstop throughout the journey on the coach, this may irritate the guests. He must balance his tongue. He should only speak as and when he feels the need to explain a particular point to his guests. He should also allow the guests to have some time on their own to see and feel the places running through the window of the coach.

BRIEFING ABOUT THE DAY'S ITINERARY

At the start of the ride on the coach, a tour manager should brief his guests about the sightseeing points which shall be covered as per the planned scheduled for the day. A tour manager must share highlights of the attractions to be visited during the day. He must also provide instructions, if required to be followed, to the guests about the places to be visited. He must also tell his guests the approximate time that they shall spend at each of the attractions being visited.

ADVISING THE TIME DURATION

It takes time to reach from one point to another. It is essential for the tour manager to communicate the approximate timings and distance of travel from one location to another to his guests so that they are mentally prepared for the journey.

INTRODUCING THE TOUR GUIDE

At many sightseeing points or for a full-day and half-day city tour, local guides are hired by the tour operator in particular destinations. The tour guide, being a local resident of the place, is a specialist in showcasing his destination and has the competence to share the information about the points of interest.

When on the coach, the tour manager must introduce the tour guide to his guests. He must share the tour guide's work experience with the guest and appreciate him for his expertise exhibited during the tour.

PLANNING REST BREAKS

Generally, during long journeys, rest breaks/refreshment breaks are planned for the guests after every 1.5–2 hours for using public conveniences. These hiatuses may last from 10 to 20 minutes. The idea is that the guest may want to use this time for the restroom/relax/stretch/have tea or coffee etc. The rest break is also required for the driver who may have been driving continuously. In some countries around the world, it is a mandate for the driver to take rest for a specific number of hours during the journeys. Also, the refuelling of the vehicle and other necessary checks, if required, can be done during these rest breaks.

Therefore, at the beginning of the tour for the day, a tour manager must communicate about the rest breaks to his group members. However, it is often noticed that tourists tend to stretch these rest breaks and take long breaks spending time in shopping at the stores or having snacks and so on. He must, therefore, explicitly specify to his guests about the time to get back to the coach. He must reinstate the importance of punctuality to his guests so that the group may remain on schedule and the itinerary may be executed as planned. Even then, if guests do not listen to the tour manager and do not report on time, then he may introduce some kind of light penalties for the latecomers that may discomfit them. He may, for example, ask the latecomer who boards the coach last to sing a song for the whole group. This kind of punishment may mortify that guest and other guests too, who may then onwards try to be on time to escape the humiliation.

ALLOCATION OF SEATS

Sitting in front is the priority of every guest on a coach. The significant advantage is that the guests sitting in front can get better views from front and also have better interaction with the tour manager who sits in front. This sometimes becomes a bone of contention between the guests. It would always happen that in every group there would be a bunch of guests who may ever wish to occupy the front seats. Such guests try to monopolise the front seats by placing their bags or keeping their handkerchiefs to reserve these seats well in advance. This may initiate discord among the guests. Therefore, to avoid such kind of tiffs, a tour manager must have a rotation policy in place for his guests. At the very outset of the tour, he may

ask his guests to rotate their seats every day with other guests so that no single person can patronise the front seats.

Alternatively, before boarding the coach, tour managers may assign the seat numbers to his guests calling their names and the seat number that has been allocated to them or alternatively giving them chits with seat numbers mentioned. This may be also helpful in handling this situation as it does not creates unnecessary tiffs between the guests as the seat numbers have been already assigned to the guests.

SAFETY OF GUESTS

Every place has specific road safety norms which must be adhered to by the guests. Abiding by the road safety measures is also a legal requirement. However, these road safety norms may also vary from country to country. Therefore, a tour manager must brief his guests about the safety procedures required to be followed by the guests while on the coach.

He must request his guests to cooperate in adopting safety measures as the safety of guests is of paramount importance for the tour manager while on a tour. The safety instructions for the guests on the coach by the tour manager may include the following:

- He must remind the group to wear safety belts after sitting in the coach, wherever is compulsory to wear. In case the guests are not able to fasten the seat belt, he may assist them with the same.
- He must also request his guest not to stand or walk in the aisle area of the coach when the coach is in motion.
- He may also request the children and the adults not to take their arms/face out of the window while the coach is moving.
- He should also ask his guests not to stand in front of the doors.
- On reaching a stoppage, he may ask his guests to remain seated unless the bus completely stops and is safely parked.

INSTRUCTIONS FOR BAGGAGE

A tour manager may ask his guests to keep their purses and small bags in the overhead bins. The big suitcases may be placed at the designated storage compartment of the coach behind or below the coach.

He must also remind the guests to carry all their belongings with them before disembarking the coach to visit attractions. The purses, wallets, cameras, passports and other belongings, if any must remain in the custody of the guest at all times.

ARRANGING ON-BOARD ENTERTAINMENT

The guests spend a substantial time of their travel on the coach while moving from one place to another. Sometimes, long journeys may range from 3–4 hours to 8–10 hours or even more. This can become very boring for the guests. The tourists might get fatigued and report lack of energy. Therefore, it is essential for a tour manager to keep his guests engaged all the time by taking care of his guests' entertainment on the coach. To do this, he may pep up his guests with games such as Tambola (Housie), organise quizzes on the attractions visited or crack jokes to keep them energised and charged up. He may also ask his guests to sing songs, or he may play songs on the audio system for his guests. Sometimes, the guests may give their own collection of songs which they would like to be played on the audio system of the coach. However, it is advisable that the tour manager must have a good collection of songs with him so that he can play the music according to the taste of his group members.

Many coaches have TV facility as well. In that case, a tour manager can play movies depending on the choice of the audience. Therefore, he must have a collection of entertaining videos with him too. However, this might also become a source of a tiff as the different audience in the coach may have different preferences to see the film. Children may like to see a cartoon or animated movies while senior citizens might want to see a classic cinema. Some guests might want to see action movies while some women might wish to watch romantic movies, and some others might prefer comedy movies. He must very tactfully handle such situations and keep in mind the interest of the majority of the audience and the composition of the group members. A tour manager must understand the vibes of his guests and act accordingly. It is advisable for him, if possible on extended tours, to try to show such movies which show the same destination that the guests are visiting so that the guests can connect and be excited to explore the destination. Another good option is to play educative documentaries about the destination to be visited.

FACILITATING FAMILIARISATION OF GROUP MEMBERS

At the start of the tour or whenever the tour manager gets a chance, especially during a long journey, he must organise an ice-breaking session for his guests. This gives the group members an opportunity to know about each other— names, hobbies and lives. These are also moments of social cohesion. A tour manager may suggest that his group members gel with and know more about each other so that they become more comfortable as early as possible on the trip.

FACILITATING A CONGENIAL ENVIRONMENT

Overall, a tour manager is responsible for maintaining a friendly atmosphere within the coach. The accompanying passengers become like a family during the trip. Therefore, he must request his guests to come in a family mode as soon as possible.

COLLECTING GRATUITIES

Giving tips to the driver is customary in many countries. In most of the package tours, the gratuities are part of 'extras' which are to be paid directly to the tour manager in the destination being visited. Generally, in a coach, every day, the tour manager collects gratuities for the driver at the beginning or end of each day. Alternatively, he may collect the 'tips' for the whole duration of the tour at the beginning or end of the trip.

As the driver may sometimes assist in stacking luggage inside the coach and then unloading it again for the guests at multiple destinations, tipping becomes essential to keep the driver in good humour.

SELLING OPTIONAL TOURS

Optional tours are included in the package tours but have not been paid for in advance by the guests. The optional tours may range from excursions to amusement parks, adventure activities and famous shows. The guests have the option of taking the optional trip depending on their taste and preference. Optional tours are operational subject to the minimum numbers of passengers ready to take up the tour/option.

It is the job of the tour manager on the coach to sell these optional tours to his guests. The tour manager may give a detailed explanation about the kind of optional excursions available and also the advantages of taking these optional trips in the coach. He may even then collect the payments in the coach for optional trips on behalf of his company.

ASSISTING THE GUESTS WITH SPECIAL REQUIREMENTS

In a tour, there might be some elderly people and some people with special needs. Therefore, a tour manager must assist such guests in boarding and deboarding the coach. To facilitate such guests, he may have to request the driver to align the ramp for the physically challenged guests in a wheelchair, or he may help such guests in keeping their luggage inside the coach. He must always extend a helping hand to such guests and must do everything to make such guests comfortable on the coach.

TIPS FOR A TOUR MANAGER ON A COACH

A tour managers must consider the following:

- Report 15–20 minutes before the arrival of the guests.
- Physically examine the coach to see if it is neat and clean.
- Meet the driver and initiate a dialogue with him and exchange pleasantries with him, and also take his contact number for further coordination.
- Discuss the days' itinerary and stoppages with the driver.

- Confirm the best possible routes for the tour, and ensure that the roads are not blocked or closed due to any reason. In case the roads are blocked on a specific route, an alternative route should be discussed beforehand with the driver and then followed.
- Check the brakes, tyres and fuel, and confirm from the tour driver if the coach is in order.
- Identify beforehand the emergency exits, emergency windows, fire extinguisher and first aid box inside the coach.
- Locate and check the microphone facility inside the coach.
- Inspect the working of audio system and television, if available on the coach.
- Before the guests claim their seat, the tour manager must claim his seat in the front of the coach. He may claim it by keeping his belongings such as a bag, a jacket or a notebook if required.
- While boarding the coach every time after any sightseeing attraction, he must do a headcounts. He must ensure that all the passengers have boarded the coach.
- On long journeys, he may suggest that his guests take small naps to refresh themselves.
- Remain vigilant all the time of the speed of the driver.
- Frequently talk to the driver on long journeys as the driver has a tendency of falling asleep on long trips that may put the security of the whole group in trouble.
- Remain assertive with his guests.
- Speak slowly to be clearly heard.
- Try to involve all the guests for entertainment, but should not force them to participate.
- Always keep a check on the temperature of the coach for the comfort of his guests.
- While deboarding the coach, he must thank the driver publicly in front of the guests for taking care of the safety of guests.
- While ending the day tour, he may also thank his guests for cooperating with him for the day on the coach.

SUMMARY

A tour manager is a companion of his guests on the coach. He is also the caretaker and facilitator for them during the tour on the coach. Thus, he must be very efficient and wary while discharging his assigned responsibilities on the coach. He must make the travel of his guests very comfortable and relaxing on the coach. He must also take care of the safety of his guests besides their entertainment while on the coach. He must be very clear in issuing guidelines related to the coach to his guests. He must also ensure that he familiarises everyone with the coach on which they shall be spending the maximum time of the tour, moving from one place to another.

Activity 1 Brief your group on the coach

Create a pseudo coach by changing the seating arrangement of the class room. Now ask each student to assume the role of a tour manager and practise the briefing to be given on the coach as a tour manager when he meets his guests for the first time. You may also ask the students to cover the following points during briefing:

- Greeting and welcoming the guests
- Introducing himself and the pilot of the coach
- Introducing the local guide, if any
- Familiarisation with the coach
- Rules to be followed on the coach
- Briefing about the day's itinerary

Activity 2 Live tour

Bring seven–ten big pictures of different attractions of a particular city in your classroom. Now paste these pictures at different places in the classroom. Let us take the city of London as an example. You may choose any other city of your choice. Here you may take these pictures from magazines, newspaper, the Internet or even draw on your own. Now arrange the students in a queue and let one student take charge as a tour manager. The other students may become tourists. Now, the students may imagine they are in a coach on a panoramic view of London passing the major landmarks of the city, that is, The Buckingham Palace, The London Eye, The Tower of London, Oxford Street, Local cafes and so on. The tour manager may point out these landmarks from the coach as the coach approaches near these iconic structures and give passing remarks on these places. Eventually, others may take over as a tour manager. Few students may also enact as non-cooperative tourists who are fighting on the coach to occupy the first seat. This way every student would get an opportunity to learn how to conduct a tour on the coach.

POSSIBLE SOLUTIONS TO THE OPENING VIGNETTE

- The tour manager after failing to convince both the parties to apologize, contacted the company and requested them to make some other arrangement to proceed for the trip, to which company refused to entertain his request.
- To diffuse the situation, he then told Ali that the guests will give some extra tips if he agrees to take the take the coach to which the pilot agreed.
- He also made it clear to the group that the tour will proceed as per the agreed itinerary and the non-scheduled requests cannot be entertained as they have to make up for the lost time.

Lessons Learned

- At the beginning of a tour, a tour manager must brief his group about the itinerary along with the stopovers scheduled for the trip.
- A tour manager must always be in charge of the situation. He must establish his authority in a very subtle manner.
- He must make things very clear right from the beginning during his briefing. He must set the rules of the tour.
- He must clearly state the rules of the coach the guests need to follow failing which he may be forced to take a punitive action against them.
- He may also brief his guests not to talk to the pilot of the coach directly as it may distract him while travelling.

13

Responsibilities on Other Modes of Transportation

LEARNING OBJECTIVES

- What are the various modes of transportation available today that are widely used by the travellers?
- What is the role of a tour manager in the multiple modes of transportation?

Annie was leading a group of six NRIs in Rishikesh. It was the time of Makar Sakranti, a religious day for followers of Hinduism in India. As a part of the itinerary, Annie took his guests on a boat ride to show them the beautiful sunset on the holy river Ganges. Before boarding the boat, Annie requested his guest to wear life jackets as a safety precaution before venturing into the waters.

Narayan, a guest from the group who was a travel photographer, adamantly refused to wear the life jacket in spite of repeated requests by Annie. He boarded the boat and started clicking pictures of the views while on the boat. While the boat was moving in its full speed, Narayan abruptly stood up from his seat and went to the edge of the boat to capture some more spectacular sunset views in his camera without paying any heed to the instructions of Annie not to walk on the moving boat. In no time, Narayan lost his balance and fell in the chilling waters of Ganges. He started drowning as he did not know how to swim. He shouted and yelled at the top of his voice to seek for help. His voice started lowering down as he was close to getting unconscious due to the chilling waters and the fear of drowning. Annie was contemplating whether he should jump into the cold waters to save his client as he knew swimming. Yet, he was confused whether he would be able to take his weight as Narayan was quite heavy built. No one else was ready to jump in the waters to rescue Narayan. Also, there was no lifebuoy on the boat that could have been thrown in the waters to save Narayan.

Travel has become a fashion statement in this era. The new travel is all about gaining novel experiences. An essential component of travel is transportation as tourists use various modes of transportation to travel from one point to another. The primary modes of reaching a place may be through land, rail, sea and air transportation.

Mostly, within the destination, travelling by the guests is generally done by a coach. However, guests may use other modes of transportation too for going to places. Over a span of time, various innovative modes of transportation have been evolved that have become tourism products in themselves. These modes of transportation are an attraction for a tourist in the destinations being visited. Some of these modes of transportation are the 'must experience' tourism products for the travellers without which their trip would remain incomplete. These rides can sometimes be lifetime memories for the guests.

MODES OF TRANSPORTATION

Now let us have a detailed discussion on the different modes of transportation that are widely available and used across the world.

Air Transportation

These may be further classified into the following categories:

Travelling through airlines
For example, Singapore International Airlines, British Airways and Emirates.

Taking helicopter rides
For instance, taking helicopter tours in Grand Canyon, Nevada, USA.

Taking cable car rides
For example, cable car ride to Mt. Titlis, Switzerland (world's first revolving cable car called Rotair).

Water-based Transportation

These may be further classified into the following categories:

Cruises
For example, Huangpu River Cruise in Shanghai, China and Mandovi River Cruise, Goa, India.

Ferries
For example, Statue of Liberty cruise, New York, USA; and ferry ride from Port Blair to Havelock Island, Andaman and Nicobar Islands, India.

Water taxis
For example, water taxi tour to Fort Lauderdale, Florida.

Boats
For example, Maid of the Mist boat ride at Niagara Falls, USA, and boat tour of Varanasi, India.

Gondola rides

For example, gondola rides in Venice, Italy.

Hovercrafts

Land-based Transportation

These may be classified into the following categories:

Trams

For example, the Colonial Tramcar Restaurant, Melbourne, Australia (famous for Australian dining experience in a moving tram that has a vintage decor); trams in San Francisco, USA; and trams in Kolkata, India.

Coaches

Hop-on hop-off buses

For example, Ho-Ho Buses in New Delhi, India.

Cycle rickshaw rides

For example, cycle rickshaw ride in Chandni Chowk, New Delhi, India.

Horse carriage rides

For example, the Royal Carriage Tour, Victoria, Australia, and Central Park carriage rides, New York, USA.

Bike rides

For example, Pyrenees cycle tours, France, and Girona and Costa Brava cycle tours.

Animal safaris

For example, Camel safaris in Dubai and Yak safaris in Ladakh, India.

Jeep safaris

For example, jeep safaris in Tanzania and in Jim Corbett National Park, India.

Rail Transportation

Travelling by trains can be a great fun and a thrilling experience. Rail transportation may be of different types. These may be again be classified into the following categories:

Heritage trains

For example, The Puffing Billy Narrow Gauge Heritage Train, Melbourne, Australia; The Palace on Wheels and Maharaja Express Heritage trains, India; and the Joyride or Darjeeling Himalayan Train, Darjeeling, India.

Trains

For example, Eurostar (train that goes from London to Paris and passes through the English Channel); Scenic Railway, the Blue Mountains in Sydney, Australia (world's steepest passenger railway at 52-degree inclination); and the toy train in Vaduz, Liechtenstein, Europe.

RESPONSIBILITY OF A TOUR MANAGER BEFORE AND DURING THE TOUR

A tour manager has a significant role in facilitating the travel on the modes of transportation mentioned above. Before taking the guests on these modes of transportation, he must gather all the necessary information that may be required to be shared with the guests. He must check for the following things with the concerned local transportation authorities:

- Operational timings of the modes of transportation
- Departure and arrival gates in the embarkation/disembarkation ports/stations
- Days of operation
- Routes on which it operates
- Different classes of travel
- Interesting facts about the transportation system
- Facilities at the modes of transportation
- Total time duration of the tour on the mode of transportation and its finishing time

Now let us have an elaborate discussion on the duties and responsibilities of a tour manager on various modes of transportation.

MAKING RESERVATIONS

Travelling on any mode of transportation requires reservations. Generally, the primary reservations on trains/cruises/gondola rides may be made by the operations department of the travel company. In that case, the tour manager may collect the tickets of his group from the ticket counter of the mode of transportation. However, sometimes, for leisure rides or also for trains/cruises, when the company has not made any reservations, reservations become the responsibility of the tour manager. Through liaising with the transport authorities, a tour manager may make the reservation for his group on the mode of transportation in advance. Alternatively, when he visits the transportation site, he may check for the availability of tickets and make reservations for his guests.

DISTRIBUTION OF TICKETS

On meeting the guests, a tour manager must distribute the tickets to the passengers before boarding the trains/cruises or any other mode of transportation that may be included in the itinerary. This is important because the tickets of all the passengers may be checked by the travel authorities before boarding or during the travel on the way to the destination point.

MEETING POINT

Before travelling in any mode of transportation, the tour manager must confirm the meeting point of the group to his guests. For, example, in case of trains, the guests might be in different compartments, and on reaching a particular station, they may disperse in different directions. As a result, they might get lost. Therefore, he must in advance inform his group members about the meeting time of the group after disembarking at the station.

EMBARKATION/DISEMBARKATION

Every mode of transportation has set of procedures to be followed for embarking/disembarking. A tour manager must brief his guests as to how to use that mode of transportation. For example, while boarding the local buses/trams, the guest may have to touch the cards at a point or may have to show their tickets to the authorities. He must facilitate his guests in boarding the trains/cruises/cable cars and on other various modes of transportation.

He may also request his group members to line up in rows while boarding these modes of transportation. This will allow the tour manager to manage the crowd efficiently and, therefore, facilitate in the boarding.

BRIEFING

A tour manager must brief his guests about the rules and regulations to be followed in a mode of transportation. He may ask his guests to remain in discipline on the mode of transportations. He may ask them to follow the queues, not to push others, sit in allocated seats only, not to play loud music, etc. In some modes of transportation, taking food and beverages inside may not be permitted. The same must be communicated to the guests. Likewise, in cable cars, while they are moving, standing up from the seat is not allowed. The same may be shared with the guests.

BRIEFING ABOUT CLOTHING AND EQUIPMENT

For using specific modes of transportation, the guest may be advised to wear a particular dress code or use a particular kind of equipment. For example, in case of bicycle tours and horseback tours, the tour manager must suggest that his guests wear comfortable clothes. Tight clothes should be avoided for bicycle tours. Accordingly, hard hats may be worn by the guests for horseback tours.

LOADING OF BAGGAGE

Many transportation systems such as cruises/ferries and trains have a special compartment for stacking the heavy luggage of its passengers. Also, for keeping purses or small bags, overhead bins are provided in trains and ferries that may be used by the guests. The same may be informed by the tour manager to the guests about where to stack their luggage before the guests proceed towards their allocated seats. In fact, the tour manager may also suggest to his guests as to how to organise their luggage in the compartments. Generally, he may advise his guests to stack their bigger suitcases below the smaller suitcases.

ARRANGING MEALS

In most of the modes of transportation like trains/cruises/ferries, the guest can buy snacks from the food and beverage counter/pantry on payment basis. However, in many modes of transportation, in package tours, the companies may give the provision of packaged meals for the guests if all the meals are included in the package tour. In such cases, it is the responsibility of a tour manager to distribute the meal packets to his guests either inside the transportation vehicle or before the guests disperse in different directions before proceeding towards their seats.

Also, sometimes on the last day of the tour, gala dinners may have been organised in cruises/ferries by the travel company for its guests to make the last day of the trip memorable for the guests.

Thus, he must make all the necessary arrangements for meals in the mode of transportation if the same has been promised in the itinerary.

INFORMING ABOUT THE FACILITIES

A tour manager must be prior informed of the services available inside the mode of transportation. Accordingly, he may advise his guests about the services one can avail while travelling through the mode of transportation. These services may be FOC or on payment basis. Some of the facilities available for guests may include Wi-Fi facilities, food and beverages outlets, shopping facilities and so on. However, in case of cruises, the range of amenities offered may be extensive, such as swimming pools, spas, parlours, ice rinks, dance floors, banquet halls, restaurants and so on. Likewise, in a cable car ride in Sentosa Island, Singapore, mobile charging points are available that can be communicated to the guests for their usage.

ON-BOARD COMMENTARY

At many points of interest, a tour manager may deliver commentary to his guests while passing by them during the tour on the mode of transportation. He may provide the necessary commentary about the mode of transportation, and share its historical importance and other interesting facts with the guests. The tour manager may also discuss the routes on which the mode of transportation operates and may even highlight its uniqueness to his guests so that the guests may feel privileged for choosing to travel on that mode of transportation.

For example, while travelling on Puffing Billy Train in Victoria, Australia, he briefs his guests about the importance and uniqueness of this train as it is Australia's premium steam railway that has been given an old fashion look that adds to the thrill of the guests. While passing through the various stations, the tour manager makes necessary remarks about scenic landscapes that are just breathtaking that may leave the guests spellbound.

Alternatively, in many modes of transportation, for example, cruise ride in Singapore, pre-recorded commentary runs on-board while the boat cruises through the water. In case a tour manager is accompanying his guests on the cruise, he may ask his guests to listen to the ongoing commentary which unfolds the different facets of Singapore to its guests along with interesting facts on scenic points being passed by.

INTRODUCING LOCAL SPECIALIST GUIDES

In many modes of transportation, a travel company may hire a local tour guide who may give a running commentary about the points of interest the group may be passing by while travelling through that mode of transportation. In such cases, when the local guide is hired for a particular mode of transportation, for example, cruises/ferries/boat tours, it is the responsibility of the tour manager to introduce the tour guide to his guests.

The tours on cruises/ferries are generally guide conducted tours so as to create the 'feel' of being on that mode of transportation. While cruising through the waters, a tour guide explains the landmark buildings or spectacular sceneries to his guests so that the guests can make sense of things that they are passing by during their travel. For example the famous guided Chicago architecture river cruise on Chicago river.

COMMUNICATING ABOUT SAFETY MEASURES

The safety of guests is always a top priority for the tour manager. Therefore, a tour manager must request his guests to adhere to the safety measures adopted in the mode of transportation. Some guidelines that he may instruct his guests on are as follows:

- Request his guests to wear safety belts while travelling in the mode of transportation
- Ask his guests not to move inside the vehicle when it is in motion. This is an instruction especially given for gondola rides and cable car rides.
- Request his group members to wear life jackets for boat rides/ferries and so on.
- For cycle tours, he must ask the group to take care of their safety on roads by wearing helmets and driving slow during steep slopes and sharp curves of roads.
- The tour manager may also brief his guests about the procedures to be followed by them during emergency situations while using a particular mode of transportation.
- The tour manager may request his guests to cooperate with security during the screening of their baggage and individual frisking through metal detectors at the embarkation points.

WARNING ABOUT DANGERS

While using certain modes of transportation, a tour manager must brief his guests about the risks, if any, involved in using that mode of transportation. For instance, while travelling on cruises in deep sea waters, many people experience seasickness. They may feel certain dizziness or discomfort during travel. Therefore, a tour manager must convey in advance about the discomfort one may feel using such a mode of transportation. Also, he may suggest an appropriate preventive medication for his guest that may be taken before travelling by such modes of transportation. Thus, while going on long cruises, he may suggest that his guests take an appropriate medicine to deal with seasickness.

Alternatively, he may suggest that his guests observe certain precautions or carry certain things while travelling to deal with health issues that may happen due to tripping on specific modes of transportation. For instance, while travelling to Mt. Jungfraujoch in Interlaken, Switzerland, through the Europe's highest railway station, which is an engineering marvel by itself and an experience to travel through, many travellers on this journey feel dizzy and report headaches and vomiting on deboarding the train as there is lack of oxygen in the air due to very high altitude. In such cases, a tour manager may suggest in advance that his guests carry camphor and keep inhaling it to deal with the oxygen deficiency in the air. He may also advise his guests to eat light before travelling to such places or take some medicines to deal with motion sickness.

SUGGESTING PHOTOGRAPHY OPPORTUNITY

A tour manager must advise his guests of the viewpoints of photography from where the best views can be captured while travelling on various modes of transportation. He suggest his group to click pictures from different angles, especially when the group cruises/passes through scenic views or beautiful landscapes.

For instance, while cruising through the waters in Niagara Falls, USA, one must not forget to click pictures during the 'Maid of Mist' tour. Likewise, while cruising through the Rhine Falls, Switzerland, the most massive falls of Europe, one may click pictures of spectacular falls besides capturing the mesmerising natural views sitting on the cruise. Even, while cruising through Chicago, one may click photos at the backdrop of beautiful iconic skyscrapers that are some of the tallest buildings in the world.

ARRANGING ON-BOARD ENTERTAINMENT

Many modes of transportation such as cruises and ferries have an arrangement for entertainment of the guests. A travel company may have planned DJ nights/games/local dances or other activities during the travel on that transportation for its guest. Therefore, the tour manager must ensure that his guests are entertained during a trip in that mode of transportation as for the guests, every moment during the trip is a moment of celebration.

ON-BOARD OCCASION CELEBRATIONS

Many times, when the birthdays or anniversaries of any guest is falling during the tour dates and if the group is going on a cruise/ferry, then the tour manager may organise a small surprise party for his guests and others to celebrate such occasions on the cruise/ferry. He may organise a cake and run the party music so that everyone can have fun in the mode of transportation. Such small gestures of a tour manager can make a big difference for the guests and create lifetime memories for them.

KEEPING THE GROUP TOGETHER

A tour manager must ensure that his group remains together during travelling in the different modes of transportation. At times, the group may have seats allotted in separate compartments of the mode of transportation. However, he must try his best to keep the members together in one place.

SUMMARY

The above discussion shows that a tour manager has a significant role to play on different means of transportation used by the group during their travel. His management skills during the journey on various modes of transportation can make a lot of difference to the overall experience of the tour. It can make the travellers' experience more meaningful, joyful and memorable. A tour manager through his mediation must try to comfort his guest by familiarising them with the set-up of the transportation mode as well its system of usage.

Activity 1 The whiteboard exercise

After having gone through the responsibilities of a tour manager on different modes of transportation, divide the class into different groups. Keep six small white boards in the class and ask each group to choose one mode of transportation that should preferably not be repeated by the other groups. You may choose the following modes of transportation that the tourists might use besides a coach:

- Train
- Cruise
- Gondola ride
- Airlines
- Cable car ride
- Cycle rickshaw ride

Ask each group to brainstorm first and discuss the various responsibilities of a tour manager on these particular modes of transportation being presented by the group. After reaching a consensus within the group, enlist the number of responsibilities of a tour manager on the transportation mode chosen on the allocated white board. Let each group prepare its own list. Now, as the moderator of the class, highlight the common responsibilities of a tour manager on all modes of transportation. Also, ask students if they find any differences in the responsibilities of a tour manager for a particular mode of transportation. Clearly state the similarities and differences with respect to different modes of transportation.

Activity 2 Briefing for getting on the metro

You are New Delhi with a group of 15 Spanish women. You are about to enter the Rajeev Chowk metro station for boarding metro for visiting Chandni Chowk. Now highlight the list of things you would like to communicate as a tour manager with your group before boarding the metro.

POSSIBLE SOLUTIONS TO THE OPENING VIGNETTE

- Annie immediately reacted to the situation by taking off his life jacket and tying a rope to it.
- He immediately threw the life jacket to his guest and asked him to grab the jacket and peddle. He also asked him to stay calm.
- Narayan meticulously followed the instructions of Annie and grabbed the life jacket forcefully till the others managed to pull him out of the waters.

- Finally he was rescued, and he broke into tears thanking Annie enough for giving him a new life that would have been impossible without his presence of mind and his dexterity at situation handling.

Lessons Learned

- Always insist that your guests to adhere to the safety precautions.
- Make sure to ask all your guests to submit the indemnity form while going for any adventurous activities. The indemnity form specifies that the guest is performing the activity on his own risk, and if any incident occurs during the tour, the guests shall be himself responsible for it.
- If a guest still does not want to follow the rules, brief him about the repercussions that he might have to face as a result of non-compliance of rules.
- If possible while dealing with such non-cooperative guests, share any previous mishappenings, if any, that may have occurred with the tourists.

14

Other Responsibilities

LEARNING OBJECTIVES

- What are the other responsibilities of a tour manager besides discharging his duties at an airport, hotel, sightseeing attraction, coach and different modes of transportation?

This time it was about food. A small communication gap can make a lot of difference. This is what Rahul, the tour manager, realised while on the tour. Rosy was suffering from celiac disease. Therefore, she had requested for a gluten-free meal while on a tour to the company. However, the same was not communicated to Rahul nor to the hotel where the meal requests are forwarded through the rooming list. It was time for a dinner now. Rosy could not find any special meal arranged for her. She went to Rahul to find out if she shall be served a gluten-free meal to which Rahul responded that he was not even aware of any such special request placed by Rosy.

Whenever a tour manager conducts a tour, he is the face of his company. Whether the tourist would like to travel with the same company in the future would depend to a large extent on how the tour manager deals with his guests during the tour. If the tour manager is able to keep his guests happy, then the tourists may think of booking another holiday with the same tour operator/travel agent. Therefore, the onus of bringing future business to the company rests to a considerable extent on the shoulders of the tour manager.

A tour manager has to be committed to his assigned tasks, duties and responsibilities. From the moment a tour starts and until the time it ends, he is expected to handle a myriad of responsibilities. The duties and responsibilities that he is expected to perform are numerous and varied in nature.

In the earlier chapters, we have had an elaborate discussion on the responsibilities of a tour manager at the airport, hotel, sightseeing attractions, coaches and other modes of transportation.

In this chapter, we shall have a detailed discussion on the other roles and responsibilities that a tour manager is expected to perform while conducting the tour.

Let us have a detailed discussion on the following roles and responsibilities of a tour manager.

ENSURING THE COMPLIANCE OF ITINERARY

A tour manager is always under constant pressure to manage the itinerary on time. When a client books his holiday with a tour operator/travel agent, the company makes a lot of promises to its clients in terms of the places and activities that shall be covered during the tour.

However, fulfilling these promises is the responsibility of the tour manager. The biggest challenge for him is to cover all the points and activities as promised in the itinerary.

A tour manager may come across many challenges while operating the itinerary. There might be last minute issues or emergency situations that may lead to changes in the itinerary. Sometimes some guests may be making unnecessary delays at every point like at local markets during shopping, or sometimes the traffic or road closures or even the weather may hinder the progress of itinerary on time.

Thus, for the smooth compliance of the itinerary on the scheduled time, he must pull his guests through the sightseeing points and, from the very beginning of the tour, stick to the duration of time to be spent at a particular point of interest. This sends a clear message to the guests that the tour manager is strict on time.

DELIVERING COMMENTARY AT THE DESTINATIONS

This is one of the most essential parts of the job of a tour manager. He is expected to be a good orator who speaks and gives commentary at every notable point of the tour. His job of commentary starts when the tourists arrive at the destination. He may welcome the guest, offer necessary briefing and then present the destinations to be covered in the itinerary in a favourable and a positive tone. He is expected to give commentary at airports, hotels, sightseeing attractions, coaches and other modes of transportation. The process of daily briefing continues until the last day of the tour.

A tour manager must give the information about the destination in a fascinating, engaging and organised way. He should not deliver canned talks. It may bore the guests, and gradually the guests may lose interest in his talks. He must, however, know when to stop and exercise restraint during his commentary as the guests may not always be interested in his never-ending conversations.

BRIEFING ABOUT THE LOCAL SENSITIVITIES

Every destination has certain norms that must be followed by the guest. Some destinations are very tourist friendly and have a liberal outlook towards promoting tourism in their country. However, some destinations may be conservative in their approach and not interested in accepting alien conduct. Therefore, a tour manager must advise his guests to act locally. The idea is that the tourists must conduct themselves according to the place. Tourists must not do anything that hurts the sentiments of the local people. It is always in the interest of the guest to follow the instructions shared by the tour manager about a destination. For example, while visiting rural areas in India, the foreigners are advised not to carry beer bottles in open as this is avoided in the Indian society. Likewise, while touring rural areas of India, women are encouraged to be entirely clad as not being modestly covered can be a cultural shock for the local community of the village.

INTERPRETATION

Interpretation is an integral part of a tour manager's job. The interpretation of a destination by a tour manager on a tour helps the guests to make sense of a place. Tourists are able to connect much more with a place when the tour manager explains and builds a context of the place. Interpretation is not just confined to the attraction being visited. It may be about the whole place or the site being visited.

Also, many times when the tourists visit another country, they may not be familiar with the local language of that country. The language may become a barrier for such guests in communicating with the locals. The tourists might not be able to communicate with the local service providers who may be the staff at airlines, hotels, local restaurants, foreign exchange counters, shop establishments and etc. At such places, he may interpret for his guests and explain the requirements of his guests to the local service providers in their language, and vice versa. This interpretation amongst the guests, tour manager and local service providers facilitates the guests and makes them feel comfortable in another country.

ARRANGING MEALS AT RESTAURANTS

Most of the meals of the guests are taken care of in a package tour. Some meals may be booked for guests in a hotel, whereas mostly meals may be organised for the group at local restaurants. In such cases, a tour manager must coordinate with local restaurateurs for arranging the right meals for his guests at the right time.

In fact, there may be times when meals have not been arranged by the company. In such cases, the guests seek the assistance from the tour manager for the arrangement of meals. Accordingly, he may suggest restaurants to his guests or arrange for meals at local restaurants to facilitate his guests. He may also ask the preferences of meals from his guests before placing orders for them.

MAKING LOCAL TRAVEL ARRANGEMENTS

Sometimes, it may happen that the company has not arranged the travel of the clients on a coach as the coach may not be able to go to all places. Sometimes guests may like to visit some places on their own or take a short detour. In such cases, a tour manager may be required to arrange a mode of transportation for his guests, or alternatively, he may also suggest to his guests the possible ways of transportation for reaching a point.

ENTERTAINMENT OF GUESTS

Tourists are on holiday for fun and frolic. One of the most important reasons for travelling to another place by tourists is to be entertained. Thus, the entertainment of guests should be one of the most important concerns of the tour manager. He must ensure that his guests are entertained at every point. For the same, he may plan or suggest activities to his guests that may not have been included in the package. He may recommend that his guests experience the nightlife (only if it safe to venture out in the night), visit casinos, watch shows, visit local markets, try adventure activities and explore new areas or organise games that may keep his guest engaged during their free time. However, he should never force his opinion on his guests that may eventually make the guests feel uncomfortable.

DISTRIBUTION OF FREEBIES

Many times, tour operators/travel agents give complimentary items to their clients. These may be called as freebies. The freebies may include things such as bags, passport jackets, electric kettles, tea bags, coffee sachets, sugar cubes and milk powder to keep the guests in good humour. Accordingly, these freebies may be distributed by the tour manager to the guests on the first day of the tour.

ASSISTS IN SHOPPING

Shopping is one of the exciting activities for the tourists at a new destination. Being new to a place, the guests may not be aware of the local markets. They may seek the assistance of a tour manager who may assist his guests for shopping in the local markets or malls depending upon the interests of the guests. He may suggest his guests to buy local items of a destination that it is famous for. These are souvenirs. He may also advise his guests the marketplaces from where to shop, what to shop etc. A detailed discussion on shopping has been done in Chapter 5.

ASSISTING IN CHANGE OF TICKETS

Many times, some guest within the group might want to get their tickets rescheduled or their sectors of travel changed due to any personal reasons. In such cases, a tour manager must assist his guests in getting their tickets preponed or postponed as per the requirements of the guests.

ASSISTING IN BORDER CONTROLS

A tour manager has an important responsibility towards his guests in organising seamless travel for them. In many countries, especially in Europe where most of the journey from one country to another country is through coaches, he has an essential task of assisting his guests in border controls.

While entering another country, the guests have to pass through border controls where the tour manager must complete all the necessary formalities for his guests with the immigration officers of the country being visited. He must collect all the passports of his guests before reaching the border of another country and open the appropriate visa page to be shown to the concerned authorities at the border. He may then approach the immigration authorities and present the passports of his guests to them for stamping of their passports, and then return the passports to the guests later.

MANAGING THE GROUP

A tour manager is the leader of the group who manages and leads the group from the beginning till the end. The management of the group is a challenging task which requires a lot of patience and tactfulness on the part of the tour manager. It is the responsibility of the tour manager to ensure that all the group members comply with the set group norms. He ensures the enjoyment of his group members, but, at the same time, he must ensure that everything goes in a disciplined way. The tour manager must always be in control of the group. Details of how to manage a group has been separately discussed in Chapter 22 (Section E) of the book.

HANDLING COMPLAINTS/GRIEVANCES

A tourist can have a number of grievances on the arrangements, itinerary or any other issue that may sometimes be beyond the control of the tour manager. Thus, it is an essential part of the tour managers' job to listen to the complaints of his guests and resolve their issues. A tour manager must extend his cooperation to his guests by addressing their issues and finding solutions for them. He must be very tactful in handling their grievances. Sometimes, even the guests know that the tour manager cant' do anything about certain issues. For example, weather conditions at a destination or traffic at a place are beyond the control of a tour manager. In such situations, the guests just want to be heard empathetically by the tour manager. Thus, the tour manager must lend his ears to listen to the issues of his guest and try to calm them in every possible way. Further details on handling complaints/grievances have been separately discussed in Chapter 23 (Section E) of the book.

HANDLING QUESTIONS

The tourists may have a lot of questions in their mind about a destination that they may wish to ask from the tour manager. For them, a tour guide is like a Google search engine that has all the answers to their questions. Therefore, a tour manager must try to answer all the queries raised by his guests. Further details on handling questions have been separately discussed in Chapter 20 (Section E) of the book.

HANDLING EMERGENCY SITUATIONS

A tour manager may encounter any unforeseen circumstances that he may have never expected. Anything can happen with the tourist during the travel. The tourists may fall sick during the tour or may lose his passport or luggage during the trip. These situations are always uncalled for. However, uncertainty is the only certainty about such conditions. Therefore, when such situations arise, he must not lose control. He must get into the action mode and try to act to the best of his capacity when the situation demands. A detailed discussion of kind of emergency situations that he might have to deal with along with the solutions as to how to tackle them have been discussed in detail in Chapter 25 (Section E) of the book.

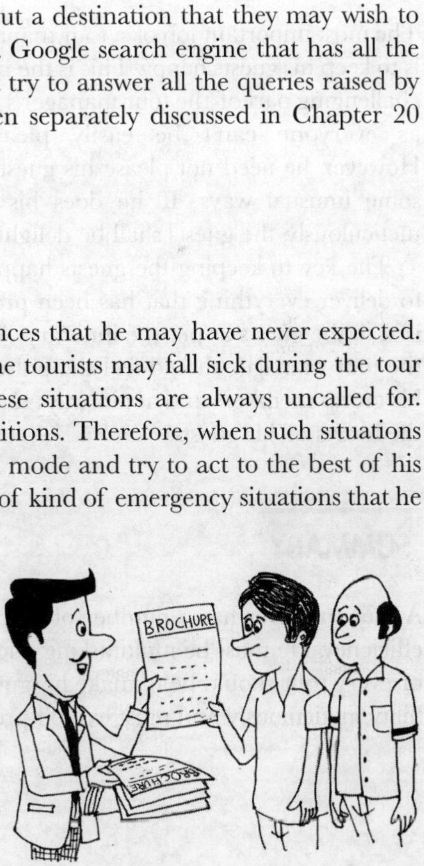

PROMOTING THE PRODUCTS OF COMPANY

A tour manager is a spokesperson for his company. During the journey, he may share information about the other tourism products offered by his company to his guests. He may talk about the various other destinations that can be explored by the guests later by booking their holidays with his company. He may also sell optional tours to his guests while on trips. In other words, he may act as a salesman for his company.

PROMOTING RESPONSIBLE TRAVEL

A tour manager must ask his group members to behave as responsible tourists in the country being visited. He must remind his guests to act responsibly towards the environment of the destination by not littering around. He should also ask his guest to be sensitive towards the local community. For instance, if the tourists want to take a picture with the natives at the destination, they may first seek the permission of the locals for taking their pictures. He must also request his guests to respect the fellow tourists during the tour and other tourists whom they may meet at the destination.

KEEPING THE GUESTS HAPPY

The most important job of a tour manager is to keep his guests happy. This is the most challenging part of the tour manager's role as everyone can't be easily pleased. However, he need not please his guests in some unusual ways. If he does his job meticulously, the guests shall be delighted.

The key to keeping the guests happy is to deliver everything that has been promised to the guests as per the itinerary. Also, the tour manager should feel the pulse of his group members and act in ways to win the hearts of his guests.

SUMMARY

A tour manager has a number of responsibilities that he must carry out with much efficacy and efficiency. He must be multitasking and must accept each assignment as a challenge. His objective of every tour should be to make his guests enjoy to the maximum. He must handle every responsibility meticulously and must exhibit professionalism in his approach.

Activity 1 What makes your group happy?

The teacher may ask a question from the students: 'Being a tour manager, what are the things that you would do to make your group happy?'

The teacher may ask the students to submit five points each to keep the information clearer. After giving 15 minutes for the write up, the students may submit it to the teacher. Now the teacher may initiate a discussion in the class based on the responses received from the students. The teacher may use white board to highlight the common points and additional points.

Through this discussion, the students get to learn through exchange of each other's ideas. This can stimulate a very interesting discussion in the classroom.

Activity 2 Roleplay

Divide your class into groups of seven–eight students each and ask each group to organise a luncheon of tourists in a local restaurant. One student may take the lead and become a tour manager, and five other members may become tourists. Few others may become the staff of the restaurant.

Now you have a situation. When you reach the restaurant with your group, the tables are not empty. Guests start feeling irritated as they are hungry. After waiting for 15 minutes, when the group gets the table, the buffet is still unfilled. Some guests leave the restaurant while some start cursing the tour manager. Now what would you do as a tour manager to pacify your guests? You only have 45 minutes for the arrangements, as you have another monument on the tour that closes soon. Suggest the appropriate course of action.

Every group may have different ways of dealing with this situation. Students may also add more such situations in the same restaurant to add more creativity and to make it more interesting.

POSSIBLE SOLUTIONS TO THE OPENING VIGNETTE

- Rahul immediately called his company staff to enquire about any such request placed by his client Rosy.
- He was informed that she did place a special request for gluten-free meals on the tour that the company staff had forgotten to apprise Rahul of during the briefing.
- Rahul immediately spoke to the restaurant manager of the hotel and asked him to arrange a special gluten-free meal for his guest.

- Throughout the tour, at every point during dining at local restaurants and hotels, Rahul made it a point to arrange a special gluten-free meal for her and always reconfirmed with Rosy if she was being served the requested meal. Rosy was very happy as Rahul took an extra step to make her feel comfortable and was taking extra care to provide her with the right food.

Lessons Learned

- Always cross-check with the company for any special requests placed by a client on a tour.
- At times, when the tourists place any special requests, a tour manager must try to meets his request and make his guests feel comfortable.

15

Closing the Tour

LEARNING OBJECTIVES

- What is the responsibility of a tour manager during the closing of a tour?
- How can a tour manager make the closing of the tour a memorable experience for his guests?

An Indian group was with Kapil, their tour manager, for 15 days in Australia. The group had a return flight from Sydney. It was the last day of the tour. After checking out of the hotel, Kapil went to drop his group at the airport to bid a final goodbye to his guests. The guests flew back happily cherishing the happy times they had during their vacation. Kapil felt very happy as the whole group went happily with good memories of the tour.

A few days later, a complaint was sent via email by one of the group members, Mr Jai Bhalla, against Kapil for being so unprofessional. He further asked for US$200 as compensation. He also mentioned that Kapil was ill-informed. Kapil was summoned by the company and asked to pay the money from his pocket to the guest. On enquiring about his fault, he was told that he had not given any such information to his guests to claim their tax refunds at the airport on the shopping that they had done in Australia. Since Mrs and Mr Bhalla were first-time travellers and had done extensive shopping, they had unnecessarily ended up paying more tax in the country on shopping. Neither had Kapil told them to keep a copy of the shopping bills with them that may be required to be produced to the authorities for claiming tax refund at the airport nor they were aware of any such tax refund policy.

Tour managers accompany and lead groups of travellers going on a vacation. In every trip, a tour manager meets a group of strangers. He stays with them for days, and then eventually these strangers become friends. While leading the groups for days, a relationship is developed between the tour manager and the guests. Sometimes these relations stay for a lifetime. Not only are these links established between the tour manager and guests but a lot of friendships are fostered during the trip between the fellow tourists. Being together throughout the journey brings everyone closer. The last day is the separation day for the guests as well as for the tour manager. The group that began as strangers parts as a family.

INTRODUCTION

Parting with guests is the most challenging aspect of a tour manager's job. As they say 'to meet and part is a way of life, but to part and meet is the hope of life'; however, there comes a time for the tour manager to bid farewell to his guests. A tour manager must end his tour on a positive note with the hope that he may again get an opportunity to meet and serve these guests sometime in the future.

Closing a tour is an art. A lot of things are required to manage the closing of a tour. Post-tour, there are many formalities to be completed by a tour manager. A detailed discussion on how to close the tour and the formalities required to be carried out by the tour manager at the end of the tour may broadly be divided into two categories:

- Formalities during the closing of the tour
- Post-tour formalities

Let us now discuss each of these.

FORMALITIES DURING THE CLOSING OF TOUR

The following things may be considered by a tour manager while closing the tour.

THANKING THE GUESTS

A tour manager must part with his guests on a positive note. He must thank his guests on behalf of his company for choosing to travel with them. He may also express his sincere gratitude towards his guests for extending their cooperation and support throughout the tour. Though some guests might have given him a tough time, yet the tour manager must not forget to thank one and all. He may also suggest his guests to make further travel bookings with his company in the future. This sets the foundation for a continued business with his guests.

TAKING FEEDBACK FROM GUESTS

An essential part of a tour manager's job before closing a group is to receive the feedback of his clients who have been on the tour with him. Eventually, many companies have replaced feedback forms with feedbacks on tabloids or requesting the guests to post their feedback on review websites such as TripAdvisor that may reach out to a number of potential travellers across the world besides building the brand of the company only if the feedback is positive. Getting feedback also means visibility for a travel company, which means more business.

Feedback is generally on two levels: one for the services offered by the company on the tour and the other for the services provided by the tour manager himself. Besides these two purposes that a feedback serves, it is also an essential yardstick for a tour manager to get rewarded from the travel companies. Many travel companies reward or declare tour managers as star performers based on the number of positive feedback they get from the tourists. The more the positive feedback for a company on review sites, the better impression it has of a tour manager and ultimately the company the tour manager is working for.

As the guests have spent sufficient time on the tour, they have a first-hand experience of using the travel services booked during the tour. They know the shortcomings in the itinerary, and they may have suggestions for making the trip better. These guests sometimes might have valuable inputs to offer to the company. The useful recommendations of such guests must not go wasted. The feedback provided by the guests should always be welcome.

A tour manager should always be receptive to new ideas and suggestions from his guests. Instead of getting defensive about the services offered by his company, he must proactively seek the feedback of his clients in the right spirit. He should not take it as an offence in any case. He must consider the input from his guests as a valuable insight that may help his company to improve its services in the future.

Also, the feedback received by the tour manager about himself may also be an opportunity for him to reflect on his demeanour and the services offered by him. These may help him to assess his weaknesses and work on them accordingly.

However, a tour manager must be able to differentiate between the genuine feedback and disingenuous feedback. Every individual has a different opinion. What may be an excellent service for one client may not hold as a first-rate service for another client. There might be a difference in their perceptions. The company might have given a coach of Mercedes-Benz whereas the guest may prefer a Volvo coach. Thus, the client may provide a negative feedback of the coach as it is not according to his personal choice. Therefore, feedback must not be taken on face value. It must be sieved by the tour manager and analysed before passing on to the company. However, the filtering by the tour manager must be done without any bias.

It may also happen at times that the guests may hesitate from giving the feedback to the tour manager. The reason could be the good relationship between the guests and the tour manager that has developed on the tour. Probably, the guests want to remain in the good books of the tour manager. Therefore, they may hesitate.

Apparently, it might also happen that the guest might have forgotten his experience of older days during long tours and thus, he may not be able to recall his exact experience. Therefore, such guests may not give accurate feedback. Therefore, a tour manager must have a mind of his own to differentiate the genuine feedback from the affected one.

PROMOTING THE TOUR OPERATOR/TRAVEL AGENT

A tour manager works for a travel company that may be offering a variety of tourism products. Therefore, it is his duty the closing of a tour to share information about the other tourism products being offered by his company. A tour manager must promote his company, but subtly. In case he is carrying the brochures of the company, he may distribute them to his guests. He must make an effort to cross-sell the products of other departments of his company.

TIPS AND GRATUITIES

The closing of the tour is also the time of accepting tips and gratuities from the guests. However, a tour manager must never demand the tips and gratuities. This creates a wrong impression on the guests. If the guests are willing to give tips to the tour manager by choice, he may not refuse from taking the tips. However, he must give his best during the tour without expecting anything in return. If he has performed his job well, the guests may themselves give tips as a gesture to return his favours.

Apparently, he may also suggest his guests about the culture of tipping in his country. Generally speaking, Americans are generous in giving tips while Indians and Australians may not be comfortable in tipping unless they are asked to. However, this is just a generalization; this may vary from person to person.

Also, in some tours, tips are also mandatory for the tour driver and the tour manager. The information about the amount of tips to be given to the driver and tour manager is clearly stated in the 'extras' section of the tour package that is known before the clients. Accordingly, a tour manager may collect the tips on behalf of the company's driver every day, or he may collect the tips on the first or the last day of the tour.

FAREWELL DINNER

The last evening of the tour must be a memorable evening of the trip for the guests. A tour manager must ensure that they have an experience of a lifetime on the tour. To make the last evening worth remembering, he may organise a gala dinner for his guests. He may use this time in sharing the experiences of his guests during the tour. He may

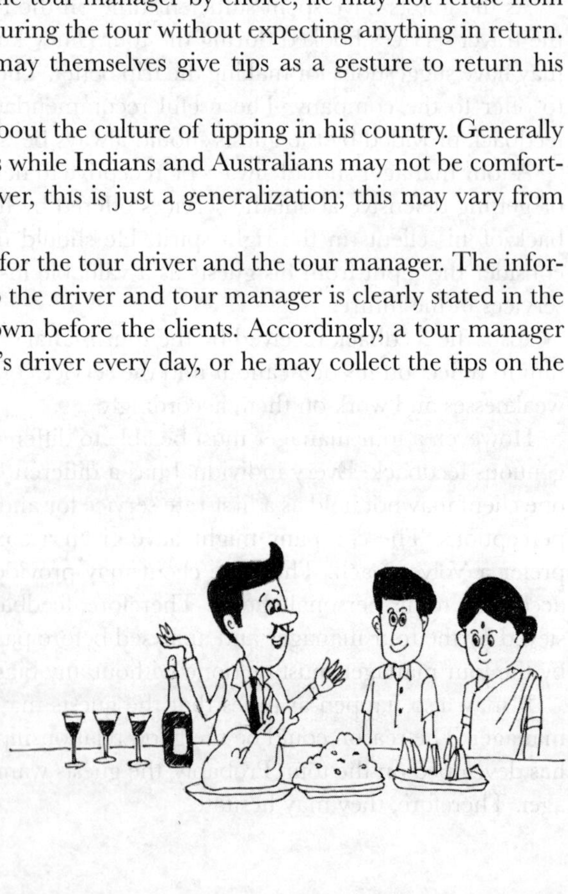

organise games for his guests or a DJ night to mark the celebrations. He may make short films and videos of the trip and show it during their get together. The idea is to bring all together to remember the happy moments spent together. A tour manager must leave his guests with some nostalgic moments.

STAYING CONNECTED

It is an era of technology. A tour manager must know how to make use of technology to stay connected with his clients. He may also keep in touch with his group members through social networking sites such as Facebook. He may even click a group picture during the trip and distribute the hard copies or soft copies among his clients on the last day of the tour as a parting memory for them.

RECONFIRMING THE DEPARTURE TIMING OF PASSENGERS

Prior to the check-out of the group for the final departure, a tour manager must reconfirm the flights/trains of his passengers with the airlines/railway authorities. In case of any delays, the same may be communicated to the guests.

TAX REFUNDS

The tour manager must remind the group to claim tax refunds at the airport for the shopping done by them. A detailed account of tax refunds has been already discussed in Chapter 8 (Section C).

POST-TOUR FORMALITIES

There are specific responsibilities that a tour manager is expected to take care of after the group has returned. Let us have a discussion on the tour manager's duties after the tour is over.

SETTLING ACCOUNTS

After the departure of the group, a tour manager must settle the accounts of the tour with his company. He must prepare a detailed expense sheet of the trip for his records. He may submit all the necessary payment receipts along with entry tickets or any other documentary proofs of expenses that he has incurred during the tour for the records of his company.

It is always advisable to settle the accounts before taking up any new assignment as the tour manager may get confused with the expenses incurred later.

THANK YOU LETTERS TO GUESTS

After the guests reach back home, a tour manager must write a thank you letter to his guests for having their holiday booked with his company and being his guests. Alternatively, a tour manager may drop an email to his guests to thank them in person.

He must thank his guests for giving him the privilege to serve them. Along with the thank you letter, he may send an invitation to his guests to get together for a reunion again to stay connected with his guests.

THANK YOU LETTERS TO TRAVEL SUPPLIERS

After completing the tour, a tour manager must write to the suppliers thanking them for the travel arrangements organised by them. He may also write about the inefficacies, in case he faced or his clients reported during the tour. This may be an opportunity for the travel suppliers to improve upon their services. If required, he must clear the outstanding bills with his suppliers or request his company to make the necessary payments.

PASSING ON THE BUSINESS OPPORTUNITY

On coming back from the tour, a tour manager must pass on the referrals/new queries given by the client to the other departments of his company. This helps him in creating a better relationship with his colleagues and also creating business opportunities for his firm, besides building his personal reputation and gaining additional incentives for cross-selling other products of the company.

SUBMISSION OF TOUR REPORT

After the completion of the tour, many travel companies expect a tour manager to present a detailed account of the tour. For this, they may ask the tour manager to submit a written report of the tour to his company. Some companies may prefer to call it a trip report or a tour report. A tour report may broadly cover the informationcovered in the subsequent subsections.

ASSESSMENT OF SERVICES OFFERED ON THE TOUR

Besides the guests, a tour manager has the first-hand experience of the services provided by the company. In fact, he has an eye for detail that can be very vital to the firm. From the first day of the tour, a tour manager uses different services such as transportation, hotels, restaurants and so on offered by the GHA and various vendors. This places him in a situation where he can form an opinion about the services provided by his company to its guests. Sharing personal feedback about the services offered by the company to the guests gives an opportunity to the company to understand the challenges faced by the tour manager and the guests during the tour. The challenge may be on account of the problems in operating an itinerary or the list of grievances related to the quality of services raised by the clients during the tour. The detailed feedback may provide valuable insights to the company to improve upon their services.

Generally, a trip report seeks the feedback of a tour manager on the following services used during the tour for the guests:

1. Services offered by the airlines
2. Services provided by the other modes of transportation such as coaches, ferries, cruises, trains, ride operators and so on
3. Type of hotel (rooms and services offered)
4. Meals offered in the hotels
5. Food provided by the local restaurants
6. Sightseeing attractions covered
7. Special arrangements for guests with special requirements
8. Other inclusions in the itinerary
9. Service of a tour guide
10. Services of a tour driver
11. Other issues related to transportation, accommodation, activity, on-tour safety, hygiene and execution of the itinerary
12. Any other issues raised by the clients

INCIDENT REPORT

Many situations are unforeseeable. A tour manager must be able to handle such cases to the best of his competency. Many companies ask the tour manager to pen down any awkward situation that he faced during the tour. He must give a detailed account of any such incidents that he encountered on the trip along with the possible way of how he dealt with it. A written report of such incidents helps the tour operator/travel agent to understand the issues that may happen on a tour. Accordingly, the company can suggest the other tour managers what situations they might encounter. Learning from these situations, the tour manager may remain prepared for such unforeseen situations in the future.

CHANGE ITINERARY FORM

Many times, there might be last minute changes in the itinerary on account of weather conditions, traffic jams or closures of the attractions due to any other unforeseen situations. In such cases, a tour manager must complete the documentation in all respects. He must fill in the Change Itinerary form that mentions the reasons on account of which he had to bring changes in the decided itinerary along with the date and change of location. It also contains the names of passengers along with their signatures that serve as a documentary evidence that the alterations have taken place with the consent of the guests. The form must be submitted at the end of the tour to his company.

RELEASE FORM

There might be some guests on a tour who want to be on their own during a trip due to any reason, or the guest may not be in a condition to continue with the group on account of his ill health. In a limiting case, some guests may be misbehaving in the group, for example, drinking excessively on the tour, abusing others and so on. In such cases, a tour manager must ask such guests to fill in the release form wherein they mention their personal details along with reasons for leaving the group and also consenting to take the own responsibility of their travel arrangements on leaving the group.

CREATING A DATABASE

A tour manager may create a database of clients who travelled with him on the tour. He may put these customers as 'preferred customers' in his database and may keep updating them from time to time about the new offers floated by the travel company.

ORGANISING A GET-TOGETHER

Post-tour, a tour manager may organise a get together for his tour members. In the get-together, he may ask his guests to take membership of the company and become preferred customers to avail discounts on packages offered by his company in the future. He may also show them the memories of the trip through a film or a video by displaying their pictures taken together at the get-together, or he may ask his group members to share their best moments of their holiday.

SUMMARY

A tour manager must handle the closing of a tour in a professional way. He must ensure to complete all the written formalities expected of him. He must end the trip on a positive note. He must use this opportunity to be grateful to his guests and also try to stay connected with his group members in the future.

Activity 1 The incidental report

Assume that Joe, one of the guests of the group, came drunk in the morning when the trip was about to start and the whole group was very excited to see and explore new places in Venice. Joe suddenly came, and in no time started unnecessarily abusing Mary, one of the tourists, in the group. In retaliation, Mary slapped Joe as she could not tolerable his unruly behaviour.

Now, being a tour manager, take this story forward with your own imagination and prepare an incidental report to be submitted to your office narrating the whole incident in your own words. Also, suggest the corrective course of action that you may have taken at that time to diffuse the matter.

Activity 2 Tour report

You were leading a group of tourists in Germany, Austria and Switzerland for 15 days from India. Now you are back and as per the mandate of the company, you are required to submit a one-page tour report to your office. Prepare a format of the same and discuss the same in the class.

POSSIBLE SOLUTIONS TO THE OPENING VIGNETTE

- Amit realised his mistake for not informing his guests due to which they had to bear a substantial monetary loss.
- To resolve this issue, he wrote an apology letter to the company as well as the guests.
- He also contacted his guests personally to apologise to them in person and asked their bank details to transfer the compensation money in his account.

Lessons Learned

- A tour manager should always be aware of his duties at all times.
- He must adequately brief his guest in detail at every point.
- During the closing of the tour, it is essential for a tour manager to inform his guests about the tax refunds at the airports in case of international travel.

SECTION D

INSIGHTS INTO GUIDING

Chapter 16 *Tour Manager as a Tour Guide*

Chapter 17 *Techniques of Commentary*

Chapter 18 *Practices to Be a Successful Tour Guide*

Welcome back learners!

Till now we have read about who is a tour manager, the pre-tour preparations he is required to make for the assignment and the on-tour responsibilities that he is required to execute while dealing with guests. However, there is one more dimension to being a tour manager. A tour manager may act as a tour guide too.

The objective of this section is to introduce the learners to from being just a tour manager to being a tour guide too. It shall orient the readers to the advantages of practising as a tour guide while also being a tour manager. As the interpretation of various touristic sites is an important part of a tour guide's profession, this section shall also highlight the various techniques and ways of giving commentary at various points of interest that is important for a tour guide to know and practise. This section shall also give valuable insights to tour guides to become successful in their profession. Chapter 18 also introduces the readers to some useful practical tips that the tour guides may practise in their daily profession to become more successful and accomplished in their jobs.

Overall, this section shall prepare tour managers to evolve as tour guides and understand the intricacies involved in executing this job as a tour guide too. After going through this section, the readers would be able to understand the following:

- Challenges involved in being a tour guide while practising as a tour manager
- Various techniques and ways of giving a commentary at an attraction
- Various practical tips that differentiate a successful tour guide from an average tour guide

So let us embark together on the journey of learning!

Happy learning!

16

Tour Manager as a Tour Guide

LEARNING OBJECTIVES

- Who is a tour guide?
- Why do tour managers prefer to work as tour guides?
- What is the nature of tour guide's job?
- What are the challenges of the tour guiding profession?

Amit was leading a group of mixed nationalities to Mauritius. The whole group was very excited to see and explore Mauritius. It was the first day of the tour. The entire group after having breakfast was waiting for Amit at the hotel lobby to proceed for sightseeing. Amit was late by only 10 minutes. He was also very dismally dressed. His clothes were not appropriately ironed, and he was not well groomed too. Everyone looked at him in annoyance and Amit felt a bit embarrassed. He rushed towards the coach indicating the group members to follow him. He was the first one to get on to the coach and occupy his seat. Others followed. As the coach started moving, he stood up from his seat facing the guests to brief them about Mauritius. Suddenly, the driver applied the brakes and Amit lost his balance. He fell tumbling into the aisle. Everybody started giggling. On arriving at the Botanical Garden when Amit stood near his guests, briefing them about the park, everybody started moving a little away from him as he was smelling foul. He was perhaps drunk. He could not even speak properly. He tottered and toddled. The guests somehow tried to accept the situation and not spoil their moods. However, while moving around the Botanical Garden, one of the guests enquired about a tree and its uses to which Amit replied, 'I am not a botanist. How can I know this?' Everybody was zapped at his blunt reply.

On coming back in the coach after the day's tour was over, he requested his guests not to complain about him to his company. He may otherwise lose his job, and he had two small children to take care of. Everybody was confused as to what should be done as he was going to be their guide for the next three days also.

The profession of leading a tour has various facets. A tour manager has a choice to be a tour guide too. The job of a tour guide is different from that of a tour manager. Both titles carry different responsibilities as they both have work in different spaces. However, many tour managers exercise the option of doubling up as a tour guide, at least in limited cases. The question that arises is, who is a tour guide? Are both a tour manager and a tour guide the same? If not, how is the job of a tour guide different from that of a tour manager's?

INTRODUCTION

Three kinds of arrangements exist in travel companies:

1. Working as a tour manager
2. Working as a tour guide
3. Working as a tour manager-cum-tour guide

This whole book has been focusing on the first kind of arrangement as a tour manager. Now in this section, we shall have a detailed discussion on the second and third arrangements. Let us first understand the difference between a tour guide and a tour manager. A tour guide is a person who conducts sightseeing tours for a limited duration of time. According to the World Federation of Tour Guides Association (WFTGA), London,

> *A tour guide is a person who guides the group of guests in the language of visitors' choice and interprets the natural and cultural heritage of a place to his guests.*

As discussed in the previous chapters, tour managers lead groups of tourists from the beginning till the end of the tour. They accompany the guest at every point of the tour, that is, at airports, hotels or sightseeing attractions. However, in the travel trade, many tour managers working for travel companies aspire to work as tour guides too. They wish to give commentary at the attractions. However, they may not provide commentary inside a monument due to restrictions imposed by authorities in various jurisdictions that may vary from country to country. In some countries, a separate permit/licence may be required to work as a tour guide.

TOUR MANAGERS AS TOUR GUIDES

Many tour managers prefer to work as tour guides too. Many tour operators also find this arrangement quite beneficial. Besides, guests are also more comfortable with the tour manager who acts as a tour guide too. Let us now understand from their own perspective, the company's perspective and the guests' perspective why tour managers want to become tour guides.

FROM A TOUR MANAGER'S PERSPECTIVE

Some factors drive a tour manager to work as a tour guide too. They are as follows:

1. As the tour manager is already on a group assignment handling his guests, he may not like to miss out on the opportunity of losing his business to a tour guide. Guiding at a

monument may mean getting more tips from the tourists as the tour guide earns money for his explanation at the monument. Knowing the techniques of tour guiding as a tour manager can mean more business for a tour manager.

2. Also, being able to guide at a monument himself reduces the dependence of a tour manager on a tour guide. Otherwise, availing the services of a tour guide at a monument is subject to his availability at the time of the tour. Also, the tour guide must be adept in the guest's language. Therefore, at times, this may become a challenge for a tour manager to arrange for a tour guide at an attraction.
3. A tour manager is in better control of the situation when he can himself act as a tour guide. He now may have less dependence on a tour guide for taking his guest on a sightseeing tour. There is no intervention of any third party at an attraction.

However, in spite of the knowledge these tour managers may have about the monument, they have to depend upon a tour guide for the commentary inside a monument. While visiting monuments, they may be restricted from giving commentary inside. This is generally due to the restrictions of the government authorities that only permit authorised guides who are licensed by the government to provide commentary at these monuments.

Therefore, to reduce his dependence on tour guides and also not to lose his share of money that the tourists may give as tips to the tour guide for providing a reasonable explanation about the monument, a tour manager may wish to take the licence from competent authorities to practise as a tour guide too. This is more prevalent in a country like India, where many inbound tour managers working as freelancers for different travel companies aspire to become a tour guide too to get more tips from foreigners.

FROM A COMPANY'S PERSPECTIVE

Now let us try to understand the benefits from a company's perspective of training a tour manager to work as a too guide too. Some of the reasons may be as follows:

1. The company does not have to spend its valuable time and other resources searching for a reliable tour guide.
2. The company may also save money that it otherwise had to spend on giving the wages to the tour guide for guiding the group on the tour.
3. At the same time, since the tour manager is working for the tour operator, a tour operator is quite aware of the competencies of a tour manager. He is already tried and tested.
4. Sometimes, it may also save the reputation of the company. It may happen that a tour guide arranged by the company may not reach on time to conduct the sightseeing tour due to an emergency, thereby delaying the whole itinerary. To tackle such a situation, if a tour manager has a licence, he may act as a substitute to the tour guide. This may help in keeping the itinerary on time, thereby saving the face of the company.

FROM THE GUESTS' PERSPECTIVE

Many tourists also prefer to explore an attraction with a tour guide who is also their tour manager. Let us discuss the reasons one by one.

1. Being with his guests for a substantial time and being already aware of the interests of his guests, a tour manager-cum-tour guide can tailor-make his commentary according to the interest of his guests. Likewise, he may also be aware of the sensitivity of his group. Therefore, he may mould the information according to the requirements of his guests.
2. Guests also feel more comfortable if their tour manager acts as a tour guide. Since the tour manager of the group accompanies the group from beginning till the end, guests may share a better rapport with him. Therefore, the guests may be more comfortable asking questions and seeking clarifications from the tour manager who acts as a tour guide as compared to a tour guide who is with the group for a decidedly shorter duration of time.

BENEFITS OF HIRING A TOUR GUIDE

We have just discussed the benefits of a tour manager being a tour guide for the guests. However, a tour guide has his own significance in conducting the itinerary of the tour. Besides the reasons mentioned earlier, following are the reasons that why tourists hire the services of a tour guide.

EXPERTISE

Guests hire tour guides to take advantage of their local knowledge that they may have by being a local person of the city. The tour guide, being a local guy, is well aware of the social dynamics of the destination and the local sensitivities to be considered while visiting the destination. Therefore, the guest has an opportunity to learn about the local sensitivities to be followed at the destination through a tour guide's expertise.

HASSLE FREE

With a tour guide, guests feel more comfortable as everything is being taken care by the tour guide. The guests do not have to do any homework as to which place to visit and which not too. Everything has already been filtered by a tour guide.

TO BE TIME EFFICIENT

A tour guide knows how much time to spend at an attraction. He expedites the purchase of entry tickets, pulls his guests through the attractions, briefs them at the attraction and makes sure that everyone in the group adheres to the time limit set for visiting the attraction. Everything is time bound. Hence, the guests get to see the maximum sites in the minimum span of time with a tour guide.

TO FEEL SAFE

Many guests feel safer in the presence of a tour guide. Guests may feel jittery and lost, especially when they are in a new country. The presence of a tour guide gives them moral support that there is someone whom they can bank upon in case of any difficulty they may face.

WORKING OF TOUR GUIDES

Now let us understand how tour guides work.

1. Tour guides generally work on full-day or half-day tours. Accordingly, they are paid per day or per half-day tour wages.
2. Tour guides may work as freelancers too. Some tour guides may work for a particular company, whereas others may associate themselves to multiple companies, taking assignments as and when they come. Alternatively, some tour guides may be chosen for handling government assignments, taking the delegates on sightseeing tours.
3. Some assignments may be FIT-based where individual guests have booked for hiring the services of a tour guide, whereas some assignments may be a big group of more than 10 travellers.
4. Some tour guides specialise in tours based on inbound tours, outbound tours or domestic tours. Within these areas, tour guides may specialise in leisure tours, nature-based tours, heritage walks, food walks, mice tours, photography tours, wildlife tours, luxury tours, rural tours, wine tours and so on. The kind of tours a tour guide conducts depends upon his interests along with the type of tours that a travel company conducts.
5. Many times, the tourist book regular brochure-guided tours in which the itinerary is already fixed, whereas in some cases, the tourists choose their own sightseeing points and requests the company to customise the itinerary according to their interests. However, in many cases, the tourists are not clear as to what they want to see. In such situations, some tours are at the discretion of a tour guide who may take his guests to places according to his own choice.

CHALLENGES OF THE TOUR GUIDE'S PROFESSION

The profession of a tour guide is very challenging. Some of the reasons that make it a challenging job are discussed in this section.

Delighting the Guests is Not Easy

Holidays are both a financial and an emotional investment. It is not easy to please anyone entirely, and that too all the tourists. The guests have spent a good deal of money and spared time to be on the tour. They may have very high hopes from the trip as well as from the tour guide. The guests must feel that they are getting value for money on a trip. Satisfying the guests is not that easy. This depends entirely upon the performance of tour guide and on how well he conducts the trip and takes care of his guests. So the pressure of performance always stays for a tour guide. Therefore, we may say it is a challenging job.

Different Types of Guests

On every tour, a tour guide is meeting a new set of tourists, except in some circumstances where the guests may have placed a request to repeat the same tour guide. Every group may have a different composition of group members. Some guests may be of different nationalities while some may be from different religions. Some groups may have expecting mothers, while some may have parents with infants who need particular attention. Some may be women travellers, while some may be elderly citizens. Some may be patients who have particular allergies, while some may have a medical history and some in the same group may be differently abled. Handling different types of such guests in the same group or even in different groups may be very challenging for a tour guide.

Always Under a Scanner

A tour guide may feel that he is being continuously monitored by the guests for his performance. He may feel pressurised and nervous as a result. To perform under pressure may be challenging for many.

Adjust to Weather Conditions

A tour guide may have to operate his tour under extreme weather circumstances for his scheduled assignments. He may have to guide his guests in scorching heat, chilly winter or on a rainy day. Saying no to the assignment means the loss of opportunity for earning money.

Working Time

A tour guide may have to work on weekends or even on public holidays. The festival time may be the peak season for a tour guide as the guest may be on holiday during that time. He may also have to work for months together during the season time without any breaks in between. Sometimes, he may have to go on back-to-back tours. This makes it a challenging profession.

Handling Questions

Guests may have a series of questions to ask the tour guide. On every tour, a tour guide may be asked different questions by different guests that he may not have even predicted. This makes his job quite challenging.

Handling Emergency Situations

The kind of conditions that a tour guide may have to face on a tour can never be predicted. While guiding his guests at a monument, someone may steal a phone from the guest or someone may even tease a female traveller in a crowd. The magnitude of situations faced by a tour guide may be myriad and entirely unpredictable. Therefore, a tour guide's job is quite challenging.

ROLES OF A TOUR GUIDE

A tour guide may perform the following roles during the tour.

CONSULTANT

It is the tour guide who would be the local guy for the guests who has an expertise in the city. He is expected to be a storehouse of information and to know the intricacies of his city thoroughly. He is supposed to direct his guests to various sightseeing points, depending upon their interest. He, therefore, acts as a consultant for his guests.

MEDIATOR

A tour guide connects the guests with the real life of his city. He may take his guests to places that have limited access, and go out of his way to bring the local community closer to the tourists. He, therefore, may act as a mediator between his guests and the local community of the destination.

CREATOR

A tour guide is a creator of experiences for his guests. He must be able to perform to the expectations of his guests. He must be able to make his guests feel the aromas, the sounds, the culture, the religion and the heritage of the city. He may involve his guests in creative experiences on the tour. For example, the Kutch district of Gujarat in India offers very impressive guided tours of different kinds. Some of these are as follows:

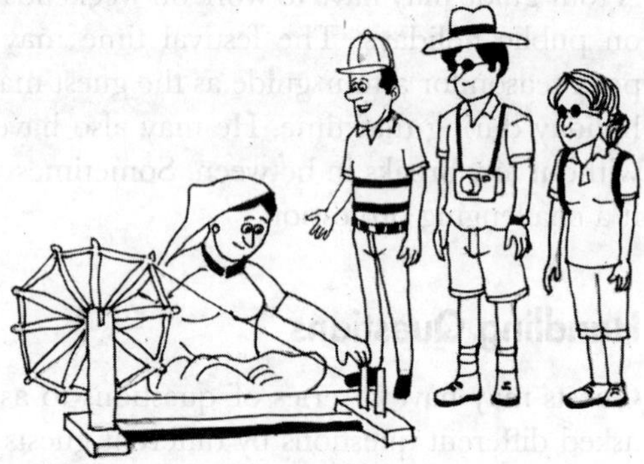

- Textile tours at Bhujodi village in Kutch which is famous for textile production with more than 1,200 inhabitants involved in textile handicraft production. It includes a visit to weavers, block printers and tie-dye artists.
- Cultural tour of Hodka village.
- Photography tours at Mandvi.

Let us take another example of New Delhi, the capital of India. It has so much to offer in terms of unique tourism experiences that mesmerizes the tourists on guided tours. Some of the experiences that the guest may be a part of during the trip may include the following:

- A cycle rickshaw ride in Chandni Chowk.
- A Segway guided tour at India Gate.
- Making rotis (bread) at the Gurudwara Bangla Sahib in the langar, the most extensive community kitchen in the world.
- Learning cooking in traditional homes of Delhi.
- Filling the tummies with local cuisines of the city during food walks.

CARETAKER

Tour guides act as custodian of groups. They are expected to take care of their guests during the sightseeing tours. Right from ensuring that all guests are together and no guests are missing to reminding them to take care of their valuables, a tour guide continuously acts as the caretaker of his guests during the sightseeing tours.

SELLER

Many tours are sold as optional tours. Generally, tour guides have a target of selling these optional tours to guests. Their incentives are linked to the number of optional excursions sold by them. Therefore, tour guides must have robust, convincing abilities and the art of selling the optional tours to their guests.

CASHIER

Many travel companies may take the booking amount on day tours and then later receive the pending balance from tourists after the trip gets over. In such cases, it becomes the responsibility of a tour guide to collect money for the trip on behalf of his company. He must be aware as to how much money has to be received from the guests. They may also know the criteria for payment collection of their company. It may be cash or cashless. In case of cashless transactions, a tour guide may carry the payment machine with him on the tour and swipe the equivalent amount to be collected from the guests.

LINK-PIN

A tour guide ensures that all his members stay together. Through his commentary and by organising different games, he tries to bring all his members closer to each other.

TRAINING OF TOUR GUIDES

Tour guides undergo training at two levels. One at the fresher level, when someone aspires to be a tour guide, and second when the experienced tour guides undergo refresher guide training to keep themselves updated on the latest practises in the trade. At entry and refresher levels, following are the general mechanisms that tour guides are generally trained under.

COMPETENT AUTHORITY

Having a valid licence is a prerequisite to becoming an authorised guide. Anyone who aspires to be a tour guide may acquire formal training from competent authorities of his domicile. Many government bodies in different countries may be the responsible authorities who provide the licence to the tour guide. In some countries, there are written examinations followed by field visits. Alternatively, many authorities may conduct practical tests to evaluate the participants. Only after the aspirant has qualified the evaluation system of the competent authority, he may be granted the licence to work as a tour guide.

TOUR OPERATORS

Working for different travel companies may be different for a tour guide as they may have different policies and regulations. Therefore, while working for a particular tour operator, tour guides may attend the formal training sessions organised by the tour operator. Courses on inputs on tourism, history, geography, architecture, trends in travel, needs of a tourist, cross-cultural differences and techniques of guiding may be imparted to tour guides by the experts.

Novice tour guides may also accompany experienced tour guides on tours to acquire hands-on training from the experienced tour guide.

ASSOCIATIONS

Tour Guide associations may also organise training sessions/seminars for the tour guides to keep them abreast about the upcoming trends taking place in the tourism industry and particularly in the field of guiding.

PERFORMANCE EVALUATION OF TOUR GUIDES

A lot depends upon the performance of a tour guide. If tour guides do not perform well, the tourists may ask for the refund of money as their holiday experience gets ruined. It may also affect the reputation of the company. Therefore, it is important for tour operators to have a mechanism to monitor the performance of tour guides continuously. Tour companies may evaluate the performance of tour guides using different tools and techniques. The mechanism of motivating the tour guides may vary from company to company. Generally speaking, the guides are rated on the following parameters in travel companies:

- Number of positive feedback generated on review sites or on feedback forms by the guests.
- Number of optional tours sold by the tour guide.
- Number of refunds of trips against each tour guide (in case the guests were not satisfied with the performance of tour guide and opted for the return of their money).

- Demand of the tour guide raised by the tourist for repeating the same tour guide on another tour based on positive personal experience and positive reviews of other guests.

To further motivate the tour guides, companies may also introduce various means of appreciating the tour guides, for example, sending appreciation letters to the performers, giving a star performer award to the best guide, giving holidays packages, giving incentives, sending them for further training, giving them promotions and so on.

SUMMARY

The roles of a tour guide are multiple. Being a tour guide requires a lot of dedication, devotion and commitment on the part of a tour guide to handle this challenging profession. A tour guide must have the art of handling people. Being a tour manager-cum-tour guide can be quiet beneficial for a tour manager, the company and the guests. Sending the tour guides for training, and evaluating their performances from time to time, is equally important.

Activity 1 Submit a report

Visit any three important sites/attractions with your group members. Identify three local tour guides and interview them. Questions may pertain to the following:

- What are the challenges that you face being a tour guide?
- What are your roles as a tour guide?
- Is there any difference between tour guiding and tour leading?
- Which is the regulatory body that has licensed you?
- Which destinations do you generally cover?
- What are the typical features of your profession?

Now submit a detailed report to your teacher on the topic 'roles of a tour guide' and submit the interviews as a separate case in the report, while also submitting photos and questionnaires, if any, in the appendices section.

Activity 2 Research the job of a tour guide

Divide the class into groups of five each and ask each group to do a small research. Ask each group to read at least seven research papers and get an insight on the roles of a tour guide. Based on the literature review, ask the students to identify the variables that define the job of a tour guide. Based on the variables, the students may prepare a questionnaire with questions related to the characteristics of a tour guides' profession. Now let each group interview five stakeholders and try to gather maximum possible information about a tour guide's job. You may choose the following stakeholders:

1. Travel company
2. Local merchandisers
3. Local attraction authorities
4. Hoteliers
5. Tourists

Interviews may be conducted of at least five respondents from each category of stakeholders. This makes gaining useful insights of at least 25 respondents. Every group may then write a research paper and then present the same in a seminar conducted in the college on the theme 'role of tour guides'. The research paper may include the introduction, objective of the study, review of the literature, research design, analysis, observations and conclusions along with references.

POSSIBLE SOLUTIONS TO THE OPENING VIGNETTE

- One of the older guests, realising the heat of the situation, called Amit in private when they reached the hotel after the sightseeing. He then warned him to mend his behaviour with the guests while on duty.
- The guests also decided to complain about Amit to the company and asked for a replacement as they did not want to retake a chance of spoiling their remaining days of vacation.
- The company sent another tour guide to conduct the rest of the tour in order to not spoil its reputation.

Lessons Learned

- A tour guide should always report to his duty before time.
- He must be well dressed and well groomed.
- He may claim his seat first, but then he should get down and let other group members board the coach. He must count the pax and then only sit at the end.
- A tour manager must not be drunk on duty.
- He must be able to learn maximum information about the attractions being visited. In case, he does not have the answer to a client's question, he may politely say that he may get back to his guest with the appropriate response in some time.

17

Techniques of Commentary

LEARNING OBJECTIVES

- What makes an excellent commentary?
- What techniques should be practised by a tour guide while giving a commentary?

Jin and Julia were very excited for a tour to India. They were a Spanish couple who wanted to witness the epitome of love, the Taj Mahal, on Valentine's Day to make their day a special one. After visiting various attractions at Delhi and enjoying its charm, the couple was very excited to visit Agra to see the Taj Mahal. To learn more about the Taj Mahal and to facilitate their overall experience, the couple decided to hire the services of a local tour guide, Jiggy, who was a licensed tour guide approved by the state government. The couple thought that now they were in safe hands and that they had someone who would help them understand the history and tell them unusual facts about the Taj Mahal. On reaching the Taj Mahal, the couple was very excited, waiting to listen to the tour guide. On entering the gate of Taj Mahal, Jiggy showed their entry tickets and in a loud tone to Jin and Julia asked them to show their passport to the authorities as a proof of identity. Both of them were shocked to see his rude behaviour. As they went inside, they lost sight of Jiggy. He had disappeared. He had gone inside the premises of officials to talk about something without informing his guests.

Then after sometime, when it had almost become a panicky situation for both, Jiggy suddenly appeared and roared 'follow me'. Without bothering to look at them, he started doling out rote information about the monument while walking towards the monument. It seemed as if he was not interested enough and was simply doing his described work without any interest. He would, at times, almost run while Jin and Julia would find it difficult to match his step. Sometimes he would not be audible as there were many other tourists and their guides. While coming out of the Taj Mahal, Jiggy took them to a local shop and almost forced to shop there. Both Jin and Julia felt very uncomfortable with Jiggy's behaviour.

The guests had an early train to catch for Delhi in the next morning. Their experience of Taj Mahal was utterly deplorable!

When the guests take a guided tour, they may be very excited to explore the destination. They may have very high expectations for the trip. They may look forward to a guide who would familiarise them with the destination and bring life to the place through his commentary.

Therefore, one of the vital aspects of a tour guide's profession is to give commentary at important points of interest. Any attraction can only make some sense to the tourists if the context of an attraction/point of interest has been interpreted to the guests in the right way through a tour guide's commentary. Therefore, the commentary given by a tour guide is critical for the guests to connect with an attraction and make sense out of it. In other words, through his interpretation, a tour guide adds life to an attraction.

INTRODUCTION

It may be understood that commentary is the soul of a tour guide's business as he earns his bread and butter through speaking. However, delivering commentary is an art that only comes with practice. The choice of words and style chosen by a tour guide for providing an interpretation matters a lot. Also, the technique of giving a commentary is equally important along with how the commentary is being delivered. Hence, a tour guide must prepare on two fronts: the content of the commentary and the style of delivery. Let us have a broader discussion on each of this one by one.

CONTENT

Content is the soul of a commentary. The quality of information that a tour guide shares about the attraction/city/country can affect the image of a destination. He, therefore, may rightly be called as the image changer of the destination. It is essential for a tour guide to present the facts and figures of his country in such a way that creates a favourable image of his country without passing on any wrong information about the destination to his guests. By putting the data in a right perspective, a tour guide may act as an image changer of a destination. While delivering the content, the following things must be borne by a tour guide.

Correct Information

The quality of the content is paramount. Giving accurate and factual information about a monument, attraction or destination is the responsibility of a tour guide. A tour guide must provide the right and authentic information to his guests while on a tour. He should always cross-check the facts before putting across any such information to his guests.

For the guests, a tour guide is the encyclopaedia of a monument, attraction, city and country. He is an expert who is expected to answer all the queries of the guests. However, a tour guide may not have all answers to all the questions raised by the guests. Therefore, to avoid this embarrassment of not knowing the answers, he may try to offset his weakness by giving false information to his guests. This must be prevented by the tour guide as the guests may cross-check the facts on the Internet that may eventually put the tour guide in a poor light and affect his feedback at the end.

Balanced Information

Too much of anything is wrong. A commentary should neither be too long nor too short. It should be just the appropriate length. Striking a balance between how much to speak is very vital for a tour guide. Giving too lengthy commentaries may bore the guests. Moreover, as itineraries are time bound and many monuments are required to be covered on the same day, a tour guide cannot afford to blabber while giving commentary to his guests endlessly.

Alternatively, speaking too less may also make guests feel that the tour guide is unprepared. A tour guide must have enough content to talk about while giving commentary at an attraction. He must not dry up so quickly.

Hence, how much to speak is an intelligent choice that a tour guide must make while also balancing the inquisitiveness of guests.

Varying Information

The commentary of a tour guide may vary from group to group. He may have to customise his commentary according to the profile and the age of the clientele he is handling. He must be able to analyse the interest of his guests and, accordingly, share information with the guest without distorting the facts of that attraction. For example, old-aged tourists while visiting a temple may be interested in learning more about the mythological stories about the temple, whereas a young group of tourists may be interested in the architecture of the temple. Therefore, he may elaborate his commentary on mythological aspects of the temple to the old-aged tourists rather than focusing on the architectural elements of the temple and vice versa.

Interesting Information

Tourists have more interests to see things rather than to listen to the commentary of the tour guide. Therefore, it is crucial to catch the attention of guests by giving them something different so that they listen to the tour guide's commentary. Hence, a tour guide must share unusual facts to attract the attention of his guests. He must be able to present the facts interestingly and engagingly to his guests. He must give new insights and novel perspectives about a destination/attraction that the guests may not find on the Internet too.

Bring in Anecdotes/Legends/Stories

Every attraction has a story to tell. A tour guide must be adept at sharing such stories of these attractions. Legends and tales make a place alive. Therefore, it is essential for a tour guide to keep his commentary unique and engaging by adding flavours of old stories/legends/anecdotes in his interpretation, wherever possible.

For example, while guiding a group of foreigners to Mathura in the state of Uttar Pradesh in India, a tour guide may narrate exciting stories of Lord Krishna's childhood and the miracles he performed on the common masses.

STYLE OF DELIVERY

The style of delivering a commentary is as important as the content of the commentary. The way a tour guide communicates with his guests makes a vital difference in the overall experience of the guests. Let us discuss the various ways in which a tour guide can improve his style of commentary.

Voice Modulation

A tour guide must not sound dull. He must sound very dynamic and exciting. Therefore, he may use his voice to his advantage. It is vital for a tour guide to modulate his voice during the delivery of commentary. Essential facts should be emphasised more by being a little loud or repeating a few words. The idea is that the narration should be like the notes of music which sometimes run high and sometimes low but always sound musical to the ears. Through his voice, a tour guide should be able to look enthusiastic and energetic that may charge the guests too. He must make his presence felt by modulating his voice.

Pace

A tour guide must keep a check on the speed of his narration. He must not speak too fast or too slow. His pitch and pace should be able to send a clear communication to the guests. He may also take pauses in between the commentary that may help not only him to make breaks and recollect, but also the tourists to understand the communication more clearly.

Body Language

The body language communicates and speaks a lot. Therefore, a tour guide must have the right body posture, gait and style while talking with his guests. His body language should neither suggest that he is arrogant by nature nor it should send a message that the tour guide is nervous to handle the group. His body language should just be upright and quite balanced. He should intelligently use his body language to convey an impression of strong personality in the minds of his guests.

Smile

A smile can be an ornament for a tour guide. A smile while giving a commentary is like a cherry on the cake. The guests feel more connected with the tour guide who keeps a smile on his face while providing narration to his guests. A cheerful looking tour guide spreads positivity and freshness amongst the group members.

EYE CONTACT

Maintaining an eye contact with the guests is essential. Sometimes, it may happen that a guide is just looking at a particular guest while giving the commentary. This may make other guests feel ignored. Therefore, this should be avoided. A tour guide must maintain eye contact with all his guests. Looking into the eyes of all the guests makes them feel important, and the guests believe that the tour guide is genuinely interested in interacting with them.

Humour

A tour guide must add some dose of fun and laughter in his commentary. Giving a monotonous narration makes it dull and boring. Therefore, a tour guide must top up his narrative with some jokes or present more humorous facts/present the information in a more entertaining way that keeps his guests more hooked to the commentary.

TECHNIQUES OF COMMENTARY

A tour guide must use the right techniques for delivering a commentary. Proper usage of techniques makes a tour guide look like a more seasoned professional in the eyes of the tourists. Following is the list of practical ways that a tour guide may adopt to make his commentary more interesting for his guests.

OPENING NOTE

As first impressions are critical, the beginning note of a narration must be fascinating. A tour guide's speech must sound very impressive. Choice of descriptive words is crucial.

A tour guide may open with a note like:

> *Good morning everyone! A hearty welcome to all in India! Dear friends, I am Raghav, your tour guide for the day. I am fortunate to be with you all witnessing Delhi 6 on a rainy day. We shall kickstart the day with the blessings of God at Gurudwara Sheesh Ganj. So, keep your minds empty and let us get going on our exciting journey of fun, thrill and surprises!*

GREETING THE GUESTS

Specially greeting the guests sets the tone of the tour. A tour guide must welcome his guests in the local language of his city or destination. Use of local words gives the guests a 'local feel' of the destination. For example, while receiving guests from a foreign country, an Indian guide may welcome his guests by saying 'namaste' with his folded hands. Alternatively, he may greet his guests in multiple languages like 'hola' in Spanish, 'ni hao' in Chinese and so on. While visiting Rajasthan, a state in India, a tour guide may greet his guests by saying *khamma ghani* which means 'many greetings'.

STRIKING A RAPPORT

A tour guide at the outset of his commentary must try to make his guests feel special. If he is meeting his guests for the first time, he must try to strike a rapport with his guests by asking them questions such as how their journey was, did they have a comfortable sleep last night and so on. This helps in breaking the ice and sets the tone for the tour.

JAZZ UP

Some jazzing up is good. A tour guide may jazz up his guests to break the monotony and make the guests' mood lighter. They may begin to feel excited about the trip and the destination. Alternatively, a tour guide, in humour, may jazz up his guests on his presence. He may make a passing remark that his guests are fortunate to be in his company.

He may start by saying:

> *A very vibrant and sunny morning to all my friends! I am Lucky, your tour guide for the day. It's a lucky day for all of you as you are in the company of Lucky! With Lucky, you will have a great kick start of the day.*

PRIMARY/STRIKING FEATURE

While guiding at a monument or an attraction, a tour guide must highlight the most visually appealing striking feature of the object/building being explained. This helps to satisfy the curiosity of guests as the striking feature of an attraction captures the eyes of the tourists first.

For example, while visiting the Lotus Temple in New Delhi, India, a tour guide must first highlight the structure of the Lotus Temple that is in the form of a lotus flower. Then the guide may highlight the number of petals in the lotus temple and the importance of lotus in different religions to his guests before proceeding to the further details of the temple.

At the same time, while delivering the commentary, if a marriage procession is going on that immediately catches the attention of all guests and distracts them from the tour guide's commentary, he must smartly shift his subject of interpretation from lotus temple to the marriage procession. Eventually, he may resume once the procession has passed by. This may be considered as a break from the commentary and a way of getting the attention back of some guests who may have lost interest in the narration about the attraction.

CHOOSING THE RIGHT POSITION

While guiding at a monument, a tour guide must ensure that he does not stand in front of the monument that may block the view of a monument for the guests. A tour guide must try to maintain a triangular formation with his tourists and the object of interest.

FIRST THING FIRST

Logic is essential while giving commentary. The flow of information must be sequential enough for the guests to comprehend. While providing a narration, it is always advisable for a tour guide to explain the most important things of a monument first followed by the less important things. If time permits, he may continue with more information, depending upon how interested the guests are in the commentary of the tour guide. He must be clear about the following:

- Must tell: The elevator pitch of the narration. It introduces the monument/attraction to the guests and generates awe.
- Should tell: Minimum information about the monument that the guide must share with the guests.

- Could tell: The add-on part of the narration that depends on the interest of the guests or their tastes.

TALK TO THE GUESTS AND NOT THE MONUMENT

Many times, a tour guide falls in love with a monument or an attraction. While giving the commentary, he keeps explaining the various aspects of an attraction by continuously gazing at the monument. He forgets to address and maintain eye contact with his guests. Therefore, the guests start losing interest in the guide's itinerary. Hence, it is advisable for a tour guide to address his guests while giving a commentary rather than to keep looking at the monument.

EXPLAINING LOGICALLY

While explaining a monument, a tour guide must not just describe it haphazardly. He either may adopt a top-bottom approach or bottom-up approach. It means that he may start explaining a monument from the top and eventually tell every aspect of the monument towards the bottom. Alternatively, he may begin to describe the monument from the base and gradually move towards the top. Likewise, he may explain the monument from right to the left or left to the right. This keeps the commentary sound more logical, and the guest can have a better understanding of the monument through the guide's commentary.

KEEPING NOVELTY ALIVE

Generally in guiding, for an experienced tour guide, giving commentary at monuments becomes repetitive in nature. Using the same chosen words (to describe) and being at the same monument every time with different groups of tourists may eventually make the tour guide's commentary like a canned speech. This may eventually make him lose interest in guiding at the particular monument which can get reflected in his narration also. This kind of commentary may ultimately bore the tourists too. Therefore, it is advisable for a tour guide to continuously work on his knowledge and style of delivering the commentary at an attraction that may keep the novelty alive in his speech. He may, therefore, continue to enjoy speaking to his guests, though he may visit the same monument again and again. As a result, the guests would also continue to enjoy the commentary.

INCORPORATE LATEST FACTS TOO

While guiding at a monument, after giving the history of the monument, a tour guide must also connect it to present. If there is any sequence of events that has recently taken place or is likely to happen in the future at the monument, a tour guide must pass on the same information to his guests. It reflects how well updated he is.

AVOID TALKING WHILE WALKING

It is advisable for a tour guide to avoid talking while walking with his guests. On the other hand, he must find a convenient point and then wait for all his guests to come together. Then, he may start his commentary when all the group members arrive.

HANDLING PILES-ON

At times, while a tour guide is at the site of guiding giving commentary to his guests, he may come across other guests who try to stand near his guests and listen to what the guide is speaking. Such unwanted guests are called as a pile-on who try to take advantage of a tour guide at the cost of others. Such guests don't pay for availing the services of a tour guide and try to pile on other group members. A tour guide must know how to tackle such unwanted guests. He must very politely request them to leave the group as it is a pre-booked group. Being straightforward to such guests is more important than later listening to tourists who may object to the tour guide for allowing them to be a part of the group.

BRIEFING AT A MONUMENT

Commentary at an attraction may also include the general briefing related to the attraction. This may consist of the instructions for the clients related to the following:

- Total time to be spent at the attraction
- Meeting time and meeting place (in case anyone loses track of the tour guide)
- Availability of amenities (e.g., washrooms, eateries, Wi-Fi facilities, locker facilities etc.)
- Camera and video policy, if any
- Things to carry and not to take (e.g., at Taj Mahal, in India, tourists are required to show their photo ID proofs to have access to the monument)

- Safety instructions, if any, like rough terrain etc.
- Asking the group to be together while moving around the monument
- Advising them of free time at the monument, including time for taking photographs.

QUESTIONS

During the narration, the tourists may pose some questions to the tour guide. They may have genuine queries about an attraction or the destination. Therefore, a tour guide must be well prepared to answer the queries raised by the guests without losing his patience. The same question may be asked differently by different tourists in the same group. A tour guide should not get agitated about this. He should instead handle such questions while maintaining his calm.

NO FRIVOLOUS EXPLANATIONS

Many times, tour guides start giving unnecessary explanations that make the commentary very lengthy. Eventually, the guests lose interest in the commentary. Therefore, while offering narration, a tour guide should not give importance to trivial things.

For example, while giving commentary at the hotel lobby, a tour guide may say:

Good morning everyone! Right now, we are standing in front of the hotel lobby. We shall be leaving in next 15 minutes.

Now, this kind of information is trivial as guests are already aware that they are standing in front of the hotel lobby. Such type of information being provided to the guests should be avoided as it prolongs the commentary unnecessarily.

USE OF LOCAL WORDS

Sometimes, a tour guide may use local words while giving commentary. For example, at a fort in Rajasthan, while referring to an overhanging enclosed balcony, a tour guide may use the local word *jharokhas* that the guest may not understand. Therefore, it is important for a tour guide to remain aware at all times of the usage of such words, if any, used by him. He may then explain the same local word in the choice of tourists' language. However, the use of local words should be avoided by the tour guide unless it is imperative to create a 'local feel' for the guests.

ENDING NOTE

A commentary must end on a positive note. The ending of a tour is as important as the beginning. Therefore, a tour guide must use this opportunity to leave a lasting impression on his guests. A tour guide may acknowledge his guests by thanking them for giving him a chance to serve them. He may also like to invite them in the future to travel with his company. He may also, if suitable, according to the situation, demand for a tip from his guests if they find the service of the tour guide to be satisfactory.

SUMMARY

The given points are just indicative of how an ideal commentary of a tour guide should be like. Every tour guide may use various permutations and combinations of these techniques to make his narration sounds more exciting and more logical to his guests. An interesting commentary may keep the group together as all tourists would be attentive to listen to the tour guide's instructions and information about an attraction.

Activity 1 Outdoor activity

Choose the most popular visited monument in your area, and ask the students to read in detail about the historical importance of the monument and the important points to be taken care of before visiting the monument.

Take your class to the chosen historical monument on a decided day, and give sometime around 30 minutes to the students to be on their own to observe about the following things in the monument:

- Entry fee, if any
- Facilities available at the monument (e.g., Wi-Fi, presence of ramp or wheelchair for differently abled guests, audio-guided devices, lockers, washroom facility, drinking water facility and so on)
- Detailed layout off the attraction
- Things not allowed to carry
- Important points of interest at the monument
- Entry and exit points
- Camera fee, if any

Now when everybody has meticulously observed these points, let one student become a tour guide and the others may become tourists. Let the student stand at the entry gate of monument and brief others as a tour guide about the important things to be noted before entering the monument. Further on, each student may be given a chance to participate as a tour guide and take this activity forward by giving commentary at different points of interest of the monument.

This practical exercise may orient the students to the techniques of giving a commentary such as where to stand, how to stand, what to speak, how much to speak, how to keep the group together at the attraction and so on.

Activity 2 **Sell your city**

Give pictures of different tourism products of your city to each student and ask each student to prepare a one and a half to two-minute commentary on the picture that has been given. Invite each student as a tour guide on the stage, and ask the others to become tourists and listen to the tour guide's commentary. After the commentary is over, you may evaluate the student on the following criteria:

- Initial greeting, introduction and welcoming of guests
- Value of content delivered
- Humour, if any
- Interesting stories, if any
- Body language
- Voice modulation
- Time management

POSSIBLE SOLUTIONS TO THE OPENING VIGNETTE

- On returning home, the couple wrote a strong email to the company through whom they had hired the services of Jiggy. They complained about Jiggy and asked the company to give the complete refund to them as Jiggy had utterly spoilt their Agra trip as for them the Taj Mahal was the main attraction of their whole itinerary to India.
- They also wrote to the state government of Uttar Pradesh asking them to cancel Jiggy's licence. Besides this, they also posted about the pathetic services offered by Jiggy during their trip to Taj Mahal on TripAdvisor that could severely affect his image and his future business.
- The company paid the couple the complete refund for the fee given by them for Jiggy and sent an apology letter to them.
- The company also blacklisted Jiggy from giving him any further business and even wrote an email to other travel companies to not to take the services of this tour guide.

Lessons Learned

- A tour guide shoulders the responsibility of projecting the image of his country. He must not behave casually while on the job. He must take the responsibility of his guests and ensure that they have a pleasant experience on the tour.
- He must behave politely with his guest and should never sound rude.
- He must not make his guests wait unnecessarily around the attraction.
- He must always maintain eye contact with his guests.
- He must not talk and deliver commentary while walking.
- He must not force his guests to do shopping.

18

Practices to Be a Successful Tour Guide

LEARNING OBJECTIVES

- What are the tips to become a successful tour guide?
- What practices differentiate an excellent tour guide from an average tour guide?
- What practices should be avoided during a tour?

Mehul was leading a group of 15 tourists from Thailand who were on a leisure trip to India. He was with his local tour guide Raghu, who was guiding the group in Varanasi, the spiritual capital of India. It was time for a morning boat ride—a spectacular must-do activity in Varanasi. Raghu, the local guide, briefed his group in detail about the city of Varanasi and the importance of the boat ride. He also briefed them about the instructions to be followed during the boat ride. The boat ride was planned for duration of 2 hours. Everybody had a great time on the boat. After the boat ride, Raghu took his group for breakfast to a local restaurant as planned in the itinerary. After the completion of the breakfast, he took a headcount of the guests prior to proceeding to the coach. Suddenly, he realised that a woman aged 60, Kyra, went missing. Mehul too was literally in a state of shock. He was taken aback!

The business of tourism is about managing the expectations of tourists. The day a tourist starts planning to take a holiday, he is on the journey of excitement and frolic. All he wishes for is a seamless travel experience with lots of pleasant surprises for him. He is expecting unusual, non-routinely things to happen to him on holiday. He wants to experience novelty and thrill. The primary person who is responsible for facilitating this novel experience and doubling the joy of the guest is the tour guide.

Who is a successful tour guide? This question is very subjective and subject to many interpretations. Being an excellent tour guide requires the right combination of SKAs needed to perform a job more effectively and efficiently. An excellent tour guide comes as a package who has just the right experience and the art of handling people.

INTRODUCTION

Tour guiding is one of the professions chosen by many who have a flair for travel, and an interest in history and showcasing the rich heritage and culture of their city/country. Out of many, who become tour guides, not all are very successful. Some tour guides remain average in guiding profession throughout their life, while some tour guides excel in this job. The only thing that differentiates the ordinary guide from an extraordinary guide is the 'extra' that an ordinary guide practises. A detailed discussion on certain 'extras' that a successful tour guide follows and practises in guiding scenarios have been given in the following discussion:

For the sake of understanding, we have divided the practices that a tour guide may follow under the following headings:

- Before the beginning of tour
- During the tour
- Before the termination of tour

BEFORE THE START OF TRIP

Every day is a new challenge for the tour guide. He may not know what kind of guests he may encounter, what temperament his guest may have, what expectations they may have come with, what questions/suggestions they may ask from him, what emergency situations he may encounter and so on. Therefore, on being given an assignment, preparation for a tour guide is a must. A tour guide must be mentally prepared to handle any kind of issues on tour. Hence, a tour guide must practise the following to become a successful tour guide before the beginning of a trip.

KNOWLEDGE

Basic knowledge is a must. A tour guide must prepare at every front. Be it the knowledge about a destination or a monument/attraction, be it gathering information about guests, be it learning about the distances or maps or be it learning about the standard procedures to be followed during an emergency, a tour guide must prepare thoroughly. With apt knowledge, a tour guide gains more confidence and also commands more respect in his profession.

WANDERLUST OBSESSION

Before taking any tours, a tour guide must travel every nook and cranny of his city. He must have a soul with wanderlust. He must have a hunger to discover new facets and unfold the unknown treasures of his city. His obsession with wanderlust makes him go an extra mile and break the cookie cutter type of itineraries that every tour guide may be operating.

WELL GROOMED

Personality plays a vital role in a tour guide's profession. Being presentable, by looking neat and tidy and well-groomed, can create an everlasting impression in front of the guests. As they say, after all, presentation matters. Having a good dressing sense is equally important for a tour guide.

ENSURING TOURIST DELIGHT

It is essential not just to make the guest happy on a tour but to overwhelm them. A tour guide must make sure that his guest enjoys to the maximum on the trip. He may go out of his way to make this happen. From the beginning of the journey, he must plan beforehand enjoyable means of keeping his guests engaged during the trip. Planning exciting itineraries, organising games, cracking jokes, involving the tourists in sharing their experiences and taking care of them are different ways in which a tour guide can delight his guests. Giving the tourist more than they expect from the tour is the mark of a successful tour guide.

SOME CREATIVITY IS GOOD

Giving something off the script at times works wonders. Guiding is all about being as creative as possible. It is not expected of a tour guide to be creative in distorting the information. However, creativity may be experimented with the delivery of information and, to an extent, with the content of the commentary. A tour guide may make his narration more creative by adding some voice modulation, fancy words and interesting facts, narrating stories and adding humour to his commentary.

A tour guide may experiment his creativity in providing off the best experiences for his clients that may not necessarily be included in the itinerary. He may introduce add-ons to his existing routes or customise his own itineraries to make them more exciting and engaging. The basic idea is to give the guests an experience from an insider's perspective. Some indulging experiences may include the following:

- Taking guests for a yoga session on a beach at early sunrise
- Organising a bike tour of the city for the guest
- Local food tasting
- Asking guests to have a tractor ride in lush green farms and making cow dung cakes in rural locations (more practised in a country like India)

- Inviting the guests to make pottery with their own hands
- Applying different designs of henna on the forearms/palms of the visitors
- Taking a mud bath in rural areas
- Participating in making a local delicacy
- Interacting with the local community
- Participating in local events

BEING TIME EFFICIENT

A tour guide must from the beginning be efficient and on time. He must manage his time well by being on time and covering every attraction as per the decided timing to be spent there. He should not get driven by few guests who may wish to spend more time at a monument and thereby delay the whole itinerary.

DURING THE TOUR

The conduct of a trip is essential. The success of a trip is gauged by the happy faces of the guests. Of course, there are certain things a successful tour guide does that others don't do. Let us explore these practices one by one.

BE YOURSELF

Maintaining the originality of oneself as a tour guide is very important. A tour guide must refrain from copying any of his counterparts. Generally, a novice tour guide may try to replicate the style of a successful and a more experienced tour guide. He may try to use his choice of words or may try to act in a way that has been known to be acceptable by the tourists. However, a tour guide must understand that what may work for one may not work for another. Hence, a tour guide must maintain his own style while giving a commentary to his guests. He must have his personal signature statement to start with.

BE EXCEPTIONAL

Give something that others are not offering. Create your uniqueness. It could be in the form of loading the itinerary with more activities that may be of interest to guest or telling things in a different way that may hook the attention of the guest.

BE A GOOD LISTENER

Being a good orator is not just good enough. A tour guide must be a patient listener too. A tour guide may have to listen to endless questions and grievances of his guests. Sometimes the guests may just like to share their personal stories with the tour guide. Therefore, to be an excellent tour guide, he must have good listening abilities too.

AUDIBLE

A tour guide must be loud enough to be audible to his guests. He should communicate with his guests in the right tone which is neither too high nor too low. Being loud depends on the size of the group and the number of other visitors at an attraction. For example, while guiding at a museum, there may be another group of visitors besides the guide's own group. Therefore, a tour guide must be audible amongst the crowd of other visitors present at the museum. However, guides' leading different groups cannot and should not shout over each other. Alternatively, at many attractions which are overcrowded by tourists, audio-guided devices are also provided to tourists by attraction authorities. With these instruments, guests can be in an auto mode, being apparently able to hear the commentary without any disturbance. Example, at St. Peter's Basilica Church, Vatican City, tourists are provided with audio-guided devices so that guests may be able to hear the commentary at ease without any disturbances due to lakhs of tourist visiting there.

BE A PHOTOGRAPHY EXPERT

Learning the basics of photography helps. It is advisable for a tour guide to do a basic course in photography to acquire or sharpen his skills of photography as he may be able to advise his clients in a better way to take pictures from different angles and capture the incredible moments from the best locations being visited during the tour.

BE CAUTIOUS

A tour guide must be very wary while speaking. He should avoid sensitive or controversial topics that may offend anyone in the group. Issues related with government, religion and so on should be avoided. However, on being asked about such matters, he may very judiciously give a general viewpoint without expressing his personal opinions about such issues that may hurt the sentiments of any guest in a group. He should sound more neutral rather than expressing his strong views about such controversial issues.

BE A FANTASTIC COMMUNICATOR

A tour guide must be obvious in his communication. He must not fumble when he speaks. He should be evident in his thoughts, and he must also ensure that his guests have understood his instructions correctly. Sometimes, due to language barriers, guests may not be able to follow the instructions of a tour guide clearly. In such cases, a tour guide may make an extra effort to know if the guest has understood his instructions by reconfirming from them.

ENSURE PRESENCE OF ALL

A tour guide must know when to start his commentary. He must start the commentary only when all the guests have arrived at a point. He must have the patience to wait for his guests. When he has counted all the pax, then only he should begin his commentary. However, if some guests are busy in clicking pictures it is an indication, that a tour manager should commence his commentary without letting any delay in the itinerary.

KNOW YOUR GUESTS

A tour guide must observe his group meticulously. He must try to learn as much as possible about his guests by analysing his guests as to what they enjoy doing and what they don't. Alternatively, he may candidly ask his guest through discussions and interactions about their interests, their lifestyle, what they expect from the tour and so on. This helps him to carry forward talks and conversations that may interest his guests. He may tailor-make his communication according to the likes and dislikes of his guests. With a group of women travellers, he may have different topics to discuss as compared to a group of young students who are on holiday.

BREVITY IS THE NEW TREND

Less is good. Brevity is the new trend. Tourists don't want lengthy commentaries. They want concise information in a shorter duration of time. Therefore, a tour guide must take care of this.

MODERATE THE EXPECTATIONS OF GUESTS

Resetting the expectations of the guest is another tip for a tour guide. A tour guide must be able to understand the expectations of guests and at the same time try to moderate them. It helps the guests to be ready for all kinds of experiences that may come during the tour. For example, while visiting remote areas of a destination, a tour guide may ask his guests not to expect luxurious facilities there. In some hilly terrains, guests may have to walk a lot or they may have limited food options.

Accordingly, a tour guide must prepare his guest mentally so that the guest does not feel uneasy on facing such difficulties.

BE CONSIDERATE

A tour guide must be able to adapt himself and customise things to the need of his guests. Sometimes, a few elderly guests in the group may not be able to walk fast and catch up to the pace of the tour guide and other members. Therefore, they may feel left out as they may take rest breaks in between. Likewise, in a group, there may be some guest who may be hard of hearing. Therefore, with such guests, a tour guide must show more patience and must take everyone along in the group. He must put himself in the shoes of his guests and try to remain empathetic towards them.

DO NOT FORCE SHOPPING

A tour guide should not push his guest into shopping. This leaves a wrong impression in the mind of guests. Nowadays, tourists are already aware that the guide may have a commission on the shopping done by guests, and they, therefore, may be sold at overrated prices on the shops being recommended by a tour guide. Therefore, to keep his reputation and his company's reputation, a tour guide should only recommend shopping when his guests show an interest to shop.

SELL OPTIONAL TOURS

Selling optional tours is essential for a tour guide. A tour guide must act as a good salesman who pushes his guests to buy optional excursions. Optional tours are also a way of earning commissions for a tour guide. The same may be sold to the guests as life experiences that must not be missed on by them.

SELL THE LOCAL

A tour guide has a wealth of local information about a destination that he belongs to. Since he has spent substantial time at his domicile, he is an adept in advising the best local must-do activities for the guests. For example, he may share local secrets of recipes for local dishes, suggest local events for guests to attend and stop for a tea tasting at an Indian local tea stall or for a mint tea in Morocco. He may also share his favourite places with the guests and help them to explore the sites, and also give them local treats at his favourite points.

FACILITATE INTERACTION

A tour guide must encourage communication between himself and others. He must first try to make his guests feel comfortable and strike a rapport with them. Commentary should not be a one-way process. It makes the whole process very dull and boring. Therefore, a tour guide must try to make his talks very interactive. He must allow an opportunity to his guests to ask questions and clarify their doubts about the places and attractions being visited.

Clients would not always be interested in interacting with the tour guide. Sometimes a guest may choose to be reticent if they are tired or if they generally don't talk. In such cases, the tour guide should not try to blabber. Instead, he should act according to the situation.

Also, a tour guide acts as a facilitator for interaction amongst guests. As the guests have to travel together for days, bonding is essential. Therefore, he must find ways to bring the guests closer to each other.

PAY EQUAL ATTENTION TO ALL

A good tour guide must pay same attention to all his guests. Sometimes, in a group, there may be some guests who may be interacting with the tour guide more as compared to others. Automatically, a tour guide, unintentionally, may start paying more attention to such guest who is more interactive in nature. Likewise, in some groups, the guide may be paying more attention to senior citizens or differently abled people. The others may, therefore, feel ignored. Also, sometimes a tour guide may be dealing with a group which has a composition of group members from different nationalities. In such cases, he should not be biased towards the guest from particular nationality. For him, everyone should be equal irrespective of the caste, creed, religion or colour.

Hence, it is advisable for a tour guide to pay equal attention to all his guests rather than just focusing on a few of his guests as every guest has spent the same money for the tour. He should avoid playing his favourites.

BE AWARE

It is essential for a tour guide always to keep an eye on his guests. He must ensure if all his group members are comfortable or if anyone needs any extra attention. He may also be aware of the outside environment he is operating in.

TALK FAVOURABLE ABOUT YOUR COUNTRY

A tour guide must be passionate about his country. He must take pride in presenting the culture and heritage of his country. He may show his country in a positive light.

ENSURE SAFETY

Security of the guests is the prime concern of a tour guide. A tour guide acts as a caretaker who, like a local guardian, takes care of the safety of his guest during their travel. A tour guide may advise his guest not to leave anything unattended on the coach or at a monument. He may also ask his group to remain together and not to entertain strangers who may try to approach the guests.

For example, he may admonish his guests to mind their steps while walking at the attractions unmindful of the surface.

LEARN TO SAY NO TO GUEST

Sometimes, the guest may demand from a tour guide that they wish to smoke/drink/consume drugs. Now in many places, smoking or drinking is not permitted as per the local law of a destination. Therefore, a tour guide must clearly communicate such rules to his guests. For example, while visiting a religious or a sacred site such as a memorial, a guest may desire to smoke. Such situations may become very tricky for a tour guide to handle. In order to avoid such situations, a tour guide may in advance tell about the rules related to the smoking/drinking at the attraction and may say that smoking in such places may be considered as a mark of disrespect that may invite a punitive action by the police posted there.

DURING THE COMPLETING OF THE TOUR

There are certain things that a tour guide must do before the tour ends. In this section, we will discuss the tips that a tour guide may adhere to during the closing of the trip.

THANK YOU

Thank you is the most important phrase that every tour guide must often use. The phrase has the power to connect people forever. A tour guide after the completion of the tour must always thank his guest for choosing his company to travel with. He may also use this opportunity to thank his guests for allowing him to serve them on the tour and cooperating with him on the tour.

'END' ON TIME

Some tour guides have a habit of stretching their tours. They may be driven by the fact that the more they speak, the more tips they may get from the tourists, besides getting an opportunity to establish their supremacy of knowledge. However, it is advisable for a tour guide not to stretch his tour beyond the stipulated timings except in unexpected circumstances that may arise due to traffic or any other reason. Otherwise, it may make the guests feel uneasy and bored.

FOLLOW-UP EMAIL

To engage with the customers and have a lasting impression on them, a tour guide must give something extra to his guests that others are not providing. For example, every day, once the tour is over, he may send a small write up through an email to his guests reminding them of the things that they have seen or visited during the day. For instance, on food tours, a tour guide may also share the names of food items that the guests may have tasted along with a note on each of the famous eating outlets. This one extra step of documenting the experience for the guests can help the guests always to remember their experiences on the tour for a lifetime.

DON'TS

There are certain things that a tour guide must avoid while guiding the group of guests. Here is the list of few don'ts.

NO USE OF NOTES

The mantra for a tour guide is to practise and only practise. A tour guide should know the details almost by heart. The use of handouts should be avoided.

NO DRINKING AND SMOKING

A tour guide must not be drunk while reporting for duty. Likewise, he may not drink or smoke while on duty.

NO GLARES

Avoid wearing glares while guiding as it looks casual. It is always good to maintain direct eye contact with the guests.

NO CHEWING

A tour guide must not chew anything, for example, chewing gum and tobacco, while on duty.

RESTRICT USE OF PHONE

Avoid taking any personal calls while guiding. It may distract the guests and agitate them too.

NO PERSONAL RELATIONS DURING THE TOUR

A tour guide should not make any personal advances towards any guest that he may like during the trip. Indulgence in personal relationships should be avoided entirely.

NO PRESCRIBING OF MEDICATIONS TO THE TOURISTS

A tour guide must not act as a doctor to his guest. Even if he may know the remedies or the necessary medicines to be taken for particular sickness, he may not suggest the same to his guests. The reason is that the tour guide may not know the medical history of the tourist and he is not a medical expert. Alternatively, he may request his guest to seek the opinion of a doctor at an opportune time.

SUMMARY

Guiding is a very responsible job. It involves taking care of guests and making their trip a memorable experience. Some guides may spoil the whole tour with their conduct, thereby affecting the reputation of the company they are representing. Whereas some guides with their quick wit, emotional intellect, enthusiasm, knowledge and winsome nature may win the hearts of the tourists. It is a few practices and tips that clearly delineate a successful tour guide from an average tour guide. To be successful in his profession, a tour guide must follow the right methods and learn useful tips to excel in his profession.

Activity 1 Group discussion

Organise a group discussion in the class on the topic 'Is tour guiding an inherent quality or does it come with experience'? Allow each group to speak for 5–7 minutes for or against the topic. Let each group take a position and then open the forum for discussion.

Activity 2 Script your monument

Students may be asked to think of five points that, according to them, are important to include in their guiding to become a successful tour guide. Then, the students may be asked to prepare a guiding script for a monument of their choice, and include those points in the script and demonstrate the same in the class. The same may be compared for analysis for declaring the best guiding script.

POSSIBLE SOLUTIONS TO THE OPENING VIGNETTE

- Immediately after knowing about the missing guest Kyra, Raghu and Mehul confirmed with the group if anyone knew the whereabouts of Kyra.
- After that, Mehul immediately informed his company and discussed with the local tour guide, Raghu, to help him search for her, and he also decided to call the pilot of the coach because it might have happened that the woman may have gone to the coach on her own. However, Raghu insisted that since she is a foreigner and would not be aware of the local directions, it was, therefore, highly improbable that she would have gone towards the coach. Thus, he dropped the idea of calling the pilot of the coach.
- Therefore, the tour leader took the next step and went to the local police station to file a missing report along with Raghu. However, to his surprise, instead of immediately taking action, the local police started blaming him only.
- As the situation became more and more tense, Raghu forced Mehul to first move towards the coach parked nearby and then analyse the whole situation and possible solutions in a calmer state of mind, only to realise that the old lady was sitting inside the coach. What a respite!

Lessons Learned

- A tour guide and a tour manager must not lose their cool when things go wrong. They must retain the balance of mind.
- Before and after every sightseeing or any activity, they must take a headcount to confirm the presence of everyone in the group.
- During the initial briefing, a tour manager and the tour guide must suggest that their group members to keep the tour manager informed whenever any guest want to leave the group and be on his own.

SECTION E

CALL OF THE PROFESSION

Welcome back, learners! After having gone through the various aspects of a tour manager's profession, let us further understand the call of this profession. Through this section, we would discover the facets of working in this field. This section shall broadly highlight the intricacies of what a tour manager is expected to take care of.

We begin at the outset by understanding the responsibilities of a tour manager towards various stakeholders of the tourism industry.

Working as a tour manager has its own challenges. It may be related to handling awkward tourists at times, dealing with different questions, managing groups, coping with the grievance of guests, taking care of cross-cultural differences or handling emergency situations.

So let us take each one by one and get started on with the challenges that a tour manager may have to face.

Happy learning!

19

Responsibility Towards Other Stakeholders

LEARNING OBJECTIVES

- Who are the different stakeholders for a tour manager?
- What is the responsibility of a tour manager towards the different stakeholders?

Jishan, the tour manager, was leading a group of 20 Indian guests to Jim Corbett National Park, Nainital. Before visiting there, Jishan briefed his guests on the coach about the dos and don't's to be followed at the national park. He requested his guests to behave as responsible tourists and help in the conservation of the environment. For this, he asked his guests not to litter around and throw the trash in the garbage bins only. He also asked them not to pluck flowers and leaves and also suggested to them to wear light-coloured clothes. Instructing them further, he asked them not to play any loud music or smoke inside the forest area.

Now as the group moved inside the park led by Jishan in a Jeep Safari, some of the guests started playing music on their mobile phone to entertain themselves and others. Simultaneously two children began eating potato wafers littering the wrapper all over. Then, they threw the wrapper out of the vehicle. Jishan felt very embarrassed before the local tour guide.

Managing and leading tours is a responsible job. While conducting tours, a tour manager is accountable to many stakeholders. His job involves interactions with tourists, tour operators/travel agents, tourism authorities and the host community as well as the other service providers of the tourism industry such as hoteliers, airlines, ground transporters, drivers, tour guides, shopkeepers and so on.

A tour manager does not operate in a vacuum. His functioning has a direct impact on the various other stakeholders of the tourism industry. He has a moral responsibility towards multiple stakeholders.

RESPONSIBILITY TOWARDS TOURISTS

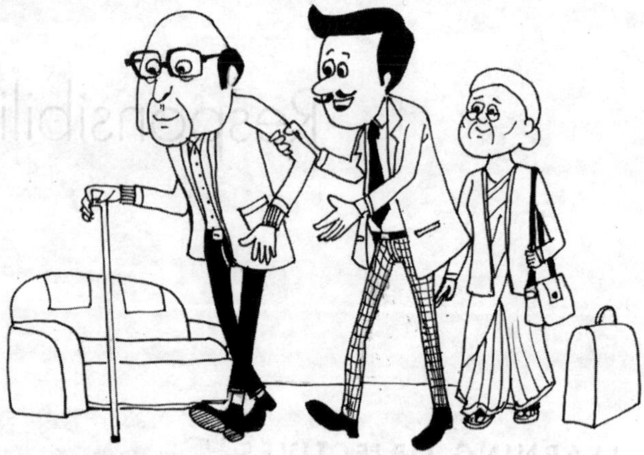

Many tourists, while choosing to travel to a place, book their vacations on group package tours. Group package tours are more popular among first-time travellers as these include the complimentary services of a tour manager. Tourists prefer these conducted tours as there is always someone who is ready to take their responsibility.

A tour manager has a significant role to play in the overall facilitation of the guests' experience. He acts as a facilitator who assists his guests with all the travel arrangements. He helps his guest at various attractions, at the airports, train stations, hotels and restaurants, and in multiple modes of transportation. He also recommends to his guests various activities that they may pursue during their free time such as shopping, experiencing nightlife or gaining more insightful experiences of a destination by going for a heritage walk, a food walk and so on. The idea is to help the tourists make the best use of their each and every minute of their holiday.

A tour manager acts as a guardian of the guests who looks after their every need and want when the guests approach him. He serves as a troubleshooter for his guests and tries to resolve every problem that his guests may face. To crown it all, a tour manager has the following responsibilities towards his guests:

- He has the duty of taking care of his guests as he ensuring the comfort of his guests 24 × 7 while he is conducting the tour.
- He is responsible for the safety of his guests.
- He is responsible for keeping his guests together.
- He is also responsible for sensitising his guests about the environment.

Overall, a tour manager is entrusted with the prime responsibility of making the vacations fun-filled and joyous for his guests so that they cherish these memories for a lifetime.

RESPONSIBILITY TOWARDS TOUR OPERATORS/TRAVEL AGENTS

Routinely, every tour manager works for a travel company unless and until he has his own business of leading groups. On tours, he is the face of the company. The company makes all the backend arrangements for the guests. However, it is the tour manager who ensures that everything goes as promised by the company.

The ultimate objective of every tour operator/travel agent is to get repeated business from the same client. For this to happen, a lot depends on the tour manager. The demeanour and the conduct of the tour manager on a tour decides whether the guests would like to travel with the same company in the future or not. Therefore, a tour manager must ensure that he takes good care of his guests so that his guests return home happy and book their next trip with the same company, thereby generating repeated business for the company.

Besides keeping the guests happy, a tour manager must also be responsible towards the travel company he is working for by being honest and transparent in his transactions with them.

The tour manager must also show his responsibility towards his company by keeping the staff updated from time to time about the progress of the group on the tour. If the tour manager comes across any problematic tourist or an uncertain situation, he must keep his company in the loop and, if required, seek necessary instructions from the company.

A tour manager must also inform his company about the pitfalls in operating an itinerary. Based on his interactions with his guests and his personal experiences, he may suggest changes in the design of an itinerary which may eventually improve the business of the company he is working for. Alternatively, he may also recommend to his company new innovative ideas that may be introduced in the itineraries to make things more interesting and exciting for the tourists.

Directly interacting with the tourists gives an opportunity to the tour manager to understand their requirements in a better way. Therefore, a tour manager may also suggest alternative tourism products to his company that the company may offer in the future to serve the tourist in a better way. The tour manager may also undertake FAM trips for his company to introduce new destinations in the future.

RESPONSIBILITY TOWARDS A DESTINATION

A tour manager is often referred to as the brand ambassador of a destination. While on a tour, the guests see a destination through the eyes of the tour manager. Their impressions of a destination are framed by choice of words that the tour manager uses to promote that destination. It is the tour manager who brings life to a destination as he connects the context of a destination to his guests. Thus, a tour manager has a moral responsibility of presenting the destination in a positive light to his

guests so that the guests feel happy about their decision of having chosen the destination for their holiday.

A tour manager is expected to showcase the heritage and culture of a destination to the tourists at its best. His fundamental knowledge of the destination can really enhance the overall experience of a tourist at a destination. A tour manager should put forward such interesting facts of a destination that may keep the tourist engaged in his commentary. For this, he must do his homework well. He must find out the lesser known facts and also the most popular facts of the destination that may amuse the guests. Every destination has a USP. A destination may be famous for its natural beauty, artificial structures, food, culture, heritage, shopping and so on. A tour manager must try to project the USP of the destination in the most favourable way. He may show the lesser known areas besides the famous attractions and also take the tourists to local markets. He may even focus on the emotional selling proposition (ESP) of his guests, that is, how his guests are feeling after having visited the destination, to remove their cognitive dissonance.

Though there would always be some shortcomings in a destination, a tour manager may subtly underplay the grey areas of a destination while also focusing on the transformations being infused to curb the negative aspects of a destination. However, he must always take pride in showcasing a destination to his guests.

RESPONSIBILITY TOWARDS ATTRACTION AUTHORITIES

A tour manager visits different types of attractions. The attractions may vary. It may be a historic site, a museum, a national park, a theme park, a pilgrimage site, a natural site and so on. Every attraction has certain norms and regulations that the visitors must abide by.

A tour manager has specific responsibilities to discharge while visiting an attraction. Before the start of a visit to an attraction, he must gather information about the rules and regulations to be followed at that attraction. Then, the tour manager must brief his guests about the rules and the appropriate demeanour that his guests must follow at the attraction being visited.

He may also sensitise his guests to keep the attraction clean and not to litter while moving around an attraction. He should ask his guests to act responsibly by not disturbing or annoying the other guests who may also be visiting that attraction.

In case he finds any challenges that a tourist is facing at an attraction, he may also bring it to the notice of the authorities of the attraction. This helps the attraction authorities to take up the corrective steps to remove the impediments that may affect the experience of tourist at an attraction.

RESPONSIBILITY TOWARDS TOURISM AUTHORITIES

A tour manager must try to establish contacts on his own with the tourism authorities of a destination he visits. He may maintain a close liaison with the national tourism organisations (NTOs), regional tourism organisations (RTOs) and local tourism organisations (LTOs) by trying to visit their offices or being in touch through social media or emails. The idea of lobbying with these agencies is to strike an opportunity for business with these authorities. At times, the government offices may give some FIT or group inclusive tour (GIT) assignments to the tour manager. This may be an additional source of revenue for the tour manager as well as the travel companies that he works for. A tour manager must consider these assignments as important. He should not refuse to take up such assignments due to fewer payments involved in them.

He may also attend their training programmes/workshops on destinations to gain knowledge about the new tourism products that might have been introduced by the tourism authorities. Besides, he may also use these authorities as a networking platform to establish a contact with other industry stakeholders.

He may also show his responsibility towards the government by sharing his real-time experiences with the government officers and apprising them of the difficulties that the tourists may face at a destination. The tourism authorities may use this opportunity to gain useful insights about the pitfalls that may exist in the tourism infrastructure and superstructure at the destination. Accordingly, the authorities may take up these issues to develop better facilities for tourists visiting these destinations.

RESPONSIBILITY TOWARDS THE TOURISM INDUSTRY

A tour manager is an important stakeholder in the tourism industry. The way he conducts himself on the tour determines, to an extent, the overall reputation of the tourism industry. Also, the kind of services he gives to his guest shall decide, to an extent, whether the tourists would like to come back to the destination, or whether the tourists would recommend their friends and relatives to visit the same destination. Therefore, this places a tour manager in a strategic position in shaping the future of the tourism industry, as the practices in the trade followed by the tour manager has a lasting impression in the mind of the tourist. If he does not give authentic information to his guests, or is dishonest in his dealings or forces them to shop from particular shops, it leads to the creation of an overall wrong impression for the tourism industry. His malpractices may adversely affect the overall brand of the tourism industry at that place.

Hence, to create a positive image of the tourism industry, he must follow a righteous behaviour and set an example for others to follow. The right practices followed by a tour manager helps in creating an overall positive impression of not only himself but also the company he is working for and ultimately the destination that he is selling.

Also, a tour manager's job involves a close liaison with airlines, hotels, restaurateurs, transport operators, GHAs, shopping establishments, tour guides and tour drivers at different destinations. He must act responsibly towards each of these service providers of the tourism industry by giving them good business during the season time and also giving them timely payments once the tour is over. A tour manager may also advise his guests to behave responsibly towards each of these service providers by taking care of the following:

- While travelling via different modes of transportation (e.g., airlines, coaches, trains, cruises and so on), guests may be reminded about keeping them clean by not throwing trash here and there.

- Guests may be asked to behave courteously with the driver when travelling on the coach.
- They may be advised to remain respectful at all times with the tour guide on a tour.
- They may be asked to conduct themselves appropriately when staying in hotels by not destroying their property at the hotel and being disciplined at all times, thereby not disturbing the experience of other guests.
- While visiting local markets, they may be requested to refrain themselves from shoplifting that may eventually tarnish the image of their country and also put the tour manager in trouble.

RESPONSIBILITY TOWARDS THE HOST COMMUNITY

A tour manager acts as a linking pin between the tourists and the host community. On a tour, a tour manager is responsible for introducing the tourists to the local community of a destination. At the same time, he carries the onus of ensuring that his guest takes care of the sentiments of the local host community.

To carry out this responsibility, he needs to educate his guests about the local sensitivities of the host community that the guest must observe at the destination.

No one likes intrusion into their privacy. Therefore, he must remind his guests to seek the permission of guests before taking their photographs. Likewise, the tour manager may suggest to his guests that they may buy local souvenirs from a place that may support the local host community economically.

RESPONSIBILITY TOWARDS ENVIRONMENT

Tourism and the environment are highly dependent on each other. Tourism is profoundly nature-dependent. A tour manager has a moral obligation towards the environment in which he operates. He is a role model for his guests. He must respect the environment before expecting his guests to respect the environment.

While conducting tours, a tour manager must educate his guests about the sensitivities that they must observe to conserve the environment while visiting an attraction. He must ask his guests to cooperate in keeping the environment clean at a destination. He may request his guests to observe the following guidelines to practise sustainable tourism:

- Do not throw the trash anywhere, except in dustbins.
- Do not spit anywhere.
- Do not urinate in the open.
- Do not make any sound while visiting national parks or wildlife sanctuaries.
- Do not spoil the walls of a monument or attraction by writing names or making graffiti. While visiting a botanical garden, do not pluck flowers.
- On hilly treks, do not trample the flora.
- Behave responsibly while you are on a tour.

RESPONSIBILITY TOWARDS ASSOCIATIONS

Associations are networking platforms. The affiliations with an association may reap many benefits for tour managers. They must register their memberships with different tour manager associations.

A tour manager may use these associations as an opportunity for socialisation besides building relationships with other tour managers. These organisations are also a platform to vent out the feelings, challenges and grievances that these professionals might be facing. The issues may pertain to wages and allowances, better working conditions for tour managers, shady trade practices and so on.

Besides this, it also increases the negotiation power of the individual tour managers. As '1+1=11', being a part of the association empowers the tour managers to negotiate with the government authorities about the difficulties that they may be facing in their profession with more conviction. The tour managers associations may also lay down a legal framework for the tour managers that may govern their working conditions. Besides, these associations may also set a code of conduct for the tour managers to follow.

The tour managers may act responsibly towards the associations they are members of by raising the real-time challenges that they face while dealing with tourist and travel companies or government bodies they are working for. In a nutshell, these associations provide a platform to the tour manager to advocate for the rights of his fraternity.

RESPONSIBILITY TOWARDS COLLEAGUES

A tour manager and his fellow mates may share common interests. Therefore, he must maintain cordial relations with other tour managers too. He must act responsibly towards his colleagues also. He may show his responsible behaviour towards them by passing on business opportunities to other colleagues. In case a tour manager is busy on particular dates for leading the groups, he may pass on that business to his other colleagues. He must exchange pleasantries with his colleagues on different occasions to stay connected with them.

RESPONSIBILITY TOWARDS FAMILY

The profession of a tour manager is very demanding. During season time, he may have to stay away from his family for days. Therefore, when the tour manager is not on the job, he must spend quality time with his family. He may take his family for vacations or just sit back home and relax with them. He must give equal importance to his family as a family can be an ultimate support system and a refuge from the daily stress of work life for a tour manager.

RESPONSIBILITY TOWARDS HIMSELF

Last but not least, a tour manager is responsible towards himself. Before taking care of anyone, he must behave responsibly towards himself. He must take care of himself. He must take care of his health as this job involves a lot of physical exertion and demands excellent fitness from a tour manager. He must maintain his physical and mental well-being.

As a tour manager's job is very taxing and stressful, he may need to stay very calm and composed. At the same time, he must maintain his physical stamina as it's a very hectic job that involves a lot of speaking and standing continuously for hours together. Therefore, a tour manager may practise meditation or yoga that gives him inner physical and mental strength to deal with situations on his job.

SUMMARY

A tour manager's job requires him to maintain harmonious relationships with different stakeholders of the tourism industry. A tour manager must act responsibly towards each of the stakeholders. He must maintain good relations and be responsible towards the tourist, tour operator/travel agent, destination, attraction authorities, host community, tourism authorities, tourism industry service providers, associations, fellow colleagues, family and towards himself. He must be professional, honest and sincere in his dealings with the stakeholders. A tour manager must keep the interest of everyone in mind while conducting the given tour.

Activity 1 What do authorities want?

Five members of the student group may visit five different attractions and interact with the attraction authorities. Try to understand from them the role of a tour manager while visiting attractions with their groups. The group may then discuss their interaction and make a presentation about what the authorities of the attractions expect form the tour managers.

Activity 2 Responsible travel

Think of your city or its attractions. Write down five points that you, as a tour manager, would brief your tourists on to promote responsible travel and take care of the environment. Write the same on a piece of paper, and let your partner read it for you and share the same with the whole class.

POSSIBLE SOLUTIONS TO THE OPENING VIGNETTE

- Jishan requested his guests very politely to switch off the music as it may disturb the fauna around. He asked them to enjoy the sound of nature that is a rare opportunity for one to experience.
- With the help of a tour guide, Jishan stopped the vehicle and picked up the wrapper himself thrown by the children and once again requested his group members to keep the environment clean.
- He once again repeated the instructions for his group members to follow.

Lessons Learned

- A tour manager must be affirmative while giving instructions to his group members.
- He may make his group aware of the penalties they may be levied with due to violation of rules.
- To ensure that his guests follow the rules, he may share prior unpleasant experiences with the guests to warn them of the repercussions they may have to face if they do not follow the rules.

20

Handling Questions

LEARNING OBJECTIVES

- What kinds of questions are asked by tourist from a tour manager?
- How should a tour manager deal with such questions raised by his guests?

Zian, the tour manager, was handling a group of Canadian tourists who were on a three-day trip to New York. On the very first day of the trip, one of the tourists, Peter, started asking questions to Zian. Zian realised that most of the questions that Peter was asking seemed genuine as they were related to the trip and it seemed that Peter was a very inquisitive tourist who wanted to know and acquire knowledge about the places he was visiting. Zian kept on explaining all the group members about the tourist places they were visiting on the day and at the same time was also trying to satisfy the inquisitiveness of Peter by paying attention to the questions being asked by him.

However, even on the next day of the tour, the same thing continued, and Peter kept posing questions to Zian. By this time, Zian had clearly understood that Peter had other intentions behind shooting questions at Zian. He wanted to test his knowledge and also seek the attention of others and show how well read he was. However, Zian still maintained his calm and tried to handle Peter's questions very gracefully on the second day too. Soon, Zian started feeling that the other guests were getting irritated with Peter's behaviour. They were also feeling neglected as they found Zian busy attending to the Peter's never-ending questions. Zian was in a fix!

Inquisitiveness of individuals is often what gets them travelling to new places. Travellers visit a destination to know and learn more about it. It is better if they have a ready support in a knowledgeable tour manager who they can ask what comes to their mind. Then there are issues of logistical arrangement and negotiating the destination that comes up. They seek answers and advice. Thus, one of the primary responsibilities of a tour manager on a tour is to answer the queries raised by the tourists. Many glorify the role of a tour manager as that of a 'living encyclopaedia', the Google search engine or the Siri of iPhone who has answers to all the questions of a tourist.

A tourist, when on a tour, may have an array of questions to ask the tour manager. The tour manager and the tourist share a mentor-mentee relationship on tour. Like an inquisitive child who has a myriad of questions in his mind, a tourist behaves in a similar pattern during the trip. For all his doubts, the tourist looks upon the tour manager as his mentee who he expects to know all.

Routinely, a tour manager gives a briefing every day during the tour and also before approaching the attractions. It has all the necessary information that is likely to be sought by the tourists. He also gives detailed information of the procedures to be followed at the airport or at the hotel. However, in spite of the scheduled, structured briefing by a tour manager to his guests, at every point, he is often required to answer some questions.

INTRODUCTION

Handling questions is an art. A tour manager must acquire two critical attributes to handle the questions of his guests: patience and diligence. A tour manager must be able to handle any kind of question gracefully without the loss of patience. He must have the ability to satisfy the curiosity of his guests calmly. He must also have the necessary diligence to handle questions smartly with basic common sense and logic.

A tour manager must not display any resistance to taking up questions from his guests. On the contrary, he must be receptive to dealing with doubts and queries raised by his guests. Sometimes a tourist may ask the same question twice. Also, the same problem may be requested by two different tourists at different timings. In such situations, a tour manager must not lose his cool. Instead, he should handle such doubts very patiently and gracefully.

While dealing with questions, a tour manager must also ensure that he gives the right information to his guest. The information must be real and authentic.

However, it may be appreciated that a tour manager may not always have all the answers to all the questions. Many times, he may lack the necessary information to answer the query raised by his guest, and as a result, he may feel embarrassed and uncomfortable. However, he must understand the fact that he is not omniscient. Knowledge is a vast ocean, and it is not possible for a person to know everything in this world.

Therefore, a tour manager must forthrightly yet politely confess that he is not aware of the looked-for information that the tourist requested. At the same time, he must not also fool his guests by passing them incorrect information. Instead, he may buy some time from his guests to find out the correct information. He may tell them that he will let them know. He may during this time search for the right information and may share the same information with his guests within the time he has asked for.

TYPES OF QUESTIONS

Clients may have different kinds of questions for the tour manager. Some questions may be very generic while others may be personal. Some questions may be debatable while some questions might embarrass the tour manager as they may be related to some not so pleasant things about the tour manager's country or region. However, a tour manager must be ready to handle these varieties of questions professionally. Generally, the questions raised by the tourists relate to the following.

ITINERARY-SPECIFIC

Tourists may have some queries associated with the itinerary of the tour. Some of the questions pertaining to itinerary by the guests may include the following:

- Which all places shall be covered during the trip?
- How long would our duration of stay be at a particular destination? (Such question may be asked by tourists in case of multiple destinations being covered on the same tour.)
- What would be the itinerary for the day?
- Which hotel properties we would be staying at?
- What are the facilities available at the hotel?
- Is the Wi-Fi facility in the hotel free of cost or chargeable?
- How far is the airport from the hotel?
- What are the things to carry at an attraction (e.g., to a beach or a mountain)?
- What are the optional activities one can undertake at a destination?
- What would be the appropriate clothing for a place?
- What are the formalities required by the guests to be done at the airport?
- What are the ingredients in the food being served? (This question may specifically be asked by people who are allergic to specific food items.)
- Are meals included in the itinerary?
- Do we need to tip you and the driver?

DESTINATION-SPECIFIC

Sometimes, the questions may relate to a destination being visited. Following are some of the questions pertaining to the destination:

- What are the exciting facts about the destination?
- What is the total population of the destination?
- What is the temperature at the destination?
- What are the weather seasons in the destination?
- What is the currency of the destination?

- What is the local language spoken by the people of the destination?
- What is the religion followed by most people in the city/country being visited?
- Can you elaborate on the political scenario of the place?
- Can you share the history of the city/country being visited?
- What is the general lifestyle of people at the destination?
- What is the local food of the people?
- What is the favourite time pass of the host community of the destination?
- What is the general occupation of people?
- What are the activities that one can undertake at the destination?
- Which company's sim card should I buy in the country that has better connectivity and offers value for money?
- Would my debit card/credit card work in the city/country being visited?

ATTRACTION-SPECIFIC

An attraction may be a monument, a garden, a theme park or any other structure that has a touristic appeal due to its historical, cultural, natural or created value.

Generally, the questions related to the attraction may revolve around the following:

- What are the exciting facts about the attraction?
- What is the history of the attraction?
- What are the things that one may carry and one may not carry at the attraction?
- How much time would be allowed to be at an attraction?
- What are the amenities available at the attraction? (e.g., An old-aged citizen may ask if the wheelchair assistance is available at an attraction or not.)

PERSONAL QUESTIONS

Some guests might ask a tour manager questions that may be very direct or 'personal' from his perspective. He may be uncomfortable in answering such questions.

Personal questions may pertain to the following:

- What is your age?
- What do you do for fun?
- Are you single or married?

- How much do you get paid to take us around to places?
- What is your height?
- What is your educational qualification?
- What is your past work experience in this field?

While dealing with such questions raised by the guests, a tour manager must know that he is not obliged to answer these questions that affect his privacy. He may choose to stay restrained. Otherwise, he may answer the guest if he wishes to or may underplay the answer in humour. He may also suggest to his guest through his stare that he is uncomfortable with such questions, or he may straightforwardly but politely tell his guest that he may not be comfortable answering such questions. However, the tour manager must ensure that he does not sound rude even while handling personal questions being asked by the clients. Alternatively, he may defer the situation by telling his guest that he would like to answer to this question later in the evening once the day's itinerary is over.

EMBARRASSING QUESTIONS

Specific questions related to the destination may be quiet embarrassing for the tour manager to answer. Especially, if the questions are about the tour manager's city/country that put his city/country in bad light, he may feel embarrassed. Questions may be related to the religion, politics, social practices, security or any other issues that may portray the destination in poor light such as issues about corruption, problems of safety and security, crime, unhygienic sanitary conditions, riots, lack of amenities at a destination etc.

Some of the embarrassing questions may be as follows:

- Why is your country so populated?
- Why is your country so unsafe for women?
- Why is your city so dirty?
- Why do people in your country spit on the roads?
- Why do men urinate in the open in your country?
- Why is corruption so rampant in your country?
- Why is dowry and child marriage a custom in your country? (This question may be more relevant for countries in South Asia such as India and Pakistan.)
- Why are women ill-treated in your country?

The thumb rule is never to paint a dark picture of one's country or of the destination being visited by the tourist. While conceding to the factual position, the tour manager must exhibit the positive aspects of the destination and try to educate his guests about the changing reforms that may be taking place in that society to deal with such issues.

Besides the above mentioned embarrassing questions related to a destination, a tour manager may feel uncomfortable with awkward questions pertaining to his travel company put up by guests. The guests may have embarrassing questions to ask such as the following:

- Why does your firm charge so exorbitantly for the tour packages?
- Why are you giving us lousy quality hotels to stay?
- How does your company allow you to ask for tips from us?

CONTROVERSIAL/SENSITIVE QUESTIONS

There might be times when a guest may like to seek the opinion of a tour manager on specific sensitive issues which may be quite controversial. Questions may be asked on sensitive issues which may affect the other group members. Questions indicative of the kind may be as mentioned further:

- Why do people fight over religion in your country? What is your opinion?
- Why do people in your country have such a dark complexion?
- What is your opinion about cow slaughter?
- Why are people so superstitious in your country?
- What is your opinion about your government?

While dealing with such questions, a tour manager must ensure that he does not hurt any sentiment of any of his group members who may belong to a different religion, sect or ethnic group. He must handle these sensitive questions very tactfully. He may refrain from expressing his personal opinion on such controversial matters. He may generalise such questions by saying that there are different opinions of different people on such issues. He may also defer such questions to some other times where he can discuss the issue in private with the particular member who has raised the question without creating tension within the group.

IRRELEVANT QUESTIONS

Sometimes, specific questions are just asked which have no connection with the tour or the destinations mentioned in the itinerary. Sometimes, the personal questions can also be categorised under irrelevant questions.

Following are the types of irrelevant questions that may be posed to a tour manager:

- What is your salary?
- Why do you drink/smoke?

- Why do you speak so much?
- Why haven't you planned my itinerary differently?
- Are you expecting tip out of me?

Such questions that are out of context may humbly be avoided by the tour manager. Very politely, a tour manager may tell his guests that such issues are not within the ambit of the tour and he may not like to answer them.

UNPRETENTIOUS QUESTIONS

Many a time, some questions posed by the guests seem too simple to be answered by the tour manager. They may sound very stupid and obvious to a tour manager. However, he must acknowledge the fact that some tourists might be travelling to a destination for the first time or they might be first-time travellers. What may be very obvious for the tour manager may be something very new for the guests. Therefore, he must maintain his sensitivity towards such guests and understand that these questions may be quite relevant from the guests' perspective.

Some simple questions asked by the clients may include the following:

- Do I need to keep my passport with me while travelling?
- What are the formalities required to be done at the airport?
- In the Continental Plan, would I be provided with lunch and dinner?
- Will you arrange transportation for us?
- Why don't you have a hospital near this hotel?
- How can I lock my room in the hotel?
- Should I carry my personal belongings with me while travelling?
- What is the check-out procedure from the hotel?
- I have lost my ticket. What do I do now?
- Do we have to pay extras for the optional activities?

A TYPOLOGY OF TOURISTS

Based on the types of questions asked, the tourists may broadly be classified under the following categories.

INQUISITIVE TOURISTS

In every group, there would be a set of tourists who would get into the details of everything. Such tourists are generally curious by nature and, therefore, yearn to gather maximum information from the tour manager about the different aspects of a destination. These tourists are genuinely interested in learning about new things at a destination and therefore pose a lot of questions on the tour manager. Everything may interest such guest.

When such tourists ask questions, the other tourists might get bored or feel agitated. Also, when the same person asks questions again and again, different tourists may think that the person is asking questions to gain the attention of others or establish his supremacy. As a result, many tourists may lose their interest in the answers being given by the tour manager as the tour manager may involve himself in a one to one conversation with that tourist who has asked the question.

Therefore, while dealing with such tourists, a tour manager must ensure that he keeps everyone engaged while answering the question raised by a particular tourist. In order to have everyone on board, a tour manager may repeat the question and transfer it to the whole group so that everyone knows about the question being asked. Also, the tour manager must maintain a thorough eye contact with all his guests' while answering the questions of a particular tourist so that others may not feel neglected.

Beyond a point, the other members of the group may not be interested in these questions and answers. A tour manager should try to restrict his responses to maintain the group's interest. He would be with the group for the entire duration of the tour. If queries of some clients appear genuine or if they are too interested to know about things in depth, he may allow an exclusive time to such guests during his free time. He can address their queries while moving from one place to another, or sometimes, stay in the hotel lobby, after the completion of the day's itinerary.

A tour manager must also make his answers more exciting and add humour to them to keep his guests engaged in his answers.

IGNORANT TOURISTS

Generally, the guests who are first-time travellers, especially to foreign countries, may be considered under this category. As first-time travellers, such tourists may be unaware of the procedures of travelling. They might seek assistance on documentation at the airport. They may also ask questions from the tour manager related to the frontier formalities needed to be done at the airport. They may ask the tour manager about the check-out procedure at the hotel, or the locking system of rooms at the hotel they are staying in that may sound very silly to a tour manager.

While dealing with such guests, a tour manager must exhibit a lot of patience. For him, these things may be very regular and mundane. However, he should not discount these questions as frivolous. For a layman, things may be very new. Therefore, a tour manager must very calmly and patiently answer the queries raised by his guests as for them every question is of relevance.

ARROGANT TOURIST

There might be some tourists who want to test the knowledge of the tour manager. This may be the hidden agenda for posing challenging questions from a tour manager. The idea of such arrogant tourists for asking the questions from the tour manager is to shrink his ego and to humiliate him in front of others and establish their own superiority.

To prove their point, they may throw difficult questions on the tour manager. While dealing with such high-headed guests, skill and tactfulness is the key.

ATTENTION SEEKERS

This may be another category of guests who just want to ask questions from the tour manager to seek his attention and the other fellow tourists' attention. Such guest may not be really interested in a tour manager, but they just have to ask questions for others to notice them including the tour manager. Sometimes, they think asking questions may make them his favourites.

While dealing with such guests, a tour manager must be able to judge the intentions of an individual, and he must not pay him enough heed all the time. A tour manager should be able to figure out if the question raised by such guest is really genuine and valid. If he feels, he is asking again and again to seek his attention; he may just defer his answer and tell him that he may answer him later in the evening.

The idea of understanding these categories of tourists is that the tour manager should be able to identify such guest from the beginning of the tour only and find appropriate ways of tackling such guests accordingly.

GENERAL TIPS FOR HANDLING QUESTIONS

To be a successful tour manager, one must adhere to the following these general tips while taking up questions from his guests:

- A tour manager must treat every question as important.
- A tour manager must have a lot of patience while handling the queries raised by his guests.
- He may anticipate the possible questions that the tourists are likely to ask and prepare accordingly. He may make an inventory of expected questions and develop their replies.
- Preparation is a tool for self-confidence. Knowledge is power. Intrinsic knowledge about the destination places the tour manager in a better situation to handle the questions. Thus, a tour manager must be thoroughly well versed with a destination before he takes up a tour.
- A tour manager is not obliged to answer every question that may intrude his privacy.

SUMMARY

A tour manager has to deal with different tourists on every tour. He may have to devise strategies accordingly to deal with his clients. Some clients may ask genuine questions out of interest and eagerness to know, while some guests might be asking questions from a tour manager to test his knowledge or to kill their time. A tour manager must be able to differentiate the genuine and valid questions from the frivolous questions. He must be able to judge the intentions behind his guests asking questions. Questions may sometimes be itinerary-specific, destination-specific, attraction-specific, personal questions, controversial/sensitive questions, irrelevant questions and simple questions. Accordingly, based on types of questions asked, tourists may be categorised as inquisitive tourists, ignorant tourists, arrogant tourists and attention seekers. A tour manager must eventually learn to deal with these types of guests and must calmly try to resolve their queries if they appear to be relevant and genuine.

Activity 1 Mock practice

Stand in a semi-circle and let each student think of any question that he/she may like to ask as a tourist from the tour manager. Questions may be personal, embarrassing and controversial or to which the tour manager has no knowledge about. Now let some other student become a tour manager and get to the centre in the position of the tour manager and answer the question raised by a tourist.

This way, every student gets an opportunity to become both a tourist as well as a tour manager. This exercise also helps the students to develop spontaneity as to how to deal with questions that a tour manager may be encountered with. The students may use the techniques mentioned in the chapter to deal with questions.

Activity 2 Group activity

Divide the class into groups and give each group a particular set of questions. For example, one group may be given to just think of personal questions while the other group may just be given the task of thinking sensitive questions. Let every group be assigned a particular set of questions. Now organise a group competition where one group questions the other and vice versa. Let the teacher and other groups judge the overall performance of group. The criteria for evaluation may be both the quality of question asked by each member of the group and the way how every member of the same group dealt with the questions posed by other groups. The grades may be accumulated accordingly and the best group may be declared. This may become a very fun-based activity.

POSSIBLE SOLUTIONS TO THE OPENING VIGNETTE

- Zian decided to handle the situation by requesting all the group members to stick to the timings at an attraction mentioned in the itinerary that was given to them. He also asked his guests not to delay the itinerary by asking unlimited questions at an attraction.
- He made it a rule that all the guests may ask limited questions from him. In case, if any guest had further queries, he/she may discuss this during coffee or lunch breaks with him. He would be more than happy to answer.
- Now all the guests felt better, as they thought that Zian was successful in tackling this tricky situation without being personal and also addressing their concern.

Lessons Learned

- Identify the attention-seeking tourist in the beginning only.
- Devise mechanisms to deal with such guests.
- Show maturity and patience while dealing with such awkward tourist.
- Announce the rules of asking questions in the beginning only.
- Ensure to pay equal attention to all the guests.

21

Handling Awkward Tourists

LEARNING OBJECTIVES

- What kind of tourist a tour manager may face while on a tour?
- What can be the possible ways of tackling such tourists?

Ruchi was leading a group of guests in Amritsar, Punjab, one of the heritage cities of India. The next day, she was supposed to take her guests to the Golden Temple, the holy place of Sikh religion, also called as the Gurudwara. Everybody was looking forward to visiting the most famous attraction of Amritsar. After dinner, before retiring to rooms, Ruchi assembled the group in the hotel lobby and shared the next day's itinerary with them. She also gave few instructions to her group members to be followed while visiting the holy shrine of Sikhs. She made it clear to guests to follow a dress code while visiting the Gurudwara. She apprised them that shoulders should be covered and shorts should not be worn. Not adhering to the guidelines meant that the guest may not be permitted to go inside the Gurudwara.

However, the next morning when everyone showed up at the restaurant of the hotel for breakfast, before leaving for the Gurudwara, everybody's eyes was hooked to Steve and Suzy, a couple from USA who chose to wear shorts and an off-shoulder dress for visiting the Gurudwara.

Ruchi still did her duty by reminding her guests about the dress code and telling them that they may not be allowed to enter the Gurudwara wearing such attire. She requested her guests that she could still wait for them to go back to the room and change their clothes. However, the couple started shouting at Ruchi and plainly refused to pay any heed to her advice. They all then left the hotel for the Gurudwara. On reaching the Gurudwara, the group was greeted by the local tour guide. Later everybody was allowed to enter, except for the couple. This left Steve and Suzy disappointed.

A tour manager's job is a people's job. It involves a high level of customer interaction with the clients as the tour manager has to remain with his guests throughout the tour. Besides management of logistics, an essential component of a tour manager's job is to manage the group of people who he meets, probably for the first time, and which comprises of people from different backgrounds and individual traits. It is more about managing the various guests, who could be unpredictable, during the tour.

Every group that a tour manager is assigned to may have a different composition of clients. The composition may vary regarding gender, nationality, religion or age. Each time the formation of the group may change. Each time a tour manager would get to meet a set of new people while handling different groups. In any group, there would always be some guests who would exhibit awkward behaviours during the tour.

One of the most significant challenges for a tour manager is to deal with such tourists who can get tough for him to handle on account of their indifferent behaviours or their snobbish body language.

Awkward tourists may be understood as those tourists who are not easy to get along with on tour. A tourist who frequently creates problems may be categorised as an awkward tourist. These tourists exhibit a particular behaviour that can become tough for the tour manager as well as other guests to handle.

Let us discuss in detail some common types of difficult tourists and the ways how a tour manager should deal with such clients.

THE CRYBABY

Such clients are quite tricky to handle for a tour manager as they show a nagging dissatisfaction over everything. These kinds of tourists are very cranky and always complain about everything during the tour. They are continually finding faults in everything. They may be further classified into two types:

- Fault finders
- Complainers

One type is the fault finders who keep finding flaws in every service/product given on tour. However, these guests may not get back to the tour manager. They keep cribbing and vitiate the mood of the group.

The other type is complainers, who make sure that they leave no chance to complain. They bring everything to the notice of the tour manager by being vocal about it. They may not like the rooms in a hotel as they may find the size of the room to be too small, the linen to be dirty or the colour of the walls too dark and depressing, and they may come back to the tour manager complaining about the room. Still some others may not get along with other group mates and complain about other group members to the tour manager. If they have to wait in queues to seek an entry in the attractions or in the public toilets, they may again get the point to complain. Further, they may complain about the food, the itinerary and virtually everything. In one case, there were cruises arranged for the guests at every destination. The complaining guest got cranky over this as well as to why the cruises have been arranged at every destination.

While dealing with such guests, it is always good to remain apathetic. Instead of taking every complaint very seriously, a tour manager may filter the complaints. He may differentiate the genuine complaint from the disingenuous complaint. He may listen to his guests and try to resolve the complaint as far as possible if he finds the problem really authentic.

But at the same time, he should be guided by the rule that he cannot afford to please everyone all the time. However, he may not brush aside every complaint as a whimper. Not attending to the complaint may also make a client too aggressive. He must ensure that such whining is addressed to keep it below a threshold.

THE TARDY

On a tour, in a group of tourists, there may be a bunch of latecomers who may always be disturbing the planned itinerary for the day. As a result, these latecomers make the whole group suffer. When the group is ready sitting in the coach to go for sightseeing, these guests might be relaxing in the restaurant of the hotel busy enjoying their breakfast. Therefore, others might suffer waiting in the coach for them to finish their meal. Sometimes, when the group is taken to the local markets for shopping, these latecomers may spend hours shopping beyond the stipulated time given for shopping. As a result, the whole group may suffer waiting for these guests. Eventually, these guests become an eyesore for everyone as everything gets delayed because of such few guests.

It is advisable for a tour manager to identify such latecomers early on the tour, preferably on the first or second day of the trip, and accordingly advise them to remain on time. He may introduce a 10-minute rule. That is if the guest is late by more than 10 minutes, the group will depart leaving these laggards behind. These latecomers may be asked to join the group later at the next point on their own. A tour manager may communicate this rule well in advance to his guests. He may also introduce some soft punishments such as asking the latecomers to sing a song when they arrive at the coach or crack a joke in front of all other group members to embarrass them subtly in front of others.

Sometimes it may also happen that due to language barriers, the guests are not able to understand the instructions issued by the tour manager and may, therefore, arrive late. Hence, the tour manager must be obvious in his communication and must ensure that everyone understands the instructions issued by him.

Thus, before exercising any such punishment, he must ensure that the individual is a perpetual laggard. He must remain sensitive to the fact that some guest might be in real trouble due to which they may not be able to show up on time.

THE UNRULY

A tour manager may land in deep trouble because of some rowdy clients on the tour. Some customers may misbehave during the trip. The following may tantamount to misbehaviour:

- Excessive drinking on the trip
- Using abusive language

- Passing personal (derogatory) remarks on others
- Sexually harassing someone on the trip
- Always criticising someone
- Humiliating someone

To deal with such guests, a tour manager must privately warn these clients to behave and mend their ways. However, depending upon the gravity of the situation, a public admonish may be desirable. However, if the tourist still repeats this behaviour again, he may suspend the client from the tour by giving him a release form that he may be carrying along with him on the trip.

It is worthy of a tour manager, at the beginning of the tour, to lay out the norms of acceptable group behaviour. He may suggest that his guests behave appropriately during the trip. He must also remind his guests of the terms and conditions they have may have signed before joining the tour that presses them to behave appropriately, failing which the tour manager has the full authority to take an appropriate action against that group member who misbehaved during the trip. In such cases, when the group member is released from the group, his money is also not refunded besides him facing public humiliation too.

THE EXPECTANTS

There would always be a set of tourists in a group who would have very high expectations of the travel arrangements from their tour. Such tourists are highly demanding. They want everything up to the mark. They want value for money. Such tourists would always expect very high levels of services and travel arrangements such as good coaches, good quality hotels, good food and so on in each and every destination planned for the tour.

Sometimes, at specific destinations during the tour, it is not always possible to give the same high-quality services due to lack of amenities available at that destination. It is suggested that a tour manager must do the initial briefing with the guests and reset their expectations. The tour manager must tell in advance to his guests to keep their expectations grounded so that they may not be disappointed later. The idea is to mentally prepare the guest for the highs and lows during the tour. In case the guests' expectations are met or are exceeded, they may be delighted. However, this does not mean that all below-par arrangements and services may be brushed aside.

THE NON-COOPERATORS

A tour manager may find it difficult to deal with such tourists. Such tourists can become a real pain for the tour manager. These tourists make things difficult for the tour manager by not following the norms and rules set by him on a tour.

Rules may be related to maintaining the local sensitivities at the destination. For example, while visiting a pilgrimage centre, the tour manager might request his guests to follow a particular dress code suitable for entering these shrines. However, some guests may not pay heed to the tour manager's advice and create problems for the tour manager. Likewise, at specific attractions, photography may be prohibited, or while taking the pictures of the local community, the guests may be advised to secure the permission of the hosts. Some guest may smoke in non-smoking areas, in spite of being told not to do so. However, these particular tourists who may be termed as non-cooperator may not follow these instructions of the tour manager and may refuse to follow the rules. This makes things difficult for the tour manager to operate. Eventually, it spoils the whole atmosphere during the tour as everything gets delayed due to unnecessary disputes that the tour manager is trying to settle down every now and then with such guests on the trip.

While dealing with such guests, it is imperative for a tour manager to communicate the conduct rules at the beginning of the tour and during the briefing at the start of the excursions. He must openly talk to his guests about the repercussions and that the fallouts will be the sole responsibility of the individual guests and not the tour company. A guest may be restricted because of improper behaviour or dress.

THE AGGRIEVED

Many visitors are sensitive. Any petty thing may hurt them. Some tourists in the group might believe that they have not been treated fairly. They may themselves feel miserable about it and go into a self-pity mode. As a result, they may choose to create distance with others.

They may think that they have not been given the first seat in the coach or they have not got a good room in the hotel as compared to other fellow tourists. They may feel that the tour manager is not giving them enough attention as compared to others. When such a feeling creeps in, a tourist may prefer to stay alone, or he may become may become more of a rebel by becoming more vocal about things. He may decide to create trouble for the tour manager by not extending his cooperation on the tour.

While dealing with such tourists, it is advisable for the tour manager to let them vent out their feelings. He must try to counsel such guests and try his best to clarify the clutter in the mind of his guest. A tour manager must also try to make that guest feel important so that he doesn't feel ignored or left out in a group.

THE ANGRY GUEST

A tour manager may confront a hostile tourist while on a tour. These tourists may get angry about anything. Hostile tourists are generally loud. They always believe that what they say is right. They may get irritated for small things. They are never ready to listen to other person's perspectives. It is hard for them to accept the other person's opinion. If a tour manager or a group member differs with them on an issue, they may get aggressive and start getting loud to prove their point.

A tour manager must be very wary while dealing with such guests. He must show a lot of patience and composure while dealing with them. He must listen to them actively and try to calm them and, if possible, try to divert their attention from the main issue. He must prevent these members from creating bad blood within the group. On seeing their repeated behaviour on certain occasions, he may take the guest in private and tactfully request them to listen to other's perspective too and avoid being too loud.

THE ARROGANTS

These are the tourists who have airs about themselves. They always try to show the group how different they are from others. They try to suggest to the tour manager that they know everything and that they have more knowledge than him. They try to monopolise the talks. They try to establish their supremacy by showing that they know everything and make sure that everyone knows this fact.

Remember you are in control of the group; the boaster will try to snatch that away from you. Never lose your cool, refuse to enter into an argument and rebuff firmly any attempts to overpower you. Should you feel that it is becoming difficult to handle such a person, seek support from the group. Group members in all likelihood may explicitly or otherwise convey their displeasure which is usually good enough.

THE ATTENTION SEEKERS

There may be some attention seekers in a group who would want to be the centre of attraction for everyone. They do everything to seek the attention of others as well as the tour manager. They may crack jokes on others, play pranks or keep tormenting the tour manager with unnecessary questions.

While some merriment is okay, it has to be in line with the sensibilities of the situation. You, as the leader of the group and controller of situations, must step in to advise them to appreciate the gravity of the situation. They are generally not harmful but must be cut in before they tread too far.

THE IRRITATING GUESTS

There might be some tourists on the tour who may always be poking the tour manager unnecessarily all the time in different ways. They may keep nagging the tour manager with their endless phone calls even during the night, keep asking irrelevant questions from the tour manager to seek his attention or keep gossiping with the tour manager to keep themselves entertained. Such guests can literally get on the nerves of a tour manager.

Therefore, to deal with such guests is quite tricky. A tour manager must know how to draw a line with such guests. He may have to start ignoring such guests or tell them straight at times without being rude that he wants to take rest or he can have the conversation later. Sometimes, it is important to be straightforward without losing one's politeness and courteous behaviour.

THE LONERS

Some tourists do not want to gel with the group. These guests stay within their own bubble and do not participate actively in the group. These people prefer their individual privacy and like to enjoy in their own circle of friends or family they have come with. To feel safe and secure, and for financial reasons, they might have chosen to be in the group package.

For a tour manager, these are awkward tourists, as these tourists don't get very well along with other fellow tourists. Besides this, they may also not be very expressive in nature. Therefore, a tour manager may stay in a dilemma if the guests are enjoying the tour or not.

To deal with such guests, he should try his best to involve such guests by organising games and other ice-breaking sessions so that they try to show up. However, if such guests still wish to be alone, a tour manager may not insist for them to get involved every time as everyone has a different way of holidaying.

THE ARGUERS

At certain times, a tour manager may confront such clients who always argue over everything. They may argue with others that they want to sit on the first seat of the bus or near the window. They may confront the tour manager and driver if the songs or movie of their choice is not played on the coach. They may also get into a tiff with the tour manager over the land arrangements such as hotels, food and so on. Issues for an argument may be umpteen.

A decent way to handle such clients is to take them in private and counsel them so as not to vitiate the atmosphere of the whole group. However, the tour manager may not put such guests in a straightjacket and conveniently blame them. He must very humbly approach such guests with patience and try to resolve the issue of the guest with a calm mind. Putting some rules in place may help. Like the roster for rotation for seats with a view.

THE PROFESSIONAL GUESTS

Professional guests may also be categorised as difficult tourists. It is not easy to deal with such guests for a tour manager as these guests always show how aware they are of their rights and laws. If anything goes wrong in the itinerary, they may suggest to the tour manager that they are aware of what legal action they may take against the tour manager if things don't go as promised.

Such guests may also flaunt their relationships with the top management of the travel company that has organised their tour and try to threaten the tour manager with their body language or sometimes may be verbally about the bad arrangements done.

A tour manager must himself be aware of the consequences. Second, he should understand that his job is to moderate the tempers of such guests, while any pitfall in the promised package is the responsibility of the company unless something goes awry on the tour. There are often recovery tactics available to the tour manager. Keeping the company in the loop, he may try to compensate the clients. However, perpetually threatening guests issues may initially be heard in private or may be ignored to some extent.

THE FIRSTS

This is another category of difficult tourist who wishes to do everything first. They may want to board the coach first and occupy the first seat on the coach. They may want to check in at the hotel first or enter an attraction first to avoid standing in queues. They may run to arrive at the restaurant first so that they may be served the food first.

The problem is not being at first but what they do to others in the process of being the first. Such tourists might push others to make their way first or use cheap tactics to come early like securing their first seat on the coach a day ahead by leaving their handkerchief or any of their belongings. As a result, they become a problem for other tourists.

The other tourists start complaining of such guests to the tour manager or may directly get into tiffs with such first comers.

Therefore, a tour manager must identify such tourists and may counsel them personally to avoid such gimmicks with others. He may come up with a specified protocol for the group.

THE IGNORANT TOURISTS

Sometimes, the ignorant tourists can pose a significant challenge for a tour manager. Such tourists are generally first-time travellers and not precisely aware of the things. However, they may also be ignorant due to the language barrier that stops them from understanding the instructions of the tour manager. These tourists may act dumb as they are unaware of things, or may feel shy or feel afraid and lack the confidence to enquire second time from the tour manager about what he said. They may also feel embarrassed about asking the simple things from the tour manager in front of others as they may fear others making a mockery of them.

For example, a tour manager may leave the whole group for shopping in the local markets and ask them to meet him at a particular point. However, these ignorant tourists after dispersing away from the group may not be able to trace the group back, leaving other to wait for them and thereby leading to a delay in the itinerary.

A tour manager must understand that these tourists may not be aware enough, may face language barriers or may just lack the confidence due to which they do not follow what the tour manager says. Hence, the tour manager must be empathetic towards such guests as he should understand that they are not doing these things intentionally but unintentionally. He may also give more atten tion to such guests and reconfirm from them if they have followed his instructions.

THE UNSOLICITED LEADERS

Some people want to lead rather than to be led. A tour manager may come across some tourists who try to dominate other members as well as the tour manager too. They may give unsolicited advice to the tour manager to make changes in the itinerary or to make changes in the food menu, or suggest some ideas as how to make the tour better. Such clients tend to become unsought leaders and try to influence others in shaping their opinions and making choices.

A tour manager must try to identify such guests and nip their advances in the bud. He may suggest openly through his choice of words and body language that he is in charge and controller of the group at all times. He must explicitly tell the group at the beginning that deviations from the promised package will not be permitted except where options have been built into the package.

THE KLEPTOMANIACS

Many tourists in a group may suffer from the habit of picking things. Stealing can be an obsessive compulsive disorder. These people cannot resist the urge of lifting things from a shop. Shoplifting is a crime. When such tourists are accompanying a tour manager, it can get very embarrassing for the tour manager when such incidents of shoplifting take place at a destination. The whole trip goes for a toss. The tour manager may have to face humiliation because of such guests, and his relations with shopkeepers may be strained as a result of this. A tour manager has to cut a sorry figure due to such guests.

To avoid such kind of incidents on a tour, a tour manager may right at the beginning of the trip share his similar previous episodes with the guests informing them of what can happen to them if they do something of this kind on tour. The idea is to make the guests well aware of the repercussions they may have to face as a result of such behaviour to prevent such incidents from happening on a tour.

GENERAL TIPS FOR DEALING WITH DIFFICULT TOURISTS

Gradually, over a span of time, after doing some groups, a tour manager is better placed to anticipate what kind of behavioural issues of tourists he might have to deal with. Accordingly, he may also evolve the strategies for coping with such guests.

A tour manager has to strike a delicate balance between being a good companion and a strict disciplinarian when the situation demands. He must know when to pamper the ego of his guests and when to draw a line with them. Always being the 'yes man' of the guests may not work for him while dealing with such difficult tourists.

A tour manager must understand that every tourist is important for his company. Retention of all the guests is his prime responsibility. He must know that he has the principal responsibility towards his guests and his company to give good memories of the trip to the guests as a return gift. On account of being awkward tourists, he cannot afford to lose the business of these guests to his competitors. A tour manager must work hard on winning the confidence of such customers. Eventually, he must learn to tackle such guests that they do not return home upset and offended after a holiday on which they may have to spend a fortune. A tour manager must be a troubleshooter for the problems that come in the way of a happy tour.

While dealing with difficult tourists, a tour manager must observe the following tips:

- Identify such guests at the beginning of the tour, and keep his company in the loop and updated about such guests on the party.
- Value each and every guest. He should give equal importance to all the group members. Perceived equity is a must.
- Listen to the guests' problems patiently.
- Allow them enough opportunity to vent out their emotions.
- Must try to understand the perspective of these awkward tourists also.
- Instead of trying to fix the blame, he must focus on fixing the problems.
- In case, he does not have a solution for his guests, he may appear empathetic towards these guests. He must demonstrate genuine concern for his guests.
- Always stay positive while handling such guests.
- Maintain his calm and stay composed while dealing with such guests.
- Choose to respond and not to react.
- Open all channels of communication with his guests.
- If the complaint of the tourist is genuine, he must try to assist his guest in every possible way. The tour manager must reassure his guests about the corrective actions being taken by him to resolve the grievance of his guest.
- To counter such stress arising out of dealing with such difficult tourists, he may practise deep breathing exercises to stay calm and relaxed while dealing with such people.

SUMMARY

A tour manager may have to deal with different types of tourists. However, he must not give up so quickly on such guests. He must try to take everyone together. However, if still some tourists do not mend their behaviours, a tour manager must remain calm and assertive. He should be diplomatic in handling such guests. He should always know that he is the sole controller and facilitator of the group. He must ensure that a small number of such guests do not spoil the overall jovial atmosphere of the group.

Activity 1 Play an awkward tourist

Divide your class into groups and let each group be asked to perform a role-play depicting a particular type of awkward tourist as mentioned in the chapter. Let every group conceptualise a situation on their own with a particular kind of awkward tourist in it, practise it and then perform it in front of the whole class. The group may also be asked to show the corrective way with one student assuming the role of a tour manager and how he dealt with the awkward tourist. Through this activity, the students would be able to appreciate the different kinds of tourists that a tour manager may have to deal with and also learn the art of dealing with such situations when their peers perform on the stage.

Activity 2 **Story telling**

Ask each student to draw a sketch of awkward tourist that may come in their mind on a white sheet of paper. Then ask them to think of an appropriate story in their mind. Also, give it a suitable caption to it. Give 7 minutes to students to draw and 7 minutes to think of a story with a caption. Now take the sheets and pick any picture at random and ask the student to come and narrate the story to the whole class.

This can be a very exciting activity for the students.

POSSIBLE SOLUTIONS TO THE OPENING VIGNETTE

- Ruchi politely requested her guests to wait for her inside the coach until the whole group comes after visiting the Golden Temple.
- She also gave them an alternative of going for shopping nearby and spending their time while the guests complete their visit inside the Gurudwara.
- She also suggested her guests that, in case they still wanted to go inside the Gurudwara, they may buy an Indian dress from outside and take it back to their country as a souvenir. She said she could help them in availing an discount too on the dress.
- Ultimately, the guests agreed to buy the Indian dress as they did not want to miss a chance of seeing the Gurudwara. Ruchi went out of her way to help them in buying the dress, and that too at a discounted price. The guests were very happy. They later apologised to Ruchi for not adhering to her instructions and creating all the inconvenience for her.
- Meanwhile, Ruchi asked the local tour guide to proceed with the group so that there is no delay in the scheduled itinerary.

Lessons Learned

- A tour manager may come across difficult tourists in the group. However, he should know how to tackle such guests calmly. Some guests may try to emulate such non-cooperative/difficult guests. Therefore, a tour manager must firmly convey his message to the guest about the local sensitivities to be observed at a destination.
- A tour manager must never forget his basic courtesies. His guests may misbehave or speak loudly, but the tour manager should choose to stay polite and smile.

22

Dealing with the Group

LEARNING OBJECTIVES

- What are the challenges that a tour manager faces while dealing with groups on a tour?
- What can be the coping mechanisms of a tour manager for managing groups?

Rocky was with a Spanish group, leading them from the railway station of Puri to catch a train for Delhi. The group was already running short of time and the coach was making its way slowly through the traffic. As the group was almost near the railway station, the coach was stuck and was not moving even a metre for the last 10 minutes. He only had next 20 minutes to board the train. On enquiring, he was told that there was a big political rally near the railway station due to which there was huge traffic jam. Assessing the situation that he was running short of time and that he had a train to catch, Rocky thought that he must do something.

Group tours are a common phenomenon in the tourism industry. Many tourists prefer to travel in groups due to the various advantages offered in GIT as discussed in Chapter 1. However, travelling in groups can be the most stressful activity for the guests in the absence of a professional tour manager.

Managing a group on a tour is the most important job of a tour manager. Though this responsibility may sound simple, it can be one of the most difficult tasks for a tour manager. Handling groups is a task in itself. Whatever may be the size of the group, handling a group of people, that too those who are in a holiday mode, calls for a lot of wit and smartness on the part of a tour manager.

Group dynamics vary from one group to another. Not having the right kind of people on a tour who get along with each other can pose a severe challenge to a tour manager. Accordingly, a tour manager must act as per the need of the situation.

A lot depends on the skills of the tour manager as to how he handles his group. A tour manager must play the role of a team leader who believes in taking every teammate together on the tour.

Now let us gain insights into the day-to-day challenges faced by a tour manager while managing the group dynamics.

MANAGING DIFFERENT EXPECTATIONS

Every tour that a tour manager has been assigned with shall always have a different composition of guests in terms of age, gender, nationality, religion, cultural backgrounds, personal interests and occupations of the group members. In group tours, the travellers come from all walks of life. Accordingly, dealing with such guests from varied backgrounds poses a significant challenge for a tour manager to take them all along. A tour manager may, therefore, use different permutations and combinations to deal with such a group of guests. His dealing with a particular group is subject to many factors. For example, while handling a group of women travellers, a tour manager must understand the sensitivities and issues involved while handling them. While dealing with senior citizens, he has to show more consideration for them.

Also, in a group, different people may have diverse interests. This may create a clash amongst the members. Youngsters may like adventure whereas the middle-aged guests might want passive sightseeing. This becomes a catch-22 situation for the tour manager as to whom to please. The rule of the game is to go by the majority without favouring anyone.

Due to the different composition of tourists in the same group, many tourists in the group may be travelling for the first time. However, some might be world class, frequent travellers. This may become very difficult for the tour manager to balance.

First-time travellers may be entirely new to the places and may not be aware of the travel procedures that may be at the airport or the hotel. Therefore, they may have different expectations from a tour manager altogether. Such travellers require briefing at every point. For such travellers, the tour manager must get into every detail of the subject. Whereas frequent travellers may feel that the information being given by the tour manager is frivolous as they may be already aware of the travel procedures.

Therefore, matching the different expectations of both kinds of travellers is a real-time challenge for the tour manager. The tip for the tour manager here is that he should not generalise the group. On the contrary, he must understand that every member of the group may have a different requirement and he may act accordingly. Although he may have to give more attention to first-time travellers, he should not ignore the other travellers.

Therefore, managing the expectations of different tourists within the same group might become a challenge for a tour manager.

ADMINISTERING DISCIPLINE

Every tour has certain norms that all group members must abide by. The discipline of a group is essential. A tour manager can't afford to be a strict disciplinarian with his guests as they are not small kids who need to be controlled all the time. He must appreciate the fact that his guests are adults who are on holiday on their own or with their family and friends to relax and chill. Yet, being too lenient with them may also become an unmanageable issue for a tour a manager later.

Thus, a tour manager must act according to a situation. Sometimes, when some guests misbehave, a tour manager may have to be assertive with them and handle the situation firmly. He can neither afford to have drunkards in the group nor can he stay silent on seeing some member abusing another member.

He must ensure that his guests follow the group norms. Therefore, a tour manager must strike an excellent balance between being a strict disciplinarian and a facilitator. He must let his group members enjoy themselves thoroughly unless it affects the joy of other group members. In the initial stage of the tour, preferably on the first day of the trip only, a tour manager may categorically communicate the group norms to his group members and the possible actions that may be taken by him in case, of extreme behaviours. This clarity removes room for ambiguity in the minds of the guests, and they may act accordingly.

KEEPING THE GROUP TOGETHER

The most significant challenge in front of a tour manager is to keep the group together. The bigger the group, the more significant is the difficulty of keeping them together. No matter whatever a tour manager may do, however, guests have a natural tendency of forming subgroups. As they say, 'birds of a feather flock together'. Therefore, guests try to be with people with whom their frequency matches and they feel comfortable with. Thus, the group dynamics start becoming visible in the first few days of the tour. Many guests of the same age or same interests may begin binding together and forming subgroups. This is very natural and can't be stopped. Sometimes, some subgroups become very dominating to others, and sometimes start politicking and bullying each other.

This can be very dangerous for the overall atmosphere of the group and can lead to the spread of negativity.

However, these subgroups should not be ignored. A tour manager must keep a check on such groups. A tour manager must try to mitigate and pretend not to cognise these subgroups. He must ensure that he is always in charge of the situation and that no one group dominates others.

Nevertheless, knowing about this fact of guests making subgroups, a tour manager should not leave a chance unturned to bring his group members together. A tour manager must create social cohesion and bonding among his group members. He may request his group members to think of the group as a part of their extended family on the tour. In order to keep the group together, he may initiate the following with his group.

Organising Ice-breaking Sessions

A tour manager may ask his group members to introduce each other. This allows them an opportunity to know more about each other and thus creates affinity amongst the group members.

Organising Games

Having fun activities together may bring group members closer to each other. When the group members play together, they might forget their individual differences. Therefore, such exercises are very beneficial for bringing the group members' together.

A tour manager may during the long journey on a coach or at the hotel after the day's itinerary gets over, may arrange activities such as Housie, a quiz, karaoke, song and dance competitions for couples and so on. This will help keep the overall atmosphere of the group light and also to break the ice between the members.

Participation in Special Events

Some events may fall during the trip dates. There might be a special event in the city like a local festival (La Tomatina Festival, Spain or a special celebration, e.g., the Canadian government celebrated 2017 as its 150th anniversary of the Confederation in different cities of Canada). These are moments of togetherness for the group members. A tour manager must take his group members around the town to show them these celebrations as these are rare opportunities and once-in-lifetime experiences for the guests to be part of the food tasting, artistic performances, musical festivities and so on at different places.

Besides these events at a destination that may be an opportunity for social cohesion, a tour manager may commemorate the birthdays/anniversaries of his guests on the tour if these special occasions are falling within the dates of the trip. The guests feel important and special, and therefore get delighted with such gestures. Other members of the party also get an opportunity to have moments of fun with each other. Such moments bring everyone closer spreading positivity all around amongst the group members.

MANAGING NON-COOPERATIVE GUESTS

Not everyone is a team player. Some tourists may be very cooperative and understanding by nature. However, some guests may be very cranky and demanding by nature. There may be still others who may not like to gel with the other group members. On the contrary, they may want to be on their own, while still being in the group. They may also create issues for a tour manager by not cooperating with others.

Therefore, it is essential for a tour manager to handle such group members in a very tactful way. At the end of the day, he has to keep everyone together. In such cases, he may request their partici pation. However, he should not force such members to participate in every activity of the group.

ENSURING PUNCTUALITY

This is one of the most critical issues for a tour manager while dealing with groups. There would always be a group of people who would be laggards in the group. They may be coming late for breakfast in the hotel and, therefore, they might delay other members for the day's itinerary. Likewise, some members may go shopping and keep shopping while other group members may keep waiting for him. Some members may continue spending their time appreciating the beauty of the attraction, thereby delaying visits to other points of attraction.

As a result, for a tour manager, operating the itinerary under the limited time constraints becomes a challenge. Skipping some part of the itinerary for a bunch of laggards would mean annoying other members of the group.

Therefore, to avoid any stress later, a tour manager at the very outset of the tour should emphasise the importance of punctuality to his guests and deal with this issue very tactfully. He may introduce creative punishments for such guests who may not offend these people also, but also tell them the importance of being punctual.

MANAGING CONFLICTS

Anything can become a source of conflict between the guests. Sometimes guests in the same group may have been given different kinds of rooms despite having paid the same amount to the tour operator/travel agent. This may become a bone of contention amongst the group members.

Sometimes the conflict may arise over occupying the first seat in the coach. Still others may fight over one person who is always coming late in the group. Reasons for conflicts between the group members can be innumerable. As a result, the guests may develop ill-will for each other.

Therefore, a tour manager must take the role of a firefighter. He must act as a troubleshooter for his guests. Through his mediation, he must try to bridge the differences between his guests. He must try to resolve their conflicts and try to diffuse the situation.

MANAGING EQUAL ATTENTION TO ALL

A tour manager must not play favourites. He must have an egalitarian approach towards his guests. Some tourists are very interactive while some are not. Interactive tourists might try to stay close to the tour manager and keep asking questions from him about a destination. They may be inquisitive to know about the place and life there. As a result, they may try to sit near the tour manager or stand with him, wherever he is. Automatically, such people in the group become the apple of a tour manager's eye. Therefore, as a result, the tour manager may start connecting with such people more over others. Others might get offended as a result.

Thus, it is essential for a tour manager, not to pay individual attention to anyone. It is quite natural that he may like such people on the tour who may try to be close to him. But this should not become evident. He should not play favourites on the trip and he must exercise an egalitarian approach towards all as everyone has paid the same amount for a holiday. He should see everyone as equal. Otherwise, it may show the tour manager in poor light as others might feel that he is biased and unfair to them.

HANDLING THE LANGUAGE ISSUE

Language can be another issue while handling a group of guests. Within the same group, people may be of different nationalities who speak different languages. Even if the group members are from the same nationality, they may not be able to communicate with each other as they may be speaking different languages being from different regions or states of the same country.

When the tour manager may be giving commentary, or briefing the group at some point, only some people may understand his instructions, whereas some of the group members may have no clue of what the tour manager is saying. Thus, language may become a barrier for the tour manager while communicating with the group. Therefore, a tour manager must try to talk in the language with his guest which is spoken by most of the guests and must try to reconfirm after his briefing if everyone has followed his instruction correctly.

TIPS FOR HANDLING THE GROUP

- A tour manager should always understand the pulse of his group. He should develop the knack of understanding what his group members expect of him.
- A tour manager should ensure that no opinion leaders are formed in the group who may try to influence others.
- A tour manager should always show his group members affirmatively that he is in charge and in control of the group.
- All the members of the group should be equal in the eyes of a tour manager.
- A tour manager should be proactive in identifying the issues that may become the cause of fights between his group members, and he should try to nip them in the bud.
- A tour manager must maintain solidarity amongst his group members at all times.

SUMMARY

Handling groups calls for a lot of wit and patience on the part of a tour manager. A tour manager may in a group have to act as a glue stick, a firefighter, a mediator and a troubleshooter for his guests. He should, therefore, be ready for all these roles. A tour manager must take the handling of groups as a challenge and must try his level best to keep the group under his control. Group dynamics may be evident from day one. However, a tour manager must know that through his wisdom and experience, he has the power to change things. To make the holiday of his guests comfortable and memorable, he must infuse positivity and good vibes amongst the group members' in spite of any harmful elements within the group. Nothing should disturb his peace of mind, and he should ensure that he is always in charge of the situation.

Activity 1 Embarrass your guest

Every student may, considering self as a tour manager, write on a piece of paper the embarrassing yet mild punishments for those tourists who come late in the group or do not cooperate with the tour manager in different ways. The teacher may then conduct the class, listen to the innovative ways of students and jot down the inventory of points on the whiteboard that comes through the class discussion.

Activity 2 Bonding exercise

You have a group of tourists from different age groups. There are five members who are senior citizens, five teenagers, five kids and five adults. Now suggest the techniques that you would initiate as a tour manager to keep your group together keeping their varied interests in mind.

POSSIBLE SOLUTIONS TO THE OPENING VIGNETTE

- The tour manager asked his clients to leave the coach and immediately start walking towards the railway station that was just 600 metres away.
- Meanwhile, he approached a local rickshaw-puller and asked him to carry the luggage with him through any short cut route to avoid the rush. He arranged for more rickshaws and shared the train details with his guests and rickshaw-pullers.
- One of the rickshaw-pullers called the local porters to be ready with a group of porters and a luggage trolley in front of railway station to carry the clients' luggage.
- Finally, the luggage reached the train successfully and the guests could board the train in just a nick of time.

Lessons Learned

- A tour manager must have a proactive approach, especially towards solving the challenges.
- He must be able to think out-of-the-box, and he must have network with locals including the local service providers. He must be aware of possible local solutions to the problems at hand.
- He must be able to take the right decision at the right time as his one decision can make or mar the overall tour experience of his guests.

23 Handling Grievances

LEARNING OBJECTIVES

- What are the kinds of grievances that a tour manager faces?
- What can be possible ways of dealing with them?
- What is the importance of grievances?

A group of 20 Swiss people were on a trip to Bombay with Harry, their tour manager. After a hectic and long journey, the guests checked into the hotel in the evening. Like every other guests, Suzy and Mary were given a key for the room as they were booked on twin sharing basis. Both of them completed the check-in formalities and proceeded to their allotted room with the room key. On opening the room, they were surprised to see two beds with different sizes instead of identical sizes. One bed was a king size bed which was quite large as compared to the other standard size twin bed. The king size bed was naturally appealing to both. Both Suzy and Mary first tried to keep stuff near the king size bed so as to secure that bed. However, it soon became a point of contention between the two.

Suzy said that she wanted to sleep on the bed while Mary said why she should allow her to sleep on that bed. Mary too claimed her occupancy over that bed. Ultimately, it turned to an ugly argument where they started cursing each other. Both needed a third party intervention. Therefore, they decided to call Harry, the tour manager, who would decide who sleeps on that bed.

No tour can be perfectly alright. A service failure at any point in time is bound to happen. There can be situations of a near miss of a service. The only person representing the company on the tour responsible for dealing with guests is the tour manager. He is the punching bag for the guests who has to face the music for every service offered during the tour. Handling grievances is an integral part of a tour manager's job profile. Pleasing the guests all the time can be tough for the tour manager. However, he has to deal with this situation every day on the tour.

When the guests are on a tour, they have spent a fortune on their vacation. They may have saved their hard-earned money to have one holiday of their lifetime. Therefore, expecting an enjoyable holiday is quite natural for them. Spending a good amount of money makes them develop high expectations from the travel company about the services to be offered on the tour.

However, sometimes, there may be a gap between what the guests expect and what they get. This may upset the guests. Therefore, the guests complain when things don't work out according to their whims and wishes. Second, they may develop grievances when things that have been promised initially before the tour in the itinerary to them are not delivered accordingly. This may again disappoint the tourists.

KINDS OF AGGRIEVED TOURIST

It is essential for a tour manager to understand first that every complaint cannot be entertained. A tour manager must be able to differentiate a genuine criticism from a disingenuous criticism. He may have to face different kinds of aggrieved tourists on a tour who have different types of grievances. They may be divided into two categories.

HABITUAL COMPLAINANTS

A tour manager is always under pressure to deal with such guests who have a nagging dissatisfaction over the status quo. These kinds of guests are frequent complainants. They have a perpetual habit of making a mountain out of a molehill for everything. They may literally have grievances on every small thing from the hotel to the tour guide. Such guests never leave a chance to complain. Also, these guests have a habit of sharing their grievances with other fellow tourists too on the tour with the intention of seeking their support against the tour manager or the travel company. This may create a precarious situation for the tour manager to handle.

A tour manager must, therefore, be able to identify such guests in the group and try to handle them tactfully. While dealing with such guests, a tour manager must remind his guests that he is just following the itinerary that was initially communicated to the guests by the company. He may tell them since they had read the itinerary before travelling, it is understood that they must have gone through the terms and conditions of the company also.

GENUINE COMPLAINANTS

Such guests only complain when they really feel something is terribly wrong with the services provided. They just complain when they genuinely think there is a gap between what has been promised and what is being delivered during the moments of truth. These disgruntled guests may feel that they have not got the real value for their money.

Since these are genuine complainants who have valid grievances, a tour manager must try to address their issues on a priority basis and, if found genuine, should try to fix their problems at the earliest. These guests can sometimes become the most loyal customers if their grievances are adequately addressed.

NON-COMPLAINANTS

These are the guests who do have grievances but they still choose not to speak about them. Such guests do more harm than good for the company. The reason is such guests may not talk about anything on the face or in the feedback form with the explicit intention of never returning and sharing their bad experience with the tour and company to others. Therefore, these guests are a permanent loss to the firm.

A tour manager must again try to identify such guests and try to read their impressions on their face. He may try to take feedback from them and try to elicit the desired response from them about the services being offered on the tour.

SOURCES OF GRIEVANCES

The grievances may be brought to the notice of the travel company by the following sources.

GUESTS

Guests are the most aggrieved party who may directly speak about their grievance to the tour manager. They may raise their objections when things do not go as promised in the itinerary or else when their expectations are not met.

FEEDBACK FORMS

Many guests may choose not to be vocal on the face of a tour manager. They may feel uncomfortable sharing their grievances directly with the tour manager. On the contrary, such guests may be better able to express their grievances in black and white on the feedback form. This may be very useful for thc company to know about the kinds of services that the company may be lacking in.

TOUR MANAGERS

A tour manager can himself be a complainant about the services being offered by the company. He may be the most useful source as he has the first-hand experience of using the tourism product or service and also of knowing the pulse of his guests, being with them all the time.

SUPPLIERS

Many local suppliers may have issues while operating an itinerary. They may bring to the notice of the company about the real-time challenges and grievances while offering their services to the guest on the package tour.

GUIDES

Sometimes, the local guides may share challenges on the domestic sightseeing tours. For example, they may have a grievance that less time was given for sightseeing or some more attractions could have been added to the trip. He may further have his complaint that the guests were not interested in listening to his commentary and that the guests were not cooperative.

TOUR OPERATORS

Tour operators may themselves face challenges while operating an itinerary. They may have their own grievances to address. For example, to make a package more attractive, a tour manager may choose to keep the price of the package low, thereby compromising on the kind of services offered. Also, at times, a tour operator/travel agent may not be getting proper services or superstructure at a destination. For example, at remote destinations, it becomes difficult for the tour manager to arrange for appropriate hotels or excellent facilities. In some destinations, where there is a monopoly of few hotel properties and transportation facilities, they may offer higher rates to the tour operator which may increase the cost of tour package for the guests. At many destinations, they may not be able to find the local agents/ground handling operators also. Such grievances or ground realities may be shared by the tour operator with the tour manager that can help him better explain the situations if his guests demand an explanation.

KIND OF GRIEVANCES

Tourism, being a service industry, is dependent on the various services offered by different service providers who may be the transporters, airlines, hotels, restaurants, attraction authorities, entertainment organisers and so on. The ideal way to keep the guests happy is to have a zero-complaint mechanism. However, this is not practically feasible. There may be service failures on the part of different service providers that may ultimately spoil the experience of the tourists besides putting the name of a travel company at stake as the guests have booked their tour with the travel company. The guests have no interests to know about the internal issues between the travel company and the local service providers that may have happened. For them, the only grievance is that the services have not been delivered up to the mark according to the money that they have paid

A tour manager may come across a variety of complaints. Broadly speaking, the types of complaints may pertain to the following.

TRANSPORTATION

Sometimes the guest may have an issue with the kind of transportation they have been booked in. For example, in the case of an airline, the guests may complain about the following:

- The services provided by the airline's staff is not up to the mark.
- The in-flight catering is not good.
- There is not enough check-in baggage allowance permitted.
- The carriers do not have an excellent reputation.
- The flight journey is very long.
- The transit hours are very long and so on.
- The seats have less leg space.

Likewise, in case of a coach, the guests might have grievances related to the following issues:

- Poor hygiene of the coach
- Ineffective cooling
- Too many stopovers
- The journeys are too long
- Rash driving by the driver
- The seats are not comfortable
- No seat rotation policy
- No food and beverages allowed inside the coach

HOTELS

Similarly, the guests may have some grievances about a hotel that may include the following:

- The standard of the hotel as promised in the itinerary is not up to the mark.
- The hotel promised to the client in the itinerary has not been given. Instead, a similar hotel has been given.

- The hotel staff is not courteous.
- The room service is not good.
- The rooms of the hotel are not very big.
- The beds are not comfortable.
- There no tea/coffee making facilities such as tea bags, kettle and so on, and refrigerator, minibar etc. in the room.
- Linen in the room is not clean.
- Food being served at the hotel restaurant is not up to the mark.
- There are fewer facilities available in the hotel. (Every hotel may not provide amenities such as Wi-Fi, swimming pool, spas, gyms.)
- Some services are chargeable, for examples, in some hotels Wi-Fi facility is chargeable etc.
- The check-in timing of the hotel is not right (e.g., in many countries, the check-in timing is 1400 hours. The guests who reach early have to wait for the check-in timing that may lead to wastage of their time).

ITINERARY

Some guests might complain about the following things in an itinerary:

- The overall itinerary is too hectic. Too many destinations have been packaged that consumes a lot of travelling time during the whole itinerary.
- The wakeup call is too early.
- There is less time provided for sightseeing at particular attractions.
- There is not enough time given for shopping.
- There is too much of walking during the tour.
- There are not enough activities offered during the tour.
- The activities are being repeated (e.g., too much of cruising has been given at every destination on the tour).
- The activities are not value for money.

FOOD

The guests might have the following complaints about the food:

- The same kind of food items is being repeated.
- The food preparation is not proper.

- The food items have not been adequately labelled.
- The food being served is not hot.
- Specific items being served earlier have exhausted for the guests who have arrived late for their meals.
- There is no proper refilling on time while the guests have their meal.
- Special requests placed by some guests such as guests with allergies, vegans and vegetarians have not been taken care at the hotel/restaurant.
- Not enough local delicacies of a destination are being served in the menu on the tour.

RESTAURANTS

The guest may have the following valid grievances about a restaurant:

- The ambience of the restaurant is not good.
- The size of the restaurant is too small to accommodate the members of the group.
- The restaurant staff is not courteous.
- The quality of service offered by the restaurant staff is not up to the mark.
- The food is not good.

TOUR GUIDE

The guests may complain about the following things about a tour guide:

- The tour guide does not have enough knowledge.
- The tour guide gives false information.
- The tour guide has an attitude problem.
- The tour guide has a language barrier.
- The tour guide is not a good time manager.

COACH DRIVER

Certain things that the guest may complain about a tour driver are as follows:

- He drives too rash and does not take care of the safety of his guests.
- He does not follow the traffic rules.
- He takes too many breaks.
- He is very rude.

TOUR MANAGER

The complaints raised by the guests sometimes may relate to the tour manager himself. These may be associated with the following issues:

- The behaviour of the tour manager is rude. He is not soft-spoken.
- He is not very friendly with the guests.
- He is not able to keep up with the itinerary.
- He does not give a proper briefing at the destination.
- He is somewhat casual in his approach.
- He is very authoritative and dominating.
- He is a strict disciplinarian.
- He has inappropriate body language.
- He is not able to manage time well.
- He is not punctual.
- He is prejudiced towards some guests.
- He has less knowledge of the destinations.
- His accent is not clear and, hence, not understandable.
- He has a language issue with his guests.
- He is not able to handle his guest well.

PERSONAL GRIEVANCES

Some guests may have complaints related to others that may be as follows:

- The other people on the tour are not cooperative and do not get along with them.
- There are differences of opinion between the guests.
- Some guests are trying to dominate the whole group and so on.
- Some guests do not gel with others. They may remain on their own or with their friends and families.
- There are too many subgroups formed within the group.
- Some guests always come late due to which others suffer.
- Some guests are always trying to brag about themselves and the riches of life that they have.
- Some frequent travellers try to show that they know more than others.
- Some guests consume alcohol and abuse others.

DEALING WITH GRIEVANCES

Whatever may be the grievances of the guests, a tour manager must be able to handle the complaints gracefully without getting panicky or anxious about them. In the first place, it is essential to take complaints seriously and then find ways to resolve them. It is critical for the company and the tour manager as clients tend to share their bad experiences with more people as compared to their good experiences. This then can seriously impair the reputation of the company.

Also, with the growing popularity of trip review sites and social networking sites, all experiences of travellers are going viral. Though they may miss on sharing their pleasant experiences, they do not hesitate in sharing their negative experiences with others. Travellers use websites such as TripAdvisor etc. where they are very vocal about sharing their experiences with the world, and more specifically, the bad ones. They can write anything about the company if they are not satisfied with the company, which can severely affect the future business of the company.

Therefore, it is essential for a tour manager to address the grievances of his guests at the right time if they seem to be genuine. Otherwise, if not appropriately handled, things can blow out of proportion that may severely damage the image of both the tour manager as well as the company he is representing.

A few things that a tour manager can do at the least to fix the grievance may be as follows:

THANKING THE CLIENT

Complaints can sometimes be good for the company. It helps a company to improve its services. A tour manager on learning about the grievance raised by his guests must first thank his guest for bringing it to his notice. It is essential for both the tour manager and company to treat grievances as a gift that can help them improvise their services. Sometimes, guests give valuable suggestions to a tour manager or on the feedback form that can be eye-openers for a company. Certain things on a tour may not have caught adequate attention of the company. When such things are brought to the notice of the tour manager, it is a time for the tour manager and the company to reflect back instead of being complacent about the services being offered. These inputs to a firm can help them make their businesses better and bigger.

LISTENING TO THE AGGRIEVED PARTY

Listening to the aggrieved guest can really work like magic for the tour manager. It is very important for a tour manager to listen to the perspective of his guest. He must give a patient hearing to his guests' grievances. Listening can soothe the angry and aggrieved guests to a great extent.

Sometimes, guests know that certain situations (e.g., a delay in flight due to a technical glitch or bad weather) are beyond the control of a tour manager. However, when the tour manager listens to the guests' frustrations and grievances, the guests feel much better and comfortable. It is, therefore, just as crucial for a tour manager to lend all his ears to his guests to give them a vent out for their emotions. The right body language of the tour manager is also equally important that shows how seriously the tour manager is listening to the grievances of his guests.

EMPATHISING

A tour manager must try to put himself in the shoes of his guests. This helps him have a better perspective of the grievances bothering his guests. He may then be able to relate much better as to why his guests are behaving in a particular way. He must genuinely show his care and concern for his guests. The guests feel much better when they see that the tour manager understands their grievance by empathising with them.

APOLOGISING

Saying sorry works at times! The guests may be appeased when they know that the tour manager is confessing his fault or the company's fault when the things go wrong. This, to a great extent, can calm the ego of the guests.

SETTING A GRIEVANCE REDRESSAL SYSTEM

For a travel company to be successful, it must have a proper grievance redressal system in its place. A company must have an appropriate department of grievance redressal or staff dedicated to resolving the grievances of the guests. Such a grievance-handling mechanism may prevent the company from facing similar complaints in the future, thereby eventually retaining the business of the company.

PROMPT REDRESSAL OF GRIEVANCES

They say 'justice delayed is justice denied'. Therefore, a timely resolution of a grievance is very importance. If a complaint is not resolved on time, the guest may feel upset, and they may be very disappointed through the tour. Their whole holiday might get spoilt. Therefore, having good decision-making ability along with the knack of taking decisions on time is really important for a tour manager. For instance, if the coach does not have an excellent cooling system, the tour manager cannot afford to keep his guests travel in the same coach throughout the tour. He must not wait for the trip to get over and tell his company about the issue later who may decide not to use the services of that local transporter in the future and may give the contract to another local carrier. This situation demands an immediate intervention of the tour manager and the company. He may immediately apprise his company about the whole situation and may request for the change of coach from the local transporter. Meanwhile, till the arrangements are being made, he may continue with the itinerary by taking his guests in an alternative vehicle so that the itinerary remains undisturbed. Therefore, a tour manager must know when to act on the grievance so that the holiday of his guests is not spoilt.

KEEPING THE GUESTS INFORMED

Sometimes specific grievances may take time to get resolved. However, it is essential for a tour manager to keep his guests informed about the things that are being done on the backend to fix the issue. This makes the guests feel that the company is seriously taking action on their grievance.

UNDERSTANDING THE PULSE OF THE GROUP

It is essential for a tour manager to understand the pulse of his group members. He must understand the expectations of his guests and what makes them happy. He must be able to anticipate the things that the guests are likely to complain about. Accordingly, he must have a solution in his mind on how to resolve such issues.

SERVICE RECOVERY

Sometimes listening, empathising and apologising to the guests do not work. Guests demand an action on the services that went wrong. Therefore, service recovery is an important mechanism to keep the situations under control and make the aggrieved guests happy. It is very important for a tour manager to identify the service failures on a tour on time. He must know to handle the service failures smartly. A timely recovery of services can save the face of both the tour manager and the company. Otherwise, the future business of the company might be at stake and it may be severely affected by the negative word of mouth spread by the aggrieved guests.

KEEPING THE COMPANY INFORMED

Certain situations, in case of service recovery, demand an intervention of the company. At times, the service recovery may have cost implications. Therefore, it is advisable for a tour manager to discuss with his firm about the valid grievances raised by his guests that demand a service recovery. He may initiate an appropriate action only after getting the necessary go ahead of his company that may have financial implications for the company.

For example, at a restaurant, the food may not be enough for the guests, and some guests may go hungry. Therefore, the tour manager must arrange an alternative meal at another restaurant for his guests immediately to resolve the grievance that may have cost implications. Before taking his aggrieved guests to another restaurant, he must apprise his company about the exact scenario and must seek a prior approval as his decision may have cost implications for the company.

Also, sometimes, in certain situations, a tour manager may have to refund the money of his guests to soothe them when services are not delivered as promised. This may again have cost repercussions. Therefore, a tour manager must take the advice from his company while dealing with such situations. He must go by the rule of the book.

TIPS FOR A TOUR MANAGER TO HANDLE GRIEVANCES

A few handy tips that can help a tour manager to address the grievances more effectively and efficiently are as follows:

- A tour manager must maintain his cool while handling grievances.
- He must know that every grievance cannot be entertained.
- He must know to differentiate the genuine grievance from the disingenuous grievance.
- He must not get defensive on hearing about the grievances.
- He must not play the blame game by putting the ball in the court of the tour operator or local suppliers.
- He must be quick enough to apologise when things go wrong.
- He must not take things personally when guests share their grievances.
- It is advisable for a tour manager to reset the expectations of his guests preferably low so that the guests are mentally prepared to face the things on the tour.
- He at no point should get aggressive while dealing with the grievances of his guests.
- He must show a lot of patience while addressing the issues of his guests.

SUMMARY

It is not always bad to receive grievances. Grievances are an opportunity for the company to grow its business. They are also a means of forging everlasting relationships with the guests. Guests who complain and get their grievances resolved are likely to become more loyal clients of the company in the future. It is essential to fix the raised issues on time to retain the guests in the future.

Activity 1 **Jot the story**

Ask students to talk to some experienced tour manager and ask him to share an incident where he came across a grievance raised by the guest. Students may write a small story depicting the situation that a guest faced on a tour and also give the possible solutions on how to deal with it. Then ask students to present the same for a classroom discussion. Other students may suggest possible solutions.

Activity 2 What do I do?

Guests booked for the tour have not liked the hotel. They were promised a stay in five-star hotel but on the reaching the hotel, they found out that it was not a five-star category hotel. The guests are very annoyed and have teamed up together to protest. All the good hotels in the city are already booked due to a conference taking place there. Now what should the tour manager do?

POSSIBLE SOLUTIONS TO THE OPENING VIGNETTE

- Harry heard from both the clients and assessed the situation in his mind.
- To play safe and neutral, he asked them to toss with a coin and the one who wins shall be given a chance to sleep for the night on the king size bed. For both of them, this sounded fair.
- He also said that for the number of nights they stay in the hotel, they would give each other an alternative chance to sleep on the king size bed. This way he resolved the issue and it was an acceptable resolution for both.

Lessons Learned

- Presence of mind pays. A tour manager must have a strong presence of mind.
- A tour manager can't afford to be biased towards his guests. He must be objective in his approach.

24

Making Sense of Cultural Differences

LEARNING OBJECTIVES

- Make sense of cultural difference that is important for the tour manager.
- Share useful tips for tour manager to handle a cross-cultural situation.

Shadab was flabbergasted. For Shadab, the tour manager of Mohan Travels, it began as a pretty cool day. A group of six Spanish men came to see Jaipur. He was very excited to show them his city. The whole day was packed with a number of sightseeing visits and activities. Guests enjoyed themselves to the core. It was around 9:00 PM in the night, and Shadab was about to bid goodbye to his guests at the hotel lobby. Suddenly, Mike, a guest, expressed his wish to Shadab on behalf of the whole group that left Shadab loose his mind. On behalf of the whole group, Mike requested Shadab to arrange men for them for obvious reasons. Shadab was in a fix. He did not know what to do. Mike clarified that they were all homosexual. The situation was the first of its kind for him to handle.

A tour manager is likely to find himself in one of the two situations—either he would be handling an inbound group of international visitors or be accompanying an outbound group to a foreign destination. In the first situation, he will be interacting with foreigners from a different cultural background. In the second case, he would be leading a group of individuals to a foreign land where he must continuously advise the group on the sensibilities of the host culture. He may also have to interact with some service providers from a different cultural background. In the case of a trip to Europe, he might be accompanying the group at various destinations with different cultural characteristics.

Negotiating cultural differences is one of the essential skills a tour manager must possess. Every day is a new day, and every group is a new challenge for the tour manager. He needs to interact with people from different countries, different cultures, diverse religious backgrounds, from different socio-economic backdrops and even with individual idiosyncrasies. As a professional tour manager, you must make sense of individual's expectations drawn from various cultural backgrounds. It is essential to understand the differences in the cultural context from which an individual comes in order to serve an individual better. For this, a tour manager must have some idea of the primary ways in which cultures around the world vary.

INTRODUCTION

While it must be appreciated that it is nearly impossible for a tour manager to understand the cultural ethos of different people, yet he should be prepared, generally, to handle the differences. A starting point for this discussion is the understanding of the term culture. There are hundreds of definitions of culture. For some, it is the communicable knowledge—learned behaviour passed on from generation to generation at a place. Over time, these patterns of learned behaviour become the distinguishing characteristics and identity of the members of a given society. Culture in that sense is something that shapes the behaviour or structures the perceptions of members of a community about the world. Culture is, therefore, how an individual relates to the world around him. However, Jan Hofstede once said, 'Culture is more often a source of conflict than of synergy. Cultural differences are a nuisance at best and often a disaster'. A tour manager must, therefore, be cautious and conscious of situations that merit intercultural interactions.

Culture is understood differently. For most, a cultural difference is a difference in language including the body language, religion, food, music, clothing, fairs and festivals and so on. However, culture has a more profound connotation than just the tangible/visible manifestations. Culture is about shared values and beliefs that the community holds based on some underlying assumptions that have passed from one generation of the community to the other over hundreds of years. These assumptions and beliefs could be a result of many things including the history, geography, ecology and so on. The foundations of a culture in terms of assumptions, consensus, ideologies, mindset, philosophy, worldview and so on are so widely shared by the members of the group that they are mostly unaware of them and do not register their presence as they grow up in a cultural milieu. This foundation is the basis of the values and beliefs that the community holds. These may not be directly observable, but can be made out of how people explain and justify things. These include the cognitive process, beliefs, commitment, ethics, feelings, values, ideologies, justifications, vision, knowledge, sentiments and so on. This is how individuals connect with the world around them. This is manifest in more physical elements such as anecdotes, arts, ceremonies, communications, heroes, habits, jargon, language, myths, norms, physical arrangements, rituals, ceremonies, dresses, crafts and so on. Together with the shared values and beliefs, a cultural experience is created which is an essential part of the tourism product. Culture is an evolving phenomenon.

DIFFERENCES THAT MATTER ON A TOUR

While understanding and interpretation of a culture could be a herculean task, we will restrict ourselves to what is more practical from a tourist's point of view and, therefore, should be the focus of a tour manager's intervention. During a limited trip, a traveller is likely to come across a difference in four dimensions—time, space, communication and religious beliefs. We will discuss them one by one.

TIME

Time is believed to be a human construction. It is interpreted differently by different cultures. People from the USA, Canada or Northern Europe consider time to be linear and a limited resource. These are monochronic cultures. Since time is linear, people in these cultures like to do one thing at a time. Time is compartmentalised and distributed among different tasks to be arranged in a sequence with no two things being done at the same time. This is perceived as orderliness. Since time is a scarce resource, it has a monetary value similar to any other commodity. Thus, to be on time at a place is a cherished value. Interruptions are despicable. People focus on the job at hand and take commitments seriously. Thus, a tour manager attending personal phone calls, say, during a briefing would be despised. Or a tour manager arriving late for the day's excursion would be the last thing that a group from the West would tolerate. If the time to gather in the hotel lobby is 8:00 AM in the morning, the tour manager must definitely be there by 7:45 AM. No excuses entertained.

People from monochronic cultures show great respect for private property. Thus, respect for hotel property, the coach and even the monuments is expected from a visiting tour party. The tour manager must advise his group from Eastern cultures to be cautious about this. They must not mishandle any property. People from monochronic cultures are reluctant to be either a lender or borrower. They have great respect for privacy and follow norms of consideration. They would adhere to plans religiously. So, as a tour manager, you may be conscious of the fact that you do not violate the privacy of a visitor from a monochronic culture. They like certainty in plans and would avoid uncertainty regarding frequent changes in programs. There should be no or least changes in the itinerary. If there is change, the tour manager must come up with a valid argument and explain it to the group.

On the other end of the spectrum is the polychronic culture where people would like to do many things at the same time. The time is spiral instead of being linear. It is elastic and is in abundance. This is just another way of looking at the concept of time. Thus, people will have plenty of time for others. Therefore, a tour manager from the polychronic background will have an open-door policy, with a guest being free to approach him any time, with no or little concept of private time and privacy. By the same argument, the guest from a polychronic culture would expect the tour manager to be available for them all the time. Lines must be drawn delicately. To make sense of the local culture, the polychronic guest might ask questions which would appear to be 'personal' to a monochronic tour manager.

Polychronic cultures will like to do many things at the same time. A polychronic tour manager will accept many guests and try to attend to them at the same time. While he may take pride in being 'multitasking', his guests from monochronic cultures would consider him to be unprofessional. For him, attending a phone call in the middle of a meeting is absolutely OK. While they appear to be distracted, they will be willing to accept interruptions and would be ready to change plans often, easily and at the guests' convenience. It is a different cultural skill. They are relationship oriented rather than being task-oriented. With their people skills, they have an inclination to develop lifetime relationships. People from the Indian sub-continent, Latin America and Africa are polychronic.

SPACE

Another crucial cultural dimension that causes confusion is the concept and use of space. Based on the works of E.T. Hall, space could be divided into four kinds—the intimate space, personal space, social space and public space. The inner space is the intimate space in which very close persons tread to hug, kiss or embrace. This is a private place. In many Eastern cultures, individuals do not allow anyone in this space in public view. Beyond that is the personal space in which people who are psychologically close to us are allowed—the friends and family. In all cultures, people are sensitive to the use of personal space. Any violation of personal space is opposed. People display discomfort, anger or anxiety when their personal space is infringed. Beyond this is the social space used for interaction with acquaintances. This space is allowed for strangers, newly formed groups and new associates. Outside the social space is the space for public interactions such as theatre or public lecture. This is called the public space. Use of these spaces conveys meaning, for example, somebody entering a personal space is an indication of familiarity and closeness.

No one is taught the magnitude of these spaces. We subtly understand these spaces as we grow up in our cultural milieus. E.T. Hall has prescribed the size of these spaces. Intimate space is up to 18 inches. Personal spaces in between 18 inches to four feet. Social space is between four feet to 12 feet. And more than 12 feet is the public space. Interestingly, the extent and scope of these spaces in different in different cultures. For example, intimate space is really short in Latin America while it could be more substantial in Asia. So, what is intimate in India could just be the personal space in Mexico. While a client is just being friendly, the tour manager from India may interpret it as being an intimate advance. Americans need more personal space than other nationalities. They feel crowded easily in India and China which are densely populated countries, and where people expect and require less personal space. In hierarchical societies, space is used to convey one's social status. Rich and mighty people occupy more space to suggest their high social standing. Some celebrities hire guards to prevent commoners from invading their personal space.

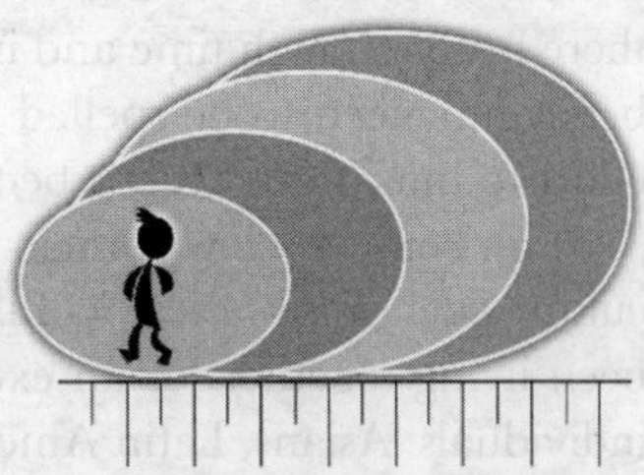

Intimate, Personal, Social, and Public Space

Spaces are situational also. On a busy day, metro trains are crowded, and people tend to be very physically close to each other. However, most people are non-acquaintances and are beyond the public space, even when they are spatially nearby. A tour manager must therefore not misconstrue the closeness of some clients as intimacy or distance of others as disinterest. He must interpret the use of space with his understanding of the cultural context of the customer. There are many reported untoward incidents of tour managers misinterpreting the use of space by visitors.

E.T. Hall coined the word proxemics in the 1950s. Proxemics is the study of space in the general sense along with its cultural interpretation. It helps to understand how the space around a person is understood by individuals at interactive and interpretive levels.

COMMUNICATIONS

Communication is best understood as high context or low context. High-context culture and low-context culture are the terms used to differentiate between cultures based on how explicit the exchanged message is or how much of context is employed in certain situations of communication.

A high context culture is when something is communicated within a context. Oriental communities with collectivistic societies tend to be high context cultures. People in these communities live closely over an extended period of time. This allows a shared understanding to develop. This is reflected in the way people communicate—fewer words and more of shared understanding. People understand what the norms are, how to think and how to behave, so the norms do not have to be explicitly stated. This makes high-context cultures challenging to navigate for those who do not understand the culture's unwritten norms. So, in a high context communication, the listener is already 'contexted' and does not need much background information. Communication involves the use of contextual elements such as body language, social status, the tone of voice and indirect messages which are not explicitly stated.

On the other hand, in low-context communication, the listener knows very little and must be told practically everything. Information is communicated clearly through language, and norms of communication are explicitly spelled out. In low context societies, people tend to form many but short-term associations with others. These relationships are in turn for some particular purpose. Thus, there is not enough time and interest to develop an understanding. Therefore, belief and norms of behaviour need to be spelled out clearly so that those entering the cultural environment expend effort to interpret it. It has been clearly stated.

High context—low context is not an either–or choice. It is situational. Even within a low context culture such as America, within the family, the communication may be high context as a family has been living together for an extended period. Generally, Americans and Germans are low context individuals. Asians, Latin American and Africans are high context people.

A tour manager's job is to communicate with the group for logistics and interpretation of the place. In both these situations, he must understand the background of his clients. A tour manager from a high context culture cannot assume the same for a German guest, who must be given specific instructions during every briefing. On the contrary, when a low context tour manager shares details with high context guests, they subject it to their own interpretation rather than taking it on face value. While on his part, the tour manager must have laid out the rules of the tour, the high context individuals will still hover around expecting departures from the stated position. They do not consider the rules as cast-in-concrete.

RELIGION

Religion is one of the elements that affect culture and is tangibly distinguishable in most cases. Religion is a codified belief system which allows or disallows certain things, thereby making it evident. There are some physical elements such as places of worship, dress code, religious symbols and motifs, architectural elements and so on. Then there are intangible elements such as rituals and religious practices. Both these elements contribute to cultural distinctiveness.

Both culture and religion are human constructs. Each is having its own symbols and manifests. Over time, the distinction between religious and cultural seems difficult to maintain. It makes more sense to think of religion as a sub-system of some cultural systems. Culture can exist outside of faith. Religion can colour the local culture but can also transcend different cultures. Culture is a way of life; religion is a belief system. Religion is one part of the culture. There are others as well.

Religion tends to be codified. It involves rituals, books or activities that are written down or taught in a particular form and preserved more or less the same. Religion, once codified, changes slowly. Culture, on the other hand, is generally not codified. It can be described and makes changes more quickly in response to external environmental forces. One such force is often the influence of religion.

Often the line between religion and culture is very fine. In practice, it is hard to distinguish between a religious and a cultural element. The two are often combined. Further, these could be sensitive issues for an individual. Tour managers are faced with many such situations. There may be persons in the group who are religious and submit themselves to certain kinds of religious–cultural restrictions. Many Indians are vegetarians. Muslims don't consume pork. Jews will have only kosher meat. A tour manager must be aware of his groups' religious preferences. They must be honoured, and personal space for adhering to religious customs may be provided to an individual as far as possible. A group, on the other hand, as part of their itinerary, would be visiting some holy places—churches, temples, mosques, synagogues and so on. The tour manager must be aware of the sensibilities of these sacred places and must advise the group accordingly. For example, he must instruct them on the proper way to dress while they visit a church or a mosque.

USEFUL TIPS FOR MANAGING THE CULTURAL DIFFERENCES

Here are some general tips to prepare to meet tourists/clients from different cultural backgrounds:

- Allow yourself time to ensure how different are your customers from you, whether they think like you or not.

- Try to read their facial expressions. Do they understand what you mean or do they despise your thoughts? In the case of the latter, retract as soon as possible.
- Watch the body movements of your guests and try to decipher what they mean.
- Start with efforts to build personal relationships through the exchange of non-business pleasantries; the earlier the better.
- Watch for and try to interpret vocalics such as laughing, coughing, yawning and so on.
- Try to learn about the differences between your guest's social, political and economic systems and yours. The tour manager will generally know about the group in advance. Some homework is desirable.
- Try to make sense of how the aforementioned differences affect his thinking, authority and methods of learning.
- Know your tourist's legal, technical and financial systems.
- Understand how these systems will affect your choice of tactics.
- Understand the effects of ethical standards (right, wrong and reasonable).
- Understand the importance of face-saving. This is paramount. Western directness is considered rude and insulting in the Eastern world. People from the oriental culture would not like to lose face. Tour managers must ensure this that they do not humiliate their guests.
- Recognise the role of status.
- Ask questions, but do not put pressure.
- Avoid using jargon. Use simple language.
- Explain in detail. Summarise. And test their understanding to ensure if the guests have understood what you have told them.
- Use both verbal and non-verbal techniques to support ideas, for example, use 'I' language to convey that the speaker accepts responsibility for what he or she is saying.
- Maintain eye contact with others as eye contact communicates sincerity, concern and involvement.
- Show a relaxed attitude towards time. Do not place unnecessary pressure on them and yourself by creating artificial deadlines that cannot be honoured. Remember tourists are here for leisure.
- Use your face to show pleasant feelings, smile or mild laugh.
- Dress elegantly; be neat and presentable.
- Demonstrate personal hygiene; be clean and have no offensive odour.

SUMMARY

A tour manager is often faced with challenges to deal with guests from different cultural backgrounds. He may try his best to serve them. However, he may not be understood or perceived differently. Since guest would be from a variety of backgrounds, it will not be possible for him to learn about any particular cultural background. Even if he claims to understand a cultural context, still, people from this background are likely to behave differently. In this chapter, we have discussed the four essential constructs of culture that are relevant to a tour manager. These include interpretation of space, the connotation of time, high versus low context communication and the difference in religious beliefs. The chapter also suggests that a tour manager, instead of trying to jump to a conclusion about the behaviour of an individual as right or wrong, should practise to make sense of the underlying difference and, thus, try to predict the behaviour of the guest.

Activity 1 Dealing with different nationalities

Identify the cultural differences between Americans and Japanese. How would you deal in a situation as a tour manager when tourists from these two nationalities are in the same group?

Activity 2 Make a collage

Divide students into groups and ask them to bring one chart each and lots of magazines and newspapers. Now ask them to sit on the floor with their respective groups and create an attractive collage depicting people from different nationalities and cultures. Now, weave a story around the pictures and give it an appropriate caption. Remember the story should relate to each and every picture depicted in the collage. The theme of the story should revolve around taking the group of guests as a tour manager to various destinations and how the tour manager comes across difficult situations dealing with people from different nationalities and how he ultimately deals with such situations.

POSSIBLE SOLUTIONS TO THE OPENING VIGNETTE

- Shadab maintained his cool and didn't react negatively. He politely told them he doesn't have any knowledge about the demand they have made and it's against his company policy.
- He contacted his company and apprised them about the client's demands. The company suggested Shadab to brief them about the LGBT scenario in India and all the legalities involved in it.
- On his company's advice, he oriented his guests about the LGBT scenario in India. He further advised his group members that it is against their company policy to indulge in such activities, that is, providing sex workers. He also told his guests that if they are found to indulge in any such activity, they might have to face legal consequences.
- On knowing about this, the group apologised to him and they actually explained Shadab that they had misunderstood the Indian socio-cultural dynamics as they saw two men holding each other's hand. They presumed that asking for sex workers may be permitted in India. Shadab oriented his guests that that holding each other's hand is common in India and doesn't mean the other way around.

Lessons Learned

- A tour manager must brief his guests about the local sensitivities of his destination at the beginning of the tour. He must explain in detail the cross-cultural differences that exist in a country.
- The tour manager must understand that his guests are from a different cultural background and hold a different cultural values and sets of beliefs. They are not necessarily wrong; they are just being different.
- The most important lesson for a tour manager is not to quickly arrive at conclusions about his guests, and judge them as 'right' or 'wrong'. They are simply 'different'.
- He must allow himself some time to make sense of the cultural ethos of his guests. The more experienced the tour manager is, the more quickly he is likely to make sense of the differences.

25

Handling Emergency Situations

LEARNING OBJECTIVES

- What kinds of emergency situations can a tour manager encounter on a tour?
- What are the things that a tour manager must take care of while dealing with emergency situations?

Sukhi, the tour manager, was very perturbed. He had never come across such a situation in his whole life! This was a group of mixed nationalities, primarily from the UK, Australia and New Zealand. Otherwise it was a day of unusual adventure. The group was visiting the Chitwan National Park in Nepal. A local guide who had local knowledge about the park was also hired to assist the tour manager. Guests were enjoying the wilderness of the park, strolling on foot and making their way to the park. They were excited to see the wildlife from up close. All of a sudden, all the fun and adventure was cut short by a scream. It was a man shouting for help. When everyone turned back to the direction of the scream, they saw something that their eyes could not even believe. A mother rhino had wildly attacked their local tour guide. Guests found themselves hardly any distance away from the incident. They ran for their own life. In no time, the local tour guide was dead. Everyone was taken aback. They were in shock. There was blood all around. Sukhi was nervous and the group looked up to him.

The job of a tour manager is not an easy cakewalk. It involves lots of challenges and difficulties that one may not even anticipate. A tour manager may have to encounter unforeseen circumstances on a tour. Sometimes it can be nerve wrecking for a tour manager.

Along with the good experiences, this profession brings along a bundle of stressful situations that a tour manager sometimes may not even be prepared to handle. A tour manager may face a variety of emergency situations in his career. However, the nature of the challenge may vary from one situation to another. A tour manager may be guided by the mantra of 'expect the unexpected' on a tour.

Emergency situations may be defined as those situations that are uncalled for. These are undesirable situations that may happen to the guests on a tour. Sometimes, not always, these circumstances may have an element of risk and danger involved with them. Every tour manager seeks that his guests have an exciting experience on the tour. However, this may not always happen. Some experiences are never even thought of on a tour that may be very unpleasant both for the guests and the tour manager to handle. However, with more experience of managing guests, a tour manager may learn to anticipate situations with the passage of time. He may able to assess the possible risks and ways of dealing with them. However, he can never be sure enough of what issue he might have to deal with in an unpredictable future.

TYPES OF EMERGENCY SITUATIONS

The emergency situations faced by a tour manager may be classified on the following basis.

EMERGENCY SITUATIONS CREATED BY CLIENTS

These kinds of situations may arise from client's side. These may further be classified as situations that may occur due to client's negligence or due to a deliberate attempt made by the client. Some cases may also be related to the client but may happen by accident. Whereas there still may be situations that may arise due to awkward behaviours of the clients. Examples of each classification are as follows.

Cases Due to Client's Negligence

- Loss of passport
- Loss of personal belongings and valuables at a destination
- Leaving things at a hotel, restaurant, sightseeing attraction etc. by mistake

Situations Created Due to Client's Deliberate Actions

- Shoplifting
- Accident of a client due to client's non-adherence to the safety procedures (e.g., a client falling from the boat accidentally and drowning as he refuses to follow the instructions to wear the life jacket)

Uncontrollable Situations with a Client

- Ill health of a client such as an allergy, diarrhoea, altitude sickness and sea sickness
- Injury or accident like an ankle twist

- Road accident of a client
- Heart attack of a client on a tour
- Death of a client on a trip
- Family issue of a client due to which he has to return home in emergency

EMERGENCY SITUATIONS BEYOND ANYONE'S CONTROL

These are the factors that are beyond the control of a tour manager. If not handled correctly, some of these situations may have massive repercussions on the life of the guests. These may be as follows:

- Natural calamities such as floods, earthquakes etc.
- Adverse weather conditions such as rain, heat, strong winds etc.
- Communal riots
- Terrorist attacks or blasts
- The outbreak of an epidemic such as SARS, swine flu, Ebola and so on
- Political instability
- Sudden change of government policy (e.g., demonetization in India in November 2016)
- Traffic jams
- Bad road conditions

EMERGENCY SITUATIONS CREATED BY VARIOUS SERVICE PROVIDERS

Some conditions may be generated due to the unforeseen circumstances or sheer negligence of the service providers. As tourism industry is dependent on all the service providers; any service not offered correctly or on time may create a bad experience for the guests. Such situations may demand an immediate intervention by the tour manager. Some of these may be classified as follows:

- Postponement or cancellation of flights/trains due to bad weather or a technical glitch by airlines/railways
- Loss of luggage/damaged luggage by carriers
- Embassy/consulate mistakes in visa issuance, for example, wrong name or passport number, visa validity and so on
- Airlines issuing the ticket with the wrong name
- Hotel rooms not ready on time
- Food not prepared in the local restaurant
- Limited meal for the guest
- Poor condition of coach
- Breakdown of bus
- Overpromising about the services by the travel company
- Increase in taxes by airlines, hotels and so on

DEALING WITH EMERGENCIES

Let us have a detailed discussion on the things that a tour manager must take care of while dealing with emergency situations on a tour.

MAINTAINING HIS COOL

Two things are critical while handling such cases. First, a tour manager must keep his cool and not panic when things go wrong. Second, he must calmly evaluate all possible alternatives and think logically as to which solution can be the most suitable for handling a particular situation. He must determine all possible pros and cons of the situation, and then make a calculative move in the light of circumstances.

He might face different challenges on the tour. Whatever be the situation, a tour manager must be guided by the principle that he has to be always ready to take things as they come on the tour. Under no circumstances should he succumb or lose his heart. He must chivalrously face an odd situation that might come his way with sheer willpower and undeterred faith during the tour. He must be gracefully able to get hold of the situation that he is likely to handle instead of panicking around. He must stay calm and poised.

INFORMING THE COMPANY

While dealing with unforeseen situations, a tour manager must apprise his company about the situation and wait for their necessary instructions. This helps him to get guidance that may help him to assist his guest in a better way, and also, the company may be able to make some special arrangements for the guests that may facilitate the tour manager in handling the whole situation in a better way. For example, if the coach is in poor condition, the company may liaison with the local transporter or local agent and arrange for an alternative coach. The tour manager may not be in a situation to assess the cost implications or legalities attached to the solutions. At times, to resolve the situation, a considerable amount of company's money may be involved. Therefore, he must be able to take his company's management approval before arriving at any decision. Also, sometimes, a tour manager might be handling a situation for the first time in which he does not have a prior experience. Therefore, he may seek guidance from his company operations team who has an earlier experience of handling such situations. Since the operations team of the company is away from the real situation, they may be better placed to think about more alternative options more objectively and rationally as compared to the tour manager who may be a bit nervous and anxious to deal with the situation.

However, he must remember that he should not disturb his company for every small issue that he might encounter. The tyre of the car may get a puncture, an attraction may be closed due to an event or the guest might report an allergy. He should not report such petty issues to his company representatives. Instead, he may resolve such small matters at his own end.

TAKING DECISIONS

A tour manager must have the capability of making spontaneous decisions that may be the demand of the situation. His timely decisions can sometimes save the life of his guests. Weighing the pros and cons of each possible alternative is essential for arriving at a right decision by the tour manager. Therefore, spontaneity and timeliness are two necessary qualities that a tour manager must have while handling emergency situations.

BEING PROACTIVE

For taking better decisions, a tour manager must be able to anticipate challenges. He must be proactive in his approach. He must have a nose for sensing the issues, and he must also find possible solutions in his mind in case, a particular situation happens. He must be able to anticipate situations and have workable solutions in his mind.

PREPARATION TO DEAL WITH A SITUATION

As they say that 'prevention is better than cure', preparing for any kind of crisis situation is a must for the tour manager to deal with them in a better way. For example, before boarding a coach, a tour manager must know the course of action in case a fire breaks out in the coach. He must imagine such expected situations in his mind. Then, he should procure himself with the right options in case any such unfortunate incident happens on the tour. For example, in this case, before he starts the trip on the coach, he must figure out the location of the fire extinguisher, emergency door, emergency window, hammer and first aid box inside the coach. He should also carry with him the local numbers of the fire station and ambulance to deal with this emergency situation, in case it happens.

KEEPING THE GUESTS INFORMED

It is also advisable for a tour manager to keep his guests informed about the situation and the possible alternatives that are being looked upon. Keeping the guests in the loop may help in seeking their favourable support and cooperation. It further helps in confidence building, and the guests also feel more comfortable that they are being involved. Besides their collaboration, the guests may sometimes have better ideas of dealing with a particular situation that may not have come to the mind of the tour manager. For example, if the coach has not arrived on time at the hotel for sightseeing, the guest may like to know as to why there is a delay in the departure for the sightseeing. Instead of offering lame excuses to the guests with different explanations', a tour manager may be honest in sharing the exact scenario that might have happened. The following may be the possible reasons for the coach getting late:

1. The driver got late as he woke up late.
2. He was stuck up in a traffic jam.
3. He went for refuelling the vehicle.
4. The tyre of the coach got punctured.
5. He went to get the coach cleaned.

Whatever be the reasons, a tour manager must share the actual reason for the occurrence of the situation and may also tell his guests the possible time required to fix the problem. This helps the guests to prepare themselves mentally so that they may not keep haggling the tour manager with individual questions as to what happened and when will they proceed with the tour and so on. Ultimately, honesty pays! For example, in this situation, if a tour manager knows it shall take two hours for the driver to reach the hotel, he may ask his guest to visit the local markets on their own. Alternatively, he may arrange another coach meanwhile from a local transporter or the GHA and proceed for the days' sightseeing tour.

INVOLVING GUESTS IN FINDING SOLUTIONS

Sometimes, the guests can also give better solutions to the problems. This makes it easier for a tour manager to get out of a situation as he actively secures the willing cooperation and support of his guests by seeking their advice. However, a tour manager must not any point of time let his guests feel that they are in charge of the situation. A tour manager must always show that he is just seeking advice from them, but his decision shall prevail final.

THANKING THE GUEST FOR THEIR COOPERATION

It is not possible for a tour manager to come out of any situation unless and until he has the support of his guests. A tour manager must, therefore, after the situation has been handled, always take a suitable opportunity to express his gratitude towards his guests for cooperating with him during the crisis that they all faced together.

COMMUNICATING THE GUESTS ABOUT THE POSSIBLE RISKS

It is always advisable for a tour manager to inform his guest about the potential risks involved in a situation. For any guest, safety is of prime concern. The same should be the top priority of the tour manager, and he should not compromise with the safety of his guest. He must inform his guests about the possible safety hazards that may occur if the tour manager does not fix a problem on time or if the guest does not abide by the rules. This helps the guest to understand the situations and appreciate the course of action initiated by the tour manager. For instance, before taking his guests for water sports and adventure, he must warn his guests about the possible dangers and the ways of dealing with them. His idea should not be to scare his guest but to give a word of caution from his end so that the guests are aware of the possible risks involved in a situation. Especially, if he feels that some people have some ailments, he must advise them of the activities accordingly, keeping in mind the health of his guests.

EMERGENCY MANAGEMENT PROTOCOL

Most of the travel companies have emergency management procedures that lay out the standard operating procedures (SOPs) on how to tackle emergency situations. The staff of these travel companies has clear-cut guidelines on addressing emergency situations that are well communicated to the tour manager during their training. At times, they are also documented in the manuals given to the tour managers by the tour operator/travel agent.

Therefore, it is expected of a tour manager to be adept in handling situations that have been already discussed in the training manual. However, some situation, besides those laid out in the company's manual and standard procedures, may arise for the first time. In such cases, a tour manager may seek the advice of operations team or speak to senior colleagues', that is, senior tour managers who may have handled similar cases earlier. A tour manager may also seek the assistance of other travel agents/tour operators who may be similarly placed at a destination. For instance, if there is a sudden flood, the tour manager may ask the other companies and their tour managers as to what they are doing in such situation. As another example, a cruise may have been booked for the guest. Due to the sudden outbreak of floods, the companies have to cancel the cruise as the safety of guests shall always come first. Now the tour manager may have to change the itinerary accordingly, and has to offer some other sightseeing attraction or activity to compensate for the cruise that could not happen due to floods for this, he may have to seek the assistance of a local agent that should be in consultation with his own company.

SUBMITTING AN INCIDENT REPORT

Many travel companies expect the tour manager to submit an incident report. An incident report has all the details of the kind of emergency situations that occurred during a particular tour led by the tour manager and the steps that were taken by him to bring the crisis under his control.

A tour manager must, therefore, give a detailed account of such emergency situations to his company after the completion of a tour. Such documentation by the tour manager facilitates the company in understanding the kind of ground realities that a tour manager faces, and also gives them valuable insights as to what can be the better solutions of handling such similar situations in the future. The company may also identify the lacunae that may help manage similar situations in the future.

CONTINGENCY PLANNING

A tour manager must also have backup plans. This is called as contingency planning. As anything can happen anytime on a tour, a tour manager must have alternatives/options available to him. For example, if Plan A doesn't work out, he must be ready with Plan B. Let us take an example here. Let us say, under the operational plan, an activity under the open skies has been planned for the guest for a day. For example, a heritage walk has been proposed for the guests to walk from one heritage site to another. Suddenly, it starts raining heavily. The activity has to be called off and replaced with another one as guests can't walk under heavy rains, though in lighter showers they may walk wearing a rain poncho or carrying an umbrella. Now, the tour manager must be able to rework out the itinerary. He may plan another activity like an indoor tour such as a visit to an indoor stadium, museum, art gallery and so on. The rule for the tour manager should be that the guests' time should not be wasted and their expectations set before the tour by the company must be met out by him at any cost.

SUMMARY

A tour manager has a duty of cure towards his guests. The safety of the guests always comes first. He carries the onus of his company's reputation. How he tackles the situation without compromising the safety and security of his guests decides his own reputation and that of the company he works for. Every tour led by the tour manager may not be a smooth ride for him. Every trip comes bundled with different situations that a tour manager may not be ready for or may have not even thought of. A tour managers' job is therefore very challenging. Every day can pose a different challenge for the tour manager that he may be uncomfortable to deal with. However, the rule of the game is to take these situations as an opportunity for learning new aspects of this profession as well as of life. Every case handled by a tour manager instils confidence within the tour manager and makes him better procured to deal with any situation in the future.

Activity 1 How would you handle this?

In Dubai while leading a group of tourists during a desert safari, a guest fainted due to a heat stroke. He requires immediate medical attention now. At the same time, there are 20 other tourists with you who are busy enjoying the safari. What will you do as a tour manager now to deal with this situation?

Activity 2 **The child goes missing**

You are leading a group of Spanish guests in the busy and overcrowded streets of Chandni Chowk. You have two children in the group too. Suddenly, as you are leading ahead, a Spanish couple in your group runs to you for help. Their child goes missing? What will you do now? What would be an appropriate course of action? Let different groups identify solutions for the same situation. The teacher may moderate the session and ask each group to make a presentation on the same.

POSSIBLE SOLUTIONS TO THE OPENING VIGNETTE

- To deal with the situation, Sukhi, the tour manager acted on the spot seeking the assistance of some forest guards who were present there. They all tried to drive away the wild animal and calm it. They also made a stretcher out of the bamboos and their clothes to take the dead body of the tour guide.
- All the tourists were immediately evacuated from the site and were taken to the safe zone.
- To deal with this trauma, the company arranged for sessions for its aggrieved guests with the psychiatrist.
- They all signed a disclaimer and paid gratuities to the deceased's family.

Lessons Learned

- A tour manager must never give up hope at any time. He must demonstrate that he is still in charge of the situation.
- The safety of his guests should be his top priority. He must do everything to save the life of his guests.
- After the emergency, at the first instance, he must share what had happened and what is that they are going to do next.

26

Some More Tricky Situations

This last chapter presents some challenging circumstances faced by the tour managers while on the job. Learners should ponder over these cases. One of the possible solutions is given. This is not even a suggested solution. Tour managers must use their creativity to offer better solutions.

THAT FATEFUL NIGHT!

Sumit was leading a mixed group of travellers who were all from different countries of Europe. He was on a tour to Rajasthan with 25 guests. It was a late night. Everyone was sleeping in their respective rooms in Kishangarh, a small town in Rajasthan. Suddenly, Evic called Sumit in the middle of the night and complained of severe pain in his shoulders and chest. At the spur of the moment, Sumit left his room to attend to Evic only to realise that Evic was no more. Sumit was in a state of shock!

Possible Solution

- Immediately, Sumit decided first to take him to the hospital and admitted him there.
- After the doctor declared the client was dead due to a heart attack, he immediately informed his company about the whole incident.
- Sumit also called the insurance company that was handling his travel insurance.
- He also informed the concerned embassy about the sad demise of its national, and he asked them to arrange a flight back home for the dead body.
- The deceased client's family was also informed by the company.
- Sumit also completed all the formalities to acquire the dead body.
- In the morning, Sumit informed the whole group about the sudden demise of the fellow client. He organised a small prayer for the departed soul and motivated his group to continue with their tour with another tour manager.
- Sumit had to take the dead body to the nearest airport and from there to the international airport where he handed over the documents and body to the embassy staff.

Lessons Learned

- A tour manager must be emotionally powerful to handle any unforeseen situation.
- He must have the know-how of the legal procedures and formalities required to be completed in such cases.
- Also, when the guest calls in the middle of the night for any issue that is bothering them, he should never go inside the room of the client alone. He must take a hotel staff along with him.

PHOTOGRAPHY THAT COSTED!

Vishal, the tour manager, was with his German group on a tour in Uttarakhand, a state in India, near the Alaknanda river for the sightseeing. Everybody was enjoying the scenic views and having great fun. A couple from the group was also randomly clicking some photographs when Vishal noticed that the male client was just standing at the corner of the cliff to get clicked. In spite of repeated instructions and warnings being given by Vishal to get off the edge of the cliff, the client did not pay any heed to it. The wife of the client was videographing the whole incident, and suddenly a mishap happened. The client suddenly fell from the cliff in to the river, and everyone was in a state of dismay.

Possible Solution

- Vishal immediately called his company staff to convey the whole incident to them.
- He also sent the footage of the video taken by his wife as evidence to reinstate that he was continuously warning the client to get off the click.
- Meanwhile, Vishal tried to find the body of client and informed the nearest police station about the incident.
- He also had a word with the insurance company as to how the travel insurance could be claimed by the wife of the client.
- Besides, he also tried to empathise with the wife in the moment of her grief.

Lessons Learned

- A tour manager must always give necessary instructions to his clients.
- He must admonish them when he sees them getting involved in any kind of dangerous activity. A word of caution from the tour manager's side can save the life of a client as well as work as a shield for him.

EDWIN LOSES HIS BAG!

Raghav was leading a group of 22 Germans who had come on a tour to India and Nepal. The group was at the Wagah border in Amritsar during the beating retreat ceremony. As usual, the place was densely crowded. After the ceremony got over and the clients were returning, one of the clients, Edwin, realised that his bag was stolen. The bag carried his passport, the most critical document for a foreign tourist. He got panicky and immediately informed Raghav, the tour manager. What can Raghav do?

Possible Solution

- Immediately, Raghav got into the action mode and first communicated to his office about this.
- Then he went with the client to lodge an FIR about the loss of passport at the nearest police station.
- He also sent the copy of FIR to his company.
- Later, all documentation and further formalities required by the German embassy were taken care of by the company in the Delhi.
- On producing the right documentation, the embassy issued a temporary passport and visa to Edwin, and this way he could continue his tour.

Lessons Learned

- A tour manager must always brief his guests to take care of their belongings at crowded places so that the guests are extra wary of their personal stuff.
- A word from the tour manager's side can help prevent pilferage or similar incidents.
- He must also be aware of the legal formalities required to be done in case of loss of a passport.
- It is essential that the tour manager carries a copy of the clients' passports as part of his group file in case of loss of passport.

THE COACH BREAKS DOWN

It was a scary night. The bus was on its way to Rishikesh from Dehradun with 30 guests who had come from USA. Most of the guests were sleeping in the coach when the coach broke down midway. There was no mechanic available nearby as it was dense forest all around. The darkness enveloped every one and animals in the jungle were howling. It was getting scary with every passing moment. All the guests, along with Sameer, the tour manager of the group, ran short of ideas. It was dark and cold, and the bus seems to be heading nowhere. Sameer knew little about what he should be doing.

Possible Solution

- Sameer immediately called his company staff and apprised them of the situation.
- However, the company asked Sameer to handle such a situation on his own.
- Immediately, Sameer called his local agent and asked him to arrange for an alternative coach. However, he was confirmed about the non-availability of the coach by the local agent.

- Immediately, to get out of this situation, Sameer asked his local agent to arrange for cabs for his group members so that they may reach the hotel safely at the earliest and get rid out of this situation.
- Meanwhile, Sameer tried to soothe his group members and apprised them about the alternative arrangements being done to ensure their safety at the earliest.
- On seeing the cabs coming in no time, guests took a respite and went to the hotel safely.
- The luggage of the guests was transferred the next day to the hotel when the coach machinery got fixed.

Lessons Learned

- A tour manager may know the basic mechanics of the coach. He should just not be dependent on the tour driver. He can be a help.
- Also, he should be able to make on-the-spot decisions.
- He should inform the company about the situation in which the party is stuck.
- Possessions such as a torch, battery backup and so on will come handy in these kinds of situations.

WHEN CUSTOMER LOST HER PURSE

A group of 50 tourists from the state of Kerala were standing at Charbagh Station, Lucknow, to board a train for Varanasi. While everyone was waiting for the train to arrive at the platform, suddenly everyone heard Mrs Joe shouting to the top of her voice. Everybody, including Shiveta, who was leading the group, was taken aback for a moment. Mrs Joe was quite an old lady, aged 78 years. It took her a moment to understand as to what exactly happened with her. She just realised that her purse was lost. A group of three burglars who were standing close to her snatched her purse instantly and ran away in no time. The purse contained her valuables such as a smartphone, voter ID and ₹10,000 in cash. Mrs Joe started crying loudly, and there was a massive crowd of passengers that accumulated all around her.

Possible Solution

- To handle the situation, Shiveta called the government railway police stationed at the railway station.
- She asked Mrs Joe to narrate the whole incident to the police and lodge an FIR.
- The police provided Mrs Joe with the lost property certificate.
- And then, Shiveta continued the tour with the group. However, the valuables lost by Mrs Joe were never retrieved by her.
- Shiveta tried to console her (client) for her loss.
- Shiveta also advised her to claim her lost valuables through the travel insurance she had done for the tour.

Lessons Learned

- A tour manager must know how to immediately respond to situations and take the right actions at the right time.
- Talking to other colleagues, the tour managers learn about such incidents and how these were handled. After that, they can remain partially conscious of such events and ways to handle it.
- He must ask his guests to remain vigilant at all times.

AN ELDERLY CLIENT GETS ILL!

An elderly Spanish couple, Mrs and Mr Fernando was on their dream destination to India. Spellbound by the rich culture and tradition of India, they chose Rajasthan as the place to visit. They wanted to experience the vibrant hospitality and royalty of Indians. Accordingly, it was decided that they visit the historic cities of Rajasthan that included Jaipur, Udaipur and Jodhpur. Sasha was their tour manager.

Upon reaching the Indira Gandhi International Airport in Delhi, they deboarded the plane with their check-in baggage and came at the arrival hall where Sasha, their tour manager was waiting with a placard and a garland of flowers to receive his guests. Due to the scarcity of time, they decided to head straight for Jaipur. Therefore, they sat in a taxi and left for Jaipur. After an hour of the journey, Mr Fernando started feeling uneasy. He was feeling feverish. On enquiring as to what precisely the guest was feeling, Mr Fernando told Sasha that he was suffering from cancer and that he had left his medicines on the plane. Sasha was taken aback for a while.

He just took a while to assess the whole situation and then decided how to deal with it. He realised that the old couple had not mentioned in the medical history that Mr Fernando was a cancer patient.

Possible Solution

- Immediately on learning about the situation, Sasha took them to the nearest hospital. However, the hospital did not have a cancer medication facility.
- Not taking any risk, Sasha decided to return to Delhi, first of all, to treat Mr Fernando before his situation could blow out of proportion.
- After getting proper treatment, when Mr Fernando felt that he was fit enough to travel and the doctor also certified that he could travel, Sasha decided to continue the trip with them.
- At every moment, he took special care of his guests and made special arrangements for them wherever required keeping in mind the health of Mr Fernando. He extended his full support and cooperation to Mr Fernando and his wife, and they both returned home with sweet memories of the trip.

Lessons Learned

- A tour manager must give top priority to the health of his clients. He should only resume the trip once the doctor certifies that the traveller is fit enough to travel.
- If his guest is not feeling well, he must not push him to travel and should instead take them to the doctor for the treatment at the first instance.

MYRA CAUGHT RED-HANDED!

It was 7:00 PM, and yes, the most awaited shopping time for the group. They wanted to not only shop for themselves but also buy some souvenirs for their family and friends. Myra and Saisha were the most excited ones about Thailand shopping. John, the tour leader, took them to their shopping destination which was a marketplace with all the wonderful fancies of the world for all kinds of shoppers. Myra and Saisha went inside a souvenir store to buy some stuff for their friends and relatives. Saisha bought certain stuff and got it billed. The moment they were about to step out of the exit gate, a siren went off. Everyone from the group ran to see what happened with the girls. The staff ran to check the items taken by these girls. It was the most embarrassing moment for Myra. She was stuck! It appeared to be a case of shoplifting! Shopkeepers insisted they call the police.

Possible Solution

- On being informed about the incident by the shopkeeper, John reached the shop where the incident took place.
- On checking by the staff, it was detected that Myra had not got two items billed.
- Further, the CCTV camera footage clearly revealed that it was a case of shoplifting.
- The shopkeeper called the local police and immediately apprised them of the whole situation. Myra was taken to the police station. Everyone was taken aback.
- The tour manager apologised to the shopkeeper on behalf of his guests.
- He also went to the police station to get bail for Myra so that she was out of the jail.
- On being released, John asked Myra to clear all his dues for getting her bail papers prepared.
- Myra felt very embarrassed as it not only humiliated John along with the group members, but it also brought a bad name to her country. Besides this, a lot of time was lost during the case investigation and preparation of bail papers by the tour manager. Myra felt very apologetic for the whole incident.

Lessons Learned

- A tour manager must necessarily share stories of such incidents with the guests that may help them to understand the sensitivities involved in the situations.
- A tour manager must ask his guests to keep the integrity of their nationality up in another country always.

LAILA HAS THE NAME WRONG ON THE TICKET!

Laila was very excited to travel to Mauritius with her husband after having visited with her group to India from Australia. The arrangements for going to Mauritius were made by an India-based travel company.

Laila woke up all excited in the morning to visit Mauritius which was her dream destination. She got nicely dressed, with pink cheeks all set to leave for the airport. Upon reaching the Indira Gandhi International airport, they all proceeded to the check-in counter. The airline's staff asked her to show her ticket and passport. After having a glance at it, the lady on the seat informed her that she couldn't travel to Mauritius. Laila was zapped for a while. Her husband was taken aback too. It was no less than a nightmare for them. Laila ran to Rajiv, their tour manager for his assistance.

Possible Solution

- On knowing about this faux pas, Rajiv immediately approached the airline's authorities and asked them about the issue. He was told that the name on the ticket was misspelled. It did not match with the name on the passport.
- Rajiv immediately informed his company about the incident and asked them to arrange another ticket for the lady in the next flight when the seats were available.
- It was an apparent mistake on the part of the company who had got their tickets issued from the airlines as the operations team did not recheck the tickets once they were issued by the carriers.
- Rajiv felt very sorry for the whole situation. He tried to empathise with her and asked her not to cry.
- He said that the company shall compensate her by giving her an extra night in Mauritius along with her husband.
- Meanwhile, he arranged for a cab and a complimentary sightseeing tour of Delhi for her the same day till she could board another available flight for Mauritius.
- The husband was asked to proceed with the tour leaving Laila alone in India. With a heavy heart, both bid goodbye to each other!

Lessons Learned

- A tour manager must request his guests to check their tickets during his briefing thoroughly.
- Any discrepancy in the ticket and the visa should be immediately reported by the clients to the tour manager so that he has enough time to get the things rectified in case there are mistakes on the part of the company.
- In case there is something wrong on the part of the company, a tour manager may offer the options to the client and help him arrange alternative arrangements.

Index